ACCESS TO JUSTICE, HEALTH INEQUALITIES AND POVERTY

Perspectives on Law and Access to Justice

Series Editors: **Jess Mant**, Monash University, and **Daniel Newman**, Cardiff University

---

This series forges a coherent field of access to justice scholarship, drawing connections between research from different disciplines such as civil and criminal law, family law, housing law, immigration law and social welfare law. It facilitates a multifaceted critique of the key issues and incorporates a diverse range of perspectives that will shape the future directions of this emerging field.

International Advisory Board:

Find out more at:

bristoluniversitypress.co.uk/
perspectives-on-law-and-access-to-justice

ACCESS TO JUSTICE, HEALTH INEQUALITIES AND POVERTY

Everyday Law in an Unequal Society

James Organ, Jennifer Sigafoos and Sophie Wickham

With a Foreword by
Matthew Ashton

BRISTOL
UNIVERSITY
PRESS

First published in Great Britain in 2026 by

Bristol University Press
University of Bristol
1–9 Old Park Hill
Bristol
BS2 8BB
UK
t: +44 (0)117 374 6645
e: bup-info@bristol.ac.uk

Details of international sales and distribution partners are available at bristoluniversitypress.co.uk

DOI: 10.51952/9781529240399

British Library Cataloguing in Publication Data
A catalogue record for this book is available from the British Library

ISBN 978-1-5292-4036-8 hardcover
ISBN 978-1-5292-4038-2 ePub
ISBN 978-1-5292-4039-9 ePdf

Cover design: Nicky Borowiec
Front cover image: RTimages/Adobestock
Bristol University Press uses environmentally responsible print partners.
Printed and bound in Great Britain by CPI Group (UK) Ltd, Croydon, CR0 4YY

FSC
www.fsc.org
MIX
Paper | Supporting responsible forestry
FSC® C013604

Bristol University Press' authorised representative in the European Union is:
Easy Access System Europe, Mustamäe tee 50, 10621 Tallinn, Estonia,
Email: gpsr.requests@easproject.com

Contents

Series Editors' Preface

Jess Mant (Monash University)
Daniel Newman (Cardiff University)

In recent years, there has been increasing global interest in issues of access to justice and how these issues relate to our increasingly unequal societies. The concept of 'access to justice' – the protection of the law that enables citizens to enforce their rights – is far from new, but has often been approached from a range of different perspectives, methodologies and disciplines. This series provides a home for socio-legal scholarship which explores issues of access to justice. It will draw important connections between research undertaken across different sub-disciplines which intrinsically involve issues of access to justice but are not routinely in conversation with one another, such as civil and criminal law, family law, housing law, immigration law and social welfare law. The series will forge a coherent field of access to justice scholarship, incorporating a diverse range of perspectives to facilitate a multifaceted critique of the key issues, debates and challenges that underpin access to justice and shape the future directions of this emerging field.

List of Figures, Tables and Boxes

Figures

Tables

Boxes

About the Authors

James Organ is Reader in Law at the School of Law and Social Justice, University of Liverpool. His research focuses on access to justice, social welfare rights and health justice, and participatory democracy.

Jennifer Sigafoos is Reader in Law and Associate Head of Department of Law, School of Law and Social Justice, University of Liverpool. Her research focuses on charity law as well as access to justice for social welfare rights and what this means for citizenship and health justice.

Sophie Wickham is Tenure Track Fellow in Public Mental Health in the Department of Public Health, Policy and Systems, University of Liverpool. Her research focuses on public mental health and mental health inequalities. She has a particular interest in the experiences of women and children, and the role that poverty and changes to the welfare system play in widening inequalities.

Acknowledgements

We would like to thank Lucy Asquith, Kathleen Sigafoos, Linda Wickham and Davara Bennett alongside the anonymous reviewer for reading and commenting on earlier drafts of this book. Your time and insights have helped enormously. Any errors remain our own.

We would like to thank the research participants, the Liverpool Access to Advice Network (LATAN) members, Councillor Jane Corbett, Martin Jungnitz, Heather Jessop and Citizens Advice Liverpool (partner organization), the LATAN Steering Committee and staff, and our research team members over the years for their roles in the project.

We would like to thank Daras Konstantinos, Research Associate in Health Data Analysis within the Department of Public Health, Policy & Systems, University of Liverpool, who created the Liverpool child poverty and index of multiple deprivation maps in Chapters 3 and 5.

Jen would like to thank Mike and Gabriel for their support and patience.

James would like to say a big thank you to his family, especially Susana, without whose support over the years this book would never have happened.

Sophie would like to thank Elliot, Amélie and Ezra for their love, encouragement and understanding during the countless hours spent writing. Your sacrifices and support have made my contribution to this book possible.

Foreword

Matthew Ashton, University of Liverpool and Director of Public Health for Liverpool

It is a privilege to introduce Access to Justice, Health Inequalities and Poverty: Everyday Law in an Unequal Society, a timely and essential exploration by James Organ, Jennifer Sigafoos and Sophie Wickham. In this important work, the authors delve into the radical transformation of legal advice funding and delivery in the UK over the past decade – a period marked by unprecedented cuts and profound changes that have left many vulnerable communities facing significant challenges.

As Director of Public Health for Liverpool, I am acutely aware of the deep connections between poverty, health inequalities and access to justice. This book takes a hard look at how the diminishing availability of legal advice has compounded the cycle of inequality, particularly in our own city of Liverpool, where these issues are most pressing. Using Liverpool as a case study, the authors examine the impact of funding cuts on access to justice, social rights and health outcomes, and they do so with a depth of insight that is both sobering and illuminating.

The authors' research, based on a comprehensive five-year socio-legal study – Liverpool Access to Advice Network (LATAN) – highlights the critical role that local advice networks and co-located services play in addressing poverty and its broader social consequences. In Liverpool, these services have become vital lifelines for those facing health inequalities, helping to break the cycle of deprivation and providing practical support to those in most need. Through their analysis, the authors make a compelling case for a more collaborative, community-based approach to rebuilding social citizenship and improving access to justice – an approach that can play a pivotal role in tackling the health challenges our city faces.

The challenges we confront in Liverpool are stark. As highlighted in our recent report, State of Health in the City: Liverpool 2040, the health of our citizens is deeply impacted by poverty and deprivation. Unless we take decisive action, by 2040, one in four adults are projected to be living with major illness, compared to one in five in England, with the burden of these poor health outcomes borne disproportionately by residents living in the most deprived areas of the city. We will see significant rises in long-term conditions, mental health issues and child poverty. The importance of providing comprehensive, accessible services that address these issues cannot be overstated.

This book underscores the need for a radical shift in how we think about justice and health. It demonstrates that when people are unable to access justice/legal support, the consequences extend far beyond legal outcomes – they ripple through every aspect of society, affecting health, wellbeing, and the very fabric of our communities. The authors advocate for a more integrated and co-located approach to service delivery, drawing on the experience of LATAN and successful examples like the Liverpool Advice on Prescription Project, which has pioneered innovative health–justice partnerships in our city. These partnerships, combining legal advice with health services, have proven to be a lifeline for many and are a model for the future.

In this book, the authors make an invaluable contribution to the conversation about how we can address health inequalities. Their fresh perspective on access to justice provides an essential framework for tackling the root causes of poverty and poor health. Their vision of a collaborative, community-based approach to rebuilding social citizenship through improved access to justice offers a clear path forward – a path that will, I hope, inspire policy makers, public services and communities to work together to create a fairer and healthier future for all.

I commend this book to anyone interested in the intersection of law, health and inequality. It is a powerful reminder that access to justice is not just a legal issue – it is a health issue, a social issue and a fundamental human right.

1

Everyday Law in an Unequal Society

This book is a (somewhat tempestuous) love story about the Liverpool Access to Advice Network (LATAN) – a long-term, highly innovative, participatory action research project. We have immersed ourselves in LATAN as researchers and participants to gain new insights into the realities of Liverpool's advice ecosystem and to strengthen and develop collaboration in it. This is the story of LATAN, of the role of free legal advice services in the everyday lives of the people of Liverpool, and of the numerous community-focused organizations in the social welfare law advice ecosystem. These organizations are connected to each other in a fragile, underfunded infrastructure trying to meet the extensive and wide-ranging advice needs of the people with whom they live and work as they wrestle with everyday legal problems. Their important collective efforts help to reduce the negative impacts of neo-liberal austerity politics and to mitigate against the rising health inequalities we see today.

A new policy approach to the delivery of social welfare law is needed. Through our depiction of the contemporary legal advice ecosystem in one of the UK's major cities, we seek to reframe the free legal advice policy environment within a broader approach to access to justice. We argue, in particular, for recognition of the central role of social rights and free legal advice in people's everyday, 'law-thick' lives (Pleasence and Balmer, 2019: 140), and how these are fundamental to combatting poverty, supporting good health and reducing inequalities in an increasingly unequal society.

How the Liverpool Access to Advice Network (LATAN) came to be

LATAN was born in 2019 out of the Liverpool City Council's (hereafter 'Council' or 'LCC') anti-poverty strategy and our long-standing research exploring access to justice, poverty and health inequalities in Liverpool. As has been a theme in the UK of late, times were hard. Poverty was rife and growing. The global financial crisis of 2007–08 had spread from the United States to the rest of the world and triggered the Great Recession. The UK Treasury made significant financial interventions to stabilize the banking sector, estimated by the Office for Budget Responsibility (OBR) to have totalled £136.6 billion (Office for Budget Responsibility, 2021: 234).

After this crisis, the UK Coalition Government (Conservative and Liberal Democrat) that took power in 2010 chose to implement a period of harsh austerity measures in public spending. This included severe cuts to free legal advice and welfare spending, local government budgets and other fundamental social and health services. David Cameron, the (then) prime minister-to-be had promised that the new 'age of austerity' would require 'some incredibly tough decisions on taxation, spending and borrowing – things that really affect people's lives' (Summers, 2009). This proved sadly prophetic, but the impact on people's lives was not felt proportionately. The heaviest burden was born by the poorest and most vulnerable in society. The United Nations Special Rapporteur on extreme poverty and human rights, Philip Alston's, assessment of the UK was very clear: 'The costs of austerity have fallen disproportionately upon the poor, women, racial and ethnic minorities, children, single parents, and people with disabilities ... Austerity could easily have spared the poor, if the political will had existed to do so' (Alston, 2018).

Changes to welfare benefits in the Welfare Reform Act 2012, such as the transition from Disability Living Allowance to Personal Independence Payments, the introduction of Universal Credit, which consolidated six previous 'legacy benefits' into one payment, increases in punitive benefits sanctions under an intensified welfare conditionality regime and other cuts such as the so-called 'bedroom tax', imposed on renters of social homes who are deemed to have more room than they require, all combined to drive up demand for social welfare law advice (Organ and Sigafoos, 2017, 2018). Sophie has produced compelling evidence of the effects of these policies on people's health and wellbeing in the UK (see, for example, Wickham et al, 2020; Song et al, 2024). The (largely temporary) increases in public spending that were a response to the COVID-19 pandemic in 2020 and 2021 were the only significant interruptions to this continued chill in public spending.

Over this same period, other Coalition Government policies reduced the availability of advice at a time when it was greatly needed and demand was rising. Cuts to legal aid in the Legal Aid, Sentencing and Punishment of Offenders Act 2012 (LASPO) hollowed out whole areas of previously funded support for people to resolve their legal problems. LASPO removed various areas of law from the 'scope' of legal aid, including most private family, employment, welfare benefit, housing, debt, clinical negligence, community care, education and non-asylum immigration law matters. It also changed the financial means test for areas of law that remained in scope for legal aid. This included ending automatic eligibility for those in receipt of means-tested benefits, and reducing the limit on the maximum income and capital an individual can have to qualify for legal aid (Organ and Sigafoos, 2018). At the same time, and even more damaging for many social welfare law areas, the cuts to local government funding led local authorities, including Liverpool, to retrench their spending for local advice services. Liverpool saw its largest provider of welfare rights advice have local authority funding cut by 90 per cent, leaving its future in a very precarious state, with most advice agencies across the region seeing cuts of more than 50 per cent (Organ and Sigafoos, 2017). One agency went from having 18 welfare benefits advisers to three, stripping services 'back to basics' (Organ and Sigafoos, 2017).

It was against this background of ever-increasing demand for social welfare law advice and well-evidenced lack of its availability, with dire financial, social and health consequences for people's lives from unresolved legal problems (Patrick, 2017; Organ and Sigafoos, 2018; Organ et al, 2021), that we began the discussion with the Council about LATAN. Poverty was increasing and so were health inequalities (Marmot et al, 2010; Wickham et al, 2016; Taylor-Robinson et al, 2019). There is plenty of evidence that austerity has not affected everyone equally. Places like Liverpool, alongside other northern local authorities, have lower life expectancy and lower healthy life expectancy than England's average, have more infant deaths, more unintended injuries, higher rates of economic inactivity due to ill health or disability and higher rates of people providing unpaid care (Munford et al, 2023). It is also important to consider the complicating effect of how the different layers of people's lives and identities can expose them to intersectional inequalities. This book considers the ways that legal advice can help to ameliorate the impacts of these inequalities in the social determinants of health on people's lives (Organ et al, 2021). The World Health Organization (WHO) described these as 'the conditions in which people are born, grow, work, live and age' (WHO, 2013). This will be discussed more fully in Chapter 3.

The findings from our study of the effects of LASPO on people's lives for the Equality and Human Rights Commission were presented to various Council anti-poverty initiatives in 2018 and 2019. This was important in launching the early conversation with the Council about LATAN. As were Jen's ongoing contributions to the Liverpool Mayoral Fairness and Tackling Poverty Strategy Group. Some vital progress had been made, including the inclusion of access to justice in the Council's basket of 'vital goods' in its anti-poverty strategy. The history of these strategies leading up to LATAN is set out in Box 1.1. We all became acquainted with one another as people working on the same problem from different angles in the same city and consequently started our research collaboration. Our research came to focus on Liverpool because we were working in a cold national political climate and we were not getting traction at that policy level with our compelling (to us) research findings. We decided to push at the door we could open.

Box 1.1: Timeline of Liverpool City Council's anti-poverty approach leading up to LATAN

2011	**The Liverpool Fairness Commission** The Council established this independent body with support and funding from the University of Liverpool. The Commission noted that Liverpool is the most deprived local authority in England, and against the background of the Great Recession and spending constraints they sought to identify practical ways of improving the lives of people in the city. This included recommendations about health, housing and education. Most notably, they made proposals for a Living Wage and embraced the campaign 'Come2gether' for private businesses and organizations to sign up to a charter based on fairness principles.
2013	**The Poverty Action Group** Chaired by Councillor Jane Corbett, the group's remit was to encourage stakeholders to work with the City Council to tackle poverty and provide support and assistance to those citizens suffering hardship. The group focused on a basic needs list or vital goods, which included food, fuel, clothing, home, income maximization, budget support, access to affordable finance, digital access, access to justice and access to essential transport, eventually incorporated into the Fair City Policy.
2014	**Real Living Wage for Liverpool City Council staff members**
2014	**Citywide Strategy Group for Fairness and Tackling Poverty** Chaired by Church of England Bishop Paul Bayes and Councillor Jane Corbett, this was a group that worked strategically to take local action focused specifically on making sure Liverpool is a strong city built on fairness. This had a diverse membership comprising business leaders, voluntary and community sector (VCS) organizations, representatives from different faiths, universities, housing associations, the Liverpool Law Society and Liverpool City Council.
2018	**Fair City Policy adopted along with a commitment to real Living Wage accreditation**
2019	**Funding for Liverpool Access to Advice Network (LATAN) and introductory work on project**
2020	**LATAN launched**

We will discuss what LATAN is in a moment, but we think it worthwhile to highlight first that despite all these local efforts things were getting worse. After eight years of austerity, the Conservative government that succeeded the Coalition announced, in 2018, 'the era of austerity finally coming to an end' (HM Treasury and Hammond, 2018). While spending on public services increased somewhat, many of the austerity-driven policies remained. This was then exacerbated by the worldwide emergency that was the COVID-19 pandemic. Although public social welfare spending increased in response, the pandemic showed that the decade of worsening poverty and health inequalities had further consequences. According to the international measure of income inequality (the Gini coefficient) the UK has one of the highest levels of inequality among European Organisation for Economic Cooperation and Development (OECD) member states. The inequality is getting worse – the latest UK data on income inequality shows that for those of us in the bottom 80 per cent of the population, income fell before housing costs, while it increased for those in the top 10 per cent. The UK's income inequality is only slightly lower than that of the US (Francis-Devine, 2024). Those same inequalities were reflected in differential rates of morbidity and mortality from COVID-19. Across the most deprived areas of the country more people died and became seriously ill. Liverpool, sadly, was one of those areas.

In response to the (perceived) out of control spending in response to the COVID-19 pandemic, and a growing UK cost-of-living crisis, subsequent Conservative governments implemented a new commitment to constraints on public spending, though this was only openly embraced as austerity by the short-lived and financially disastrous Liz Truss government. Her 49 days in office and commitment to 'Trussonomics' in the September 2022 mini-budget triggered a run on the pound, which hit a 37-year low against the dollar. There might have been a glimmer of hope from the new Labour government after the 2024 general election but, so far, their policy statements have expressed a continuing commitment to the welfare policies already in place, such as a refusal to commit to ending the two-child benefit limit. They have also emphasized the need to prioritize the constraint of public spending using language echoing that used during austerity. So here we are: poorer, more unequal and in poor health. Where can we go from here?

What is LATAN?

The LATAN project was set up by partner organizations: the University of Liverpool (School of Law and Social Justice and the Department of Public Health, Policy and Systems), the LCC and Citizens Advice Liverpool. It brings together organizations that deliver legal advice in social welfare law as well as local community organizations across the city to build a strong community of practice. That means the LATAN member organizations are engaged in a collective endeavour, and through regular interactions are learning together how to advance their common interests (Wenger-Trayner and Wenger-Trayner, 2015). LATAN's wide range of activities include holding regular forums on key issues, coordinating and delivering training and information sessions, developing a referral network, and responding to LCC consultations and funding plans. The central focus is to improve access to advice and to increase access to justice while increasing the evidence base of the impact of cuts to the free legal advice ecosystem and welfare reform in Liverpool. Further details are set out in Box 1.2.

Box 1.2: What is the LATAN project?

LATAN is an action research project, with a collaborative philosophical underpinning. Here are some of the key characteristics:

Strategic vision: 'No wrong door; advice for all'.

Our mission: To build up the relationships and to enhance collaboration between the wide range of organizations in the advice ecosystem in Liverpool. This includes 'core' advice organizations as well as smaller, neighbourhood organizations and other non-advice organizations where people might present and discuss their everyday legal problems.

Our primary goal: To build up a community of practice within the Liverpool advice ecosystem, endeavouring to improve efficiency to overcome barriers identified in previous research.

Funding: Phase one funding came from the Council and the vision of Councillor Jane Corbett and Martin Jungnitz, then Head of Revenue and Benefits in 2019, which led to the establishment of LATAN and its launch in 2020. A second phase of LATAN started with funding from the Legal Education Foundation from the start of 2023 to mid 2026.

What we explored: Participatory research since 2020 has enabled this book's detailed account of the reality of Liverpool's legal advice ecosystem and people's interactions with it. The project provides a strong evidence base to understand access to justice and provision of free legal advice, and the potential for impacting poverty and health in Liverpool and beyond.

Why we explored it: It has also enabled the provision of detailed policy recommendations that we hope will help policy makers and all those grappling with everyday legal problems in their lives, and lead to a stronger implementation of social rights and a reduction in poverty and health inequalities.

How we do this: Under the LATAN umbrella, the three initial elements to the project could be categorized, somewhat artificially, into two activities: non-research and research (which are interconnected and ever evolving).

Non-research		Research
Establish a self-sustaining legal advice network (LATAN).	Develop a system for client referrals between different agencies.	Map and understand advice services and organizational partnerships, both private and VCS, in Liverpool in relation to the socio-economic and health characteristics of different parts of the city.

Non-research	Research
Aim to improve access to advice by: • supporting partnership working between organizations; • developing training capacity (and support organizations to share best practices); • development and implementation of better referrals between services.	Research questions we ask: • What provision for legal advice currently exists in Liverpool, and how is it understood? • What are the relationships between the organizations that provide legal advice and those that connect people to them? • What is the impact of limited free legal advice provision for the people of Liverpool?

(In)access to justice

Access to justice has a long history in England and Wales, but the tendency of both policy makers and researchers has been to focus on the 'institutions of justice' and the 'justice system', on the formal court system and legal professionals, and on centralized, legal aid funding (Flynn and Hodgson, 2017; Denvir and Selvarajah, 2021; Newman and Gordon, 2023; Wilding, 2023). We urge instead a focus on the fundamental access to justice role of the community-led free legal advice ecosystem that helps people resolve their everyday legal problems.

Policy makers at a national and local government level need a new, clearer focus on the importance of all forms of legal advice and the need for stronger public legal education. As Rebecca Sandefur noted: 'the current course of focussing narrowly on lawyers' services is wrong, whether the goal is understanding the access problem or taking action to fix it. Looking only at the civil justice activity processed by lawyers misses most of the action' (Sandefur, 2019: 53). LATAN is about understanding this missed 'action'.

There have been regular calls for reinstatement of legal aid since LASPO's hatchet job in 2012. We have made them ourselves (Organ and Sigafoos, 2018; Sigafoos and Organ, 2021) and we certainly still think it is an important policy goal. But we also need to decentralize and broaden the current policy approach to free legal advice to recognize the huge number of social welfare issues that get nowhere near the justice system (Boyle and Camps, 2022; Creutzfeldt et al, 2024). This means recognizing the importance of local authority funding for advice services and reinstating it to strengthen local advice ecosystems. In the current financial environment for local authorities, this will necessarily mean national level funding to be directed to local authorities for this purpose.

We also need to implement new approaches to advice. As our focus is on social welfare law, we argue for a broad understanding of access to justice that is closely connected to people's enjoyment of the social rights that citizenship in England and Wales is supposed to promise. The story of LATAN asks policy makers to reconsider what is meant by legal advice outside and alongside formal institutions of justice and legal professions. It illustrates the difficulties involved in the journey that people take to resolve what Ab Currie called 'everyday legal problems' (Currie, 2009, 2016), and Hazel Genn called 'justiciable events' (Genn, 1999), and how these issues, if unresolved, can be cyclically reinforcing. The LATAN story shows the importance of funding the first stages of trying to understand and resolve everyday legal problems, as well as the process of referral to someone that can help. It also emphasizes the significance of this journey as an anti-poverty strategy and a means of fostering the conditions necessary to promote societal good health.

Calls for a more holistic approach to access to justice are not new but are limited in number (see Boyle, 2022; Creutzfeldt et al, 2024). There are some indications that government policy is starting to take a broader approach to legal advice, although whether this is to increase access or to save money is unclear (Ministry of Justice, 2019). The story of Liverpool's advice ecosystem tells us that decision makers need to embed these disparate, limited developments, such as the increasing experimentation with health–justice partnerships (Bearden and Genn, 2018), within the core infrastructure and make them mainstream. We need a new understanding of legal advice that includes the advice provided in the community and by organizations other than those that are regulated legal professions or recognized advice providers.

Funding models are needed that recognize the value of existing community organizations and promote their collaboration. Decision makers need to adopt policies in relation to access to advice that recognize its importance across all policy areas that relate to social rights and the development of life chances for individuals. This more strategic approach ensures that access to appropriate advice is embedded in all programmes intended to strengthen social rights and tackle poverty, raising awareness of people's rights and strengthening and enabling access to them. Policy makers must recognize the connection between free legal advice, social rights and societal health.

The story of LATAN brings up several significant theoretical questions: what do we mean by access to (legal) justice? What is social justice? What is the core of social citizenship in the UK today? The purpose of this book is not a theoretical debate about these concepts, though we will explore their development and our approach to them in Chapter 2. We are clear that access to justice is underpinned by a social understanding of justice if social citizenship is to retain any meaning in England and Wales following its dismantling over recent decades (Sigafoos and Organ, 2021). We present a manifesto for change to move forwards, towards stronger social citizenship, away from the conditional, market-based citizenship that recent welfare and justice policies have sought to develop (Sommerlad, 2018). The story of LATAN also illuminates, emphasizes and develops elements of these overarching concepts of access to justice, social justice and social citizenship. We make concluding remarks about them in Chapter 8.

Justice is not a question only of fair procedure and legal outcomes through legal institutions. It is also a question of fair social rights-focused outcomes. Elements of this are reflected, for example, in the calls for food justice (Hayes and Maynard, 2024b), health justice (Wiley et al, 2022), welfare justice (Joseph Rowntree Foundation, 2025) and other elements of a fair social citizenship settlement. The community of organizations in LATAN and the people they serve often do not think of the issues they help to resolve as legal issues (Pleasence and Balmer, 2014; Creutzfeldt et al, 2024) but are driven by other social rights-related priorities such as health, education, finance, care and so forth. An important part of the role of these organizations is to drive social justice through acting as trusted intermediaries for people in the journey to resolve issues with a legal element that crop up in people's everyday lives (Cohl et al, 2018), and which are often intertwined with other non-legal problems within the sphere of social justice.

The emphasis on the connection between free legal advice and social rights, which is inherent in social welfare law, especially for LATAN members, locates this book in the key strand of access to justice literature that began with Genn's seminal *Paths to Justice* (1999) and continues through legal needs literature (such as Pleasence and Balmer, 2014). From among the voluminous access to justice literature, the research in this area has been particularly important in three aspects for the picture we build here of Liverpool's free legal advice ecosystem. First, it focuses attention on the people experiencing the legal issues: 'Legal needs surveys investigate the experience of justiciable problems from … a bottom-up perspective, rather than from that of justice professionals and institutions (a top-down perspective)' (Boyle and Camps, 2024: 21). Secondly, this research highlights that the legal problems people face are, in many ways, part of their everyday lives. Thirdly, these issues are usually resolved with support from outside the formal legal system of courts and solicitors (Sandefur, 2019). As Pleasence and Balmer concluded from their review of legal needs surveys: 'The general picture the world over is that most [civil legal] problems are addressed through informal methods, if addressed at all' (OECD/Open Society Foundations, 2019: 143).

Legal needs surveys have been an important part of the evidence demonstrating that 'disputes occur and are mostly resolved outside the purview of both courts and lawyers', and that this has already led to a policy shift in some jurisdictions, but they are not best-suited to analysing specific service provision (OECD/Open Society Foundations, 2019: 155). The LATAN project helps fill this gap. One of our key messages is that policy must be developed from a service-user and voluntary and community sector (VCS) organization perspective that recognizes the range of specific everyday issues that these informal (in a strictly legal sense) services help address. The blurred lines between legal and social justice, and the need for policy makers to recognize these points, are explored in this book with a specific focus on the link between justice and health. In Chapter 9, we offer a manifesto to help makers think through how they might tackle this.

There is a growing body of research in the academic literature that underlines the connection between legal advice and health (Beardon and Genn, 2018; Genn, 2019; Organ et al, 2021; Aregawi et al, 2025). The legal needs surveys noted earlier have also been important in providing evidence of the connection between legal issues and health. For example, the 2024 legal needs survey of England and Wales found that 53 per cent of respondents reported stress as a result of their contentious legal issue, and 16 per cent became unwell as a result, rising to 20 per cent in those with lower incomes (YouGov, 2024).

LATAN was established as an interdisciplinary law and public health project just before the COVID-19 pandemic exposed the grim consequences of the policies that had widened health inequalities. Access to free legal advice has the capacity to be highly influential across multiple (if not all) social determinants of health. We will introduce this properly in Chapter 3. Free legal advice is fundamental to the development of health–justice partnerships, which are being explored increasingly as an important policy response to the connection between advice and health (Reece et al, 2022; Gilboe and Curran, 2025). We will demonstrate the value of developing these and other forms of co-location of advice and social rights-related services. We discuss these in detail in Chapter 6.

The COVID-19 pandemic and its impact on advice services and their clients needs to be acknowledged because it was the background to the first two years of the LATAN project. The pandemic experience has informed this book. Most fundamentally, it exposed just how fragile everything is now. People's lives are often lived right on the edge; just a temporary reduction to working hours offered under their zero-hours contract, an accident or a benefit sanction away from hunger and cold homes. Services themselves are fragile. In some cases, they are cobbled together from volunteers being willing to give what support they can. Even this is a pressure, though, as volunteers are not free. They need space to sit and lighting and a warm(ish) office and a phone and a computer (usually) and, crucially, supervision, which is desperately short in the wake of LASPO (Organ and Sigafoos, 2017, 2018). In all cases, services are inadequately funded and in very high demand.

LATAN is a case study in the UK's best city. Home to and shaped by some of the most influential bands and musicians – the Beatles, Elvis Costello, Frankie Goes to Hollywood, Gerry and the Pacemakers come to mind, but the list goes on. It was the European Capital of Culture in 2008 and is home to some of the best performers past and present (the likes of Paul O'Grady, Cilla Black, Kim Cattrall, Stephen Graham and Jodie Comer), and two

Premier League football clubs (Everton and Liverpool) and a Women's Super League team. A city that loves a spectacle – we all remember the triumph of hosting the Eurovision Song Contest in 2023.

It is also a city of social connection, innovation and action. It was a pioneer in public health: among other achievements it had the country's first Medical Officer of Health, William Henry Duncan (we regularly walk by the University of Liverpool building named for him) (Halliday, 2003), and the Liverpool School of Tropical Medicine was the world's first. Liverpool has continued to innovate in this area: it now has the Children Growing Up in Liverpool (C-GULL) study, a longitudinal birth cohort that strives to be the largest family study in the UK. Liverpool also has one of the first and longest running health–justice partnerships: the Citizens Advice on Prescription project run by Citizens Advice Liverpool (Aregawi et al, 2025).

Liverpool has long been an innovator for people coming together to start VCS organizations to help their fellow Liverpudlians. The Liverpool Society for the Prevention of Cruelty to Children was founded in 1883, beating London by more than a year to be the first of its kind in the country, and eventually giving rise to the National Society for Prevention of Cruelty to Children (National Centre for Social Research, nd). We are exploring advice in the city where the Citizens Advice Bureau (CAB) organization was born. Liverpool's Personal Service Society, which was the forerunner to CAB, was established in 1919 by Dorothy Keeling and Eleanor Rathbone, MP (whose namesake building we also walk past daily). As well as being a city of significant social and health innovation, Liverpool is a highly relevant city from which to understand and analyse the value of advice services and the connection between social rights and justice.

These are only examples of the unashamed solidarity, loyalty and resilience of the city. With deep apologies to the Evertonians reading this, it really is a city where 'you'll never walk alone'. There is a reason we have all chosen Liverpool as the place to live, grow our families and work – the people here are the best. And yet, the city faces significant challenges. Using official government data, Liverpool is recorded as one of the most deprived cities (explored further in Chapter 3). This is a Liverpool (love) story, but it will resonate across all local authority areas and provide clear policy considerations for everyone trying to maximize council services in relation to housing, anti-poverty, immigration and so on. Other cities have a similar rich tapestry of community organizations and advice agencies providing the advice that helps people to navigate their lives and the services they rely on. We believe that the lessons from Liverpool can transform the approach to free legal advice policy across the country, strengthen social protections, reduce poverty and combat health inequalities.

2

Access to (Social) Justice and Everyday Legal Problems

In this chapter we situate the Liverpool Access to Advice Network (LATAN) project and our analysis of Liverpool's free legal advice ecosystem in the relevant theoretical environment. We set out our position in terms of access to justice, social justice and social citizenship. In doing this, we explain the relationship between access to (legal) justice and social justice that underpins the analysis of LATAN throughout the book. We also explain the meaning of 'everyday legal problems', which is a central concept in our evaluation of the valuable role played in people's lives by LATAN's 100-plus member organizations.

What is access to (legal) justice?

Access to justice has a long history as a civil right in England and Wales. There is a lot of academic research on the subject (Cappelletti et al, 1976, 1982; Cappelletti and Garth, 1978). In recent years, it has been approached from the perspective of various communities of interest, including disadvantaged communities (Mayo et al, 2015), rural communities (Newman and Gordon, 2023) and young people and children (Stalford, 2024). Access to justice research encompasses a wide range of topics relating to people's ability to resolve legal issues and to receive a fair outcome. These include issues such as the impact of court architecture (Duncanson and Henderson, 2021), the rise of digital means to access advice (Mant et al, 2024) and the courtroom (Denvir and Selvarajah, 2021), and effective participation in courts and tribunals (Jacobson and Cooper, 2020).

Our community of interest is all people using or needing social welfare advice services in Liverpool. Our research explores how effective the free legal advice ecosystem is in helping people towards a fair outcome in relation to their social rights, and, in turn, reducing poverty and health inequalities, and how this ecosystem could change. Our analysis of LATAN extends to questions of free legal advice beyond the predominantly private sector providers of services funded through the centralized legal aid scheme, and beyond the formal court and tribunal system. This is underpinned by a broad approach that connects the civil right of access to justice to the social rights that are the subject of social welfare law.

Access to justice has both a normative and a descriptive aspect (Cornford, 2016). Our focus here is analysing and understanding more fully the descriptive component of access to justice; that is the services that facilitate people's ability to enforce their rights. We have an empirical starting point when considering questions of the relationship between law, social change and justice. In recent years, our participatory research has focused on the collaboration through LATAN of Liverpool voluntary and community sector (VCS) organizations involved in people's journey towards resolving everyday legal problems. This is not to say, of course, that we reject thinking about these ideas from a normative perspective starting with key principles. We will progress from our empirical analysis to discussion of these bigger ideas (particularly in Chapter 8) that are based on the belief that access to justice and social justice are foundational to society. We will explain how these ideals are necessary to address the huge societal issues of poverty and heath inequalities. The starting point for doing this is based on understanding the experience of people grappling with everyday legal problems and of the organizations they turn to, and the impact this has on their lives.

Natalie Byrom, previously Director of Research and Learning at the Legal Education Foundation, sets out a typical definition of access to justice as one that in relation to the formal legal system provides access to an effective hearing, access to a decision in accordance with substantive law, and access to remedy (Byrom, 2019). Here, while recognizing the importance of these elements of access to justice, we extend beyond this definition to include the vast number of issues with a legal component and the people who experience them that never come into contact with the formal legal system when seeking advice or a remedy. As Ab Currie described it, we deal with 'justice writ large … as a social institution, not limited to the formal laws and system of justice' (Currie, 2009: 2).This broad understanding of access to justice, which is less common in academic literature but not unique (see, for example, Creutzfeldt et al, 2024), is necessary if we are to design an effective free legal advice ecosystem that will maximize access to (social) justice.

Limiting the focus in policy making to the formal legal system leads to a significant amount of unmet legal need and reduced access to social and legal justice. One specific issue that highlights this problem is the £23 billion of welfare benefits that people are entitled to as part of their social rights but do not claim (Ghelani et al, 2024). Another is the high (and rising) number of people who are homeless – according to the latest statistics, 358,370 households in England in 2023–24, an increase of 10.4 per cent from 2022–23 (Ministry of Housing, Communities and Local Government, 2024).

People's inability to claim or receive these social rights is both a legal and a social justice issue. The non-fulfilment of rights that are underpinned by the legal framework of the welfare state is a legal issue, despite the fact that most social welfare claims never get to a legal professional or the court system. When they do, there is a 'very strong feeling of reluctance' for the courts to decide on these matters, as 'the UK national discourse is aligned with a narrative that assumes social rights are non-justiciable' (Boyle et al, 2022: 65). This non-fulfilment of rights leads to greater inequality – both generally and in terms of health, unfairness, a lack of dignity and basic needs being unmet. This means that the non-fulfilment of rights is an issue of access to social as well as to legal justice.

There is support for this broad approach to access to justice from legal needs research. The Organisation for Economic Co-operation and Development (OECD) and the Open Society Foundation, in their report on legal needs surveys, defined access to justice in a way that fits our broad approach to legal advice and justice: 'Access to justice concerns the ability of people to obtain just resolution of justiciable problems (a problem that raises legal issues) and enforce their rights, in compliance with human rights standards; *if necessary, through impartial formal or informal institutions and with appropriate legal support*' (OECD/Open Society Foundations, 2019: 24; emphasis added). Their report recognizes at several points that the formal legal system and specialist legal advice funded by legal aid is only one part of access to justice: 'only a minority of surveys have found that courts or tribunals resolved more than 10% of justiciable problems with some suggesting a rate of 5% or lower' (OECD/Open Society Foundations, 2019: 33). We believe it is very important for policy makers to recognize that access to justice is not only access to a hearing, decision and remedy in the formal legal system, and that it is not only legal professionals that can provide the services needed for a just resolution. It is about people's ability, more broadly, to understand and enforce their rights and to get support to resolve a problem with legal dimensions.

The narrower 'courts and lawyers' approach to access to justice leads to the description of the provision of legal information and advice prior to engaging a legal professional as a necessary precursor to access to justice (Byrom, 2019). Our approach is that the provision of legal advice and information services are an important part of access to justice, rather than just a precursor to it. The use of the court and tribunal system and/or legal advice from a legal professional can be an important phase in a person's journey to try to resolve an issue with a legal component. It is not, however, the most common path for social welfare issues. The legal advice that people receive can come from various sources within and outside of the formal legal system: Worldwide, '[o]nly a minority of people facing justiciable problems obtain assistance from a lawyer, with a median reported rate of around 12%' (OECD/Open Society Foundations, 2019: 33). In the United Kingdom, appropriate support can come from a wide variety of sources: friends, colleagues, general practitioners (GPs) (the entry point for healthcare support to the National Health Service [NHS]) and the range of community-focused organizations that make up much of the advice ecosystem.

Support can come at several different time points in a person's efforts to resolve a problem in their everyday lives that relates to social rights. For example, in welfare rights law, support could come at the point when a person wonders if they might be entitled to state support, or when they are short of money. It could also come during the various application stages for that state support, at each of the appeal points in the process, or at a tribunal to challenge a decision. In housing, the support could be to help someone understand that they have an enforceable right, such as getting their landlord to carry out repairs to their home, to help them navigate and negotiate a local council's system for bidding on a social home, or in relation to a court case. This includes activities recommended or required in the pre-action protocols for civil claims, which set out and explain the steps that should be taken to help resolve disputes without resorting to litigation, for example the tenant's letter of claim and the landlord's response in relation to a housing condition claim (Ministry of Justice, 2022). There are many points when advice is needed but not available and often a social welfare issue is tangled up in a bundle of connected issues that need sorting out. These are the snares of a life lived in poverty.

What is social justice?

Access to free legal advice is central to the normative ideal of equal access to justice (Cornford, 2016). In turn, legal justice is essential for the fulfilment of social justice. This means that the legal system and social justice are intrinsically connected. As Cappelletti and Garth stated, following their groundbreaking access to justice study, 'First, the [legal] system must be equally accessible to all; second, it must lead to results that are individually and socially just ... Indeed, a basic premise [is] that social justice, as sought by our modem societies, *presupposes* effective access' (1978: 182). Similarly, our focus in the LATAN research project is on the practicalities of free legal advice as a means of increasing the equality of access to legal justice and its role as a prerequisite for social justice.

In myriad ways, the members of LATAN are trying to achieve justice through enabling social rights. Often these organizations are trying to ensure that people access the social rights they are promised and the resources they need. For example, support with access to food, access to available housing, help when recovering from an accident, assistance in finding educational opportunities for their children, advice for paying their bills, or support while waiting for immigration decisions. For these organizations justice is social in nature. Their objectives relate to increasing equality, dignity and providing basic needs, not specifically the provision of free legal advice to increase the effectiveness of the justice system. Many of these areas of support, though, involve or are connected to issues that have a legal element. This places the work of LATAN organizations at the interface between social rights and the broad understanding of legal justice that underpins our research.

As an academic concept, social justice is complex and highly contested. Although 'social justice is in the province of politics' (Sommerlad, 2018: 285), there are important elements around which many commentators coalesce, and which are representative of the LATAN approach. The core elements of a standard approach to social justice (adapted from Craig's survey of the literature, 2018: 6) are:

- fairness, equality and dignity for all;
- meeting at least basic needs – a 'safety net';
- reducing inequalities and addressing their negative impact;
- full participation for all.

We see some tension between the first two of these. The idea of 'at least' a safety net is a problem unless that safety net is set at a high enough level. Fairness, equality and dignity for all require that everyone has a decent, not just a minimum, standard of living. The NHS is an example that is closer to the level of service we aspire to, as it promises healthcare for all, free at the point of delivery that promises to resolve the health issue fully.

This understanding of social justice depends on the provision of social rights. The state largely took on responsibility for social rights with the birth of the welfare state after the Second World War. This delivery of social justice through a new socialized form of citizenship – adding social rights to the pre-existing political and civil rights – sought to tackle substantive inequalities, such as in income, education and health. Fulfilment of fundamental social rights in a comprehensive manner was promised to all, and fairness and equality placed at the heart of justice. At the same time, the state promised delivery of free legal advice to those that needed it through the Legal Aid and Advice Act 1949. This has meant that access to justice/free legal advice and access to social rights have evolved together and become co-dependent, further blurring the distinction between legal and social justice.

As is discussed in detail in Chapter 3, during the period of Conservative-led governments from 2010 to 2024, poverty and inequality rose across a range of health outcomes, and access to justice and social rights reduced. Many of the LATAN members' services exist because of the lack of state provision of services to ensure social justice for all in society. The rise in food bank usage in the UK to several million food parcels distributed annually and increased homelessness during this time are just two examples of this reduction in social justice and limited vindication of social rights.

LATAN members are working to address this lack of social justice. Issues with a lack of fairness, dignity, equality, participation and access to even a minimum, acceptable standard of living are common among the people they help. To varying degrees, there is a rise in the five 'great evils' that the Beveridge Report promised to tackle: poverty, poor health, lack of education, poor housing and lack of employment (Beveridge, 1942). We focus here on the first two of these: poverty and health inequalities.

We are not trying to engage in detail in the debate about the meaning of (social) justice. Nevertheless, we are not neutral in terms of justice. We certainly believe that justice has a social component, and our project is working towards advancing this.

What is social citizenship?

Arendt's well-known conceptualization of citizenship is that it is the membership of a political community that entails the right to have rights, so that one's actions and opinions count (Arendt, 1998; Kesby, 2012). We leave aside the question of whether there is a right to belong to a particular community, and the many issues associated with the inherent nature of citizenship as an exclusionary concept (Takle et al, 2023). It is problematic enough to consider, as we do here, whether those that have a recognized right to belong are enjoying the rights that this membership promises (or should promise). Citizenship, as such, is one of the core doctrines of legitimate modern states. Its normative basis is that all citizens have a single legal status and equal possession of a set of rights.

Through the establishment of the welfare state, the set of rights promised by citizenship was broadened to include social rights (Marshall and Bottomore, 1992) and linked to equal access to justice through their co-evolution with legal aid. The inclusion of access to free legal advice in this new form of social citizenship meant there was a means to enforce, not just proclaim, these new social rights. Our participation in and research through LATAN sits at this juxtaposition between civil and social rights in Britain today and highlights the need to understand the free legal advice ecosystem in this social citizenship context.

While acknowledging the importance of T.H. Marshall to today's understanding of social citizenship, our framing of social citizenship was developed from Taylor-Gooby's theoretical frame that uses three key values of social citizenship: reciprocity, inclusion and trust (Taylor-Gooby, 2008; Sigafoos and Organ, 2021). Access to justice, particularly access to free legal advice, is a critical element of social citizenship as an enabler of the social rights that social citizenship promises. Furthermore, 'the limited availability of legal advice reduces the extent to which reciprocity and inclusion are an expected or intended outcome of access to justice and welfare policy. In turn, this undermines trust in the welfare system, on which social citizenship and, more broadly, political legitimacy rely' (Sigafoos and Organ, 2021: 364). Here, we focus on providing a deeper empirical understanding of access to justice in community settings and how this impacts policy related to social citizenship. However, following the presentation of our research findings and analysis of the free legal advice ecosystem, we develop in Chapter 8 the theoretical meaning of social citizenship in two key aspects: the link to effective participation and the re-evaluation of the role of trust.

The LATAN experience highlights the impact of policies on these values of social citizenship and of the subsequent increase in demand for free legal advice. Trust is particularly important to social citizenship. As Taylor-Gooby stated: 'in relation to social citizenship, it is institutional trust writ large, trust not only that the legal and regulatory framework will work but also that the behaviour of those involved will be such that the institutions of welfare will deliver the goods to the trusting citizen' (2008: 11).

Importantly, the LATAN research indicates how people's identification of everyday legal problems can be improved, how the efforts towards resolution of those issues can be made more effective and the centrality of trust in this process. As such, LATAN is a case study of how social citizenship is operationalized and experienced in the UK today, and specifically how trust is fundamental at all levels and between all stakeholders.

Our participation in LATAN evidences the importance of the network of trust relationships, for example between service users and organizations, and between organizations of different sizes and with different approaches and objectives. A large part of the work with LATAN, and one of the benefits of a participatory approach to the research and the development of LATAN, has been to develop stronger trust relationships, which are important in building our evidence base and in finding effective solutions to the issues facing the sector. It is essential, however, that a huge caveat is attached to this claim: issues of capacity must also be addressed. Even with very strong trust relationships and effective, collaborative networks, if there is nowhere for people to actually get the advice they need, building trust will achieve very little. We would go further and say that without the delivery of a reasonable quantity of appropriate advice at a reasonable standard, it is not possible to have strong trust between people and the state. If people cannot get the advice they need, the promise of social rights will not be met, and trust in the system breaks down as people perceive that they are not getting what they deserve and were promised.

One of the aims of this book is to clearly link free legal advice policy to the concept of social citizenship, particularly the link between justice and health. This will enable the identification and implementation of more effective solutions to the current crisis in social justice, as well as the rising health problems and widening health inequalities facing Liverpool, England and beyond. Marshall famously describes the social rights promised as 'the whole range from the right to a modicum of economic welfare and security, to the right to share to the full in the social heritage and to live the civilized life according to the standards prevailing in society' (Marshall and Bottomore, 1992: 8). The idea of people maintaining a standard of living that befits the 'civilized life' is central to Marshall's conceptualization of social citizenship, but has become today a more minimalist promise of *just* a safety net, which does not keep people out of poverty, let alone give them full participation in society or be based on policies that strive for equality of outcomes. The evidence from the LATAN research project is that welfare and justice policies in recent years have led to the position where many people are excluded from the social and other rights that they should enjoy as part of their membership of a political community based on ideas of social citizenship. Destitution has become an increasing reality for people in the UK (Simpson et al, 2023) and health inequalities are widening (see Chapter 3). Full participation in society is a pipe dream when so many people spend all their time fighting to manage the everyday challenges in their life: feeding the family, heating the home, managing finances, relying on uncertain and low-paid work and so on.

We are presenting the case that access to advice is an anti-poverty and pro-health strategy. The process of making this case in Liverpool has not been straightforward. In 2022, we collaborated with other LATAN organizations to draft Liverpool's access to advice strategy. We worked with the Liverpool City Council (Council or LCC) and received political sign-off for the new strategic approach in 2023 (Chapter 9 explains the principles in detail). Just as we went to press with this book in late 2024, however, a new Council housing strategy was drafted. When we asked whether advice had been included, as is required under the provisionally agreed advice strategy, we were told that no advice was provided in the new housing strategy, but we were not to worry because the information on the website had been updated. Despite the progress made with the LCC, there is still some way to go before access to free legal advice is fully understood and recognized as a key determinant of success for strategies seeking to strengthen social rights, such as housing, and embedded in interventions to drive positive change.

What are everyday legal problems?

We use the 'everyday legal problems' paradigm to focus attention on the people experiencing the problems, rather than those delivering services, and on the wide range of everyday situations in which people find social welfare law influencing their lives (Currie, 2009). This reflects the formal establishment of social rights that brought millions of people in direct contact with situations in their everyday lives that were regulated and/or promised in primary legislation (Currie, 2009).

These problems are 'everyday' in the sense that they are part of events experienced by a wide range of people at different stages in their lives, that they are a possibility for almost everyone in society, and that many people somewhere will be experiencing them at any given point in time. Problems that need legal advice do not occur every day for everyone, but law relating to social welfare underpins elements of everyone's life at home, work and in public. Our understanding of 'everyday' issues is not that the issues themselves are everyday – in that they are mundane or occur all the time for everybody – rather that they are connected to activities that are unexceptionally a part of a large majority of people's lives (or could be) at any given time, such as employment, marriage, having children, renting a home, claiming welfare benefits and so on. The practical focus that the use of 'everyday legal problems' is intended to bring to the approach to resolving 'justiciable issues' is also reflected in the phrase 'pragmatic justice' that Barnard et al (2024) use in the context of community services for European Union migrant workers.

Social welfare law is most prevalent for those with limited resources. The nomenclature 'poverty law' used elsewhere in the world is very apt. The everyday legal problems include welfare benefits applications, disputes at work, debt management, immigration status and special educational needs and disabilities (SEND). The legal needs in any particular area vary according to the prevailing policy in that area and the public resources allocated to avoiding social problems. For example, housing issues such as disrepair, eviction notices, inability to access housing and so on have increased significantly in recent years and were regularly referenced by our interviewees as a priority. Whatever the policies, though, people on lower incomes are more likely to experience social welfare law-related issues (Pleasence and Balmer, 2019). Despite this, many of these issues are also experienced by a much wider demographic. For example, anyone with children will have the potential for numerous and significant 'everyday legal problems' such as child protection cases and divorce, issues related to SEND or maternity rights disputes at work.

Finally in this section, we explain the *legal* in everyday legal problems. All justiciable problems are legal problems. Genn defines a justiciable 'event' as 'a matter experienced by a respondent which raised legal issues, whether or not it was recognized by the respondent as being "legal" and whether or not any action taken by the respondent to deal with the event involved the use of any part of the civil justice system' (Genn, 1999: 12) In other words, they are everyday legal problems as soon as they involve a person's rights. This is true at their inception as well as at any stage of their enforcement. It is true whether or not any action needs to be taken or is actually taken. It also does not matter what the level of complexity is of the matter itself or the law that underpins it. Even when no action is taken the matter should be viewed as one with a legal need, whatever the cause of the inaction: be it lack of resources, lack of awareness of the legal element of the issue or inertia. This broad definition of everyday legal problems means that we have a similarly broad approach to free legal advice, which includes the full range of advice work from matters such as advice about potential welfare benefits entitlement, for a welfare benefit application or for a low-complexity employment dispute through to advice and drafting for a tribunal claim, and all the way up to a solicitor or barrister to represent you in court.

The framing of legal issues as 'everyday legal problems' means a broad understanding of access to justice that highlights the close connection between social and civil rights. This framing of legal issues as everyday legal problems has important policy implications. It requires policy makers to focus on the people experiencing these matters in their lives rather than the legal profession. It requires a realization that social welfare matters are multifaceted, with legal and non-legal influences and outcomes. It emphasizes the preventative role of legal advice. It recognizes the interconnected nature of legal and non-legal matters in the complexities of people's lives. This framing also allows us to further develop thinking about the connection between legal advice and the social determinants of health, as these everyday legal problems clearly implicate employment, housing, education and so on. The resolution of an employment issue, for example, often without any recourse to the courts, may avoid a problem with health, reduce the need to claim benefits and avoid difficulties in housing. The 'everyday legal problems' paradigm turns policy away from management of individual dispute resolution in the courts towards resolution in people's everyday lives through negotiation, mediation and empowerment, and a more systemic focus on social rights as part of the fabric of society as a whole.

What is legal advice?

To capture the broad range of advice that people get in relation to their everyday legal problems (that are rooted in the social determinants of health), we define 'free legal advice' as advice that impacts on people's rights or entitlements, or that helps resolve a dispute with a private or public body. This is distinct from 'legal activities' as set out in section 12 of the Legal Services Act 2007, which identifies activities reserved to the legal profession, such as conducting litigation and probate. Legal advice will at times involve the legal profession, usually paid for, and the courts or tribunals, but often it will not be paid for, especially for social welfare issues, which are more likely to affect those that cannot afford to pay for advice. Advice may be for disputes between parties but will also include advice on people's legal entitlements and how to navigate systems relating to the enforcement of and application for social rights.

Free legal advice may be provided by a solicitor but does not have to be. Increasingly, especially in social welfare law, legal advice for everyday legal problems is provided by someone working in a voluntary and community sector (VCS) organization. In the years following the Legal Aid and Advice Act 1949 free legal advice was almost entirely provided through legal aid, and this was regulated and delivered by the legal profession. This has changed over time. The widening of legal aid contracts to be available to organizations outside traditional law firms, the introduction of Community Legal Advice Centres (CLACs) and Community Legal Advice Networks (CLANs) in the 1990s and the Legal Aid, Sentencing and Punishment of Offenders Act 2012 (LASPO) are just three examples of major steps that have changed the nature and significance of legal aid and, as a result, the delivery of free legal advice. We have now arrived at the point where hundreds of thousands of free legal advice cases every year are managed by people who are not regulated by the legal profession (other quality of advice standards usually apply to them), and whose services are not funded by the Ministry of Justice.

The juridification of social rights since the Second World War (Magnussen and Nilssen, 2013), and the fact that legal advice is an essential part of the civil rights that give meaning to the social rights promised by social citizenship, is part of the reason why this broad approach to defining legal advice and legal advice providers is necessary. The definition of free legal advice is not limited by who delivers, regulates or funds the advice. Broadly speaking, if an issue engages a person's rights and considers their personal circumstances in the context of applying for or enforcing those rights, then the advice they receive is legal in nature. In practice, this could come from a friend or neighbour as well as a legal professional, but the free legal advice services within scope of our research project are those delivered through organizations.

The level of advice does not need to be specialist casework or support for appeals at a court or tribunal, it can include all the levels of advice that we asked organizations to identify that they provide. This is supported by the definitions used by the Ministry of Justice and the Legal Services Board, which are not limited to legal aid funding or activities reserved for the qualified legal profession under the regulation of the Solicitors Regulation Authority (SRA). The level of advice just needs to be more than the provision of information.

This makes it clear that advice can be the regular, early legal advice that many LATAN members offer and which could be a one-off piece of casework or advice. The type of activities this could include are advice on filling out a welfare benefits form, understanding whether a person should receive holiday pay or is receiving the minimum wage, whether there are benefits that someone could receive, or the lawfulness of a landlord's demands of their tenant and so on. This has important policy implications in terms of the need to fund every stage of a person's journey towards resolution of a problem or claim. This need for the funding of 'early advice' has been duly recognized. For example, the Ministry of Justice started a small early legal advice pilot project in 2022 to offer holistic advice without means testing for a limited period of time per person. How organizations and services are delivering this early legal advice is part of the gap that we are exploring here and in our continuing research. One concern from the advice sector is that the focus on early legal advice is accompanied by a lack of recognition of the significance, seriousness and potential complexity of social welfare issues even at this early stage. The concern is that this could lead to funding limited to early advice as an alternative to funding casework and tribunal support to save money and lead to less effectiveness in fully resolving issues.

The Legal Services Board and the Law Society, in their jointly commissioned research into the legal needs of individuals in England and Wales, defines a legal issue as: 'A problem, issue or question that can be resolved or answered by law' (Legal Services Board and the Law Society, 2024: 5). In their research, the most common legal issues that people face fall in to the category of 'employment, finance, welfare and benefits'. The legal issues reported include those that involve a dispute between two parties, which is often the situation where casework and more complex legal advice is needed. It also, however, includes non-contentious legal advice that includes 'advisory work', which would be common in early legal advice in social welfare law delivered by VCS organizations. The point is that this acknowledges that the advice that VCS organizations offer is legal in nature and should be treated as such by policy makers. Its value to ensuring social rights and delivering anti-poverty and other similar initiatives, as well as access to justice more broadly, needs to be recognized in policy decision making at local and national political levels.

It is important to be clear about the distinction between information and advice. Information is a more autonomous and much lower-level service for clients than advice and will only be of limited assistance to many people with everyday legal problems. It may help with identification of legal issues, and help some sections of the population to address problems, such as those with higher social capital, education levels and legal capability. Information is of limited assistance, however, to those that have low levels of legal capability or complex and multifaceted social welfare problems, such as disputes with landlords, navigating welfare benefits processes, disputes about pay, immigration status or family law cases.

Having described and set out our understanding of these key foundational questions, in Chapter 3 we will introduce a further set of concepts about how free legal advice can break the cycle of health inequalities.

3

Bridging the Inequalities Gap: Addressing Poverty for Better Health

> We've seen quite a few single parents who have children under 16 and so many of their anxieties are attached to trying to get to work, usually on a zero-hours contract and get somebody to look after the kids for a couple of hours here and there. So, the anxieties and their health is suffering as a result of being in employment. So, they will be going to the GP [general practitioner], saying that I've got this headache, I have got this stress, I've got a rash, I have got this ... (Interview O3)

In this chapter we lay the groundwork (and there is a lot to lay) for our main argument that access to justice, health inequalities and poverty are bound up together. We present the UK's health inequalities and poverty context, which is essential for understanding the Liverpool Access to Advice Network (LATAN) and its wider significance for the policy recommendations we make.

Health and health inequalities

Who is responsible for your health? For ensuring you stay healthy? That was a question posed to a portion of the general population in 2021. It seems that most of us think we hold the keys to maintaining our health status (96 per cent). This makes sense to us. We feel like we have control over when, where and how we eat and exercise, things that we are often told are important for living healthy lives. Beyond the individual, we attribute responsibility for our health in the following order: the government (80 per cent), the National Health Service (NHS) (71 per cent) and finally, local authorities (64 per cent) (Kane et al, 2022).

Life expectancy at birth is an estimate of the number of years people are expected to live, assuming that the current levels of mortality will continue for the rest of someone's life. It is a robust measure of how healthy we are as a population, and clearly demonstrates health inequalities. Drawing on the latest available data in April 2025, the average life expectancy for newborn baby girls in England is 83.0 years and 79.1 years for newborn baby boys (ONS, 2024a). That is not terrible, but we are still some way off the pace of Japan, Switzerland and Korea, which have life expectancies above 85 for women and 80 for men (OECD, 2024).

We see large inequalities in life expectancy by region in England. For example, the South West is the best place to be born if you are a newborn baby girl, with a life expectancy of 84.0 years. If you are a newborn baby boy, you have won the life expectancy lottery if you are born in the South East, with a life expectancy of 80.3 years. Both are above England's average.

The region at the other end of the league table is the North East, where a newborn baby girl's life expectancy, on average, is 81.2 years and for boys it is 77.2 years. That is a difference of almost three years across the country for both girls and boys, simply based on your region of birth. To show the context locally, Liverpool is in the North West, which has a slightly better life expectancy of 81.4 years for girls and 77.4 years for boys, though still well short of the nation's best.

These are not small differences. Alarmingly, they are even greater when you consider life lived in good health (ONS, 2024b), that is, our estimated lifespan spent in either very good or good health, based on contemporary mortality rates and how people report their general health. The average *healthy* life expectancy for newborn baby girls is 61.9 in England, and 61.5 for newborn baby boys. For both girls and boys, the South East is the winner of most years lived in good health, with an average health life expectancy of 64.4 and 63.6 years respectively. Again, at the other end of the table is the North East, with average health life expectancy for newborn baby girls and newborn baby boys set at just 57.5 and 56.9 years, respectively.

That is quite something – that where you are born, specifically what part of the country, changes your expected life (and health) span. It seems that the majority of us who believe we, as individuals, are the determinants of our own health (Kane et al, 2022) are missing the bigger picture. The full league tables can be seen in Table 3.1 and Table 3.2, which describe both the average life expectancy at birth for women and men alongside healthy life expectancy at birth for the years 2021 to 2023. The tables also present the change in months from data collected before the COVID-19 pandemic (2017–19). From this, and looking at a longer time trend, research shows that the life expectancy in England has stagnated and started to decline. It has started to decline fastest for certain groups: women, who are now living longer in poorer health, and those living in deprived areas (Inquiry Panel on Health Equity for the North of England, 2014; Munford et al, 2023; Bambra et al, 2024).

Table 3.1: Average life expectancy (LE) and healthy life expectancy (HLE) at birth for women 2021–23 alongside the change in months from 2017–19 for England and regions

Region	Women			
	LE	Change (months)	HLE	Change (months)
England	83.0	−3.1	61.9	−22.3
North East	81.4	−4.4	57.5	−20.8
North West	81.6	−5.4	59.9	−27.0
Yorkshire & Humber	82.1	−4.2	59.3	−31.8
East Midlands	82.6	−3.7	60.2	−21.6
West Midlands	82.5	−4.9	60.0	−30.7
East of England	83.6	−2.1	63.2	−22.0
London	84.1	−2.7	64.0	−0.7
South East	84.1	−1.9	64.4	−22.9
South West	84.0	−1.1	62.9	−32.4

Source: ONS (2024a, 2024b)

Table 3.2: Average life expectancy (LE) and healthy life expectancy (HLE) at birth for men 2021–23 alongside the change in months from 2017–19 for England and regions

Region	Men			
	LE	Change (months)	HLE	Change (months)
England	78.9	−9.6	61.5	−20.1
North East	77.2	−9.6	56.9	−29.9
North West	77.3	−13.2	59.1	−31.0
Yorkshire & Humber	77.9	−1.8	58.8	−28.2
East Midlands	78.6	−10.8	60.4	−20.2
West Midlands	78.1	−12.0	60.3	−17.2
East of England	79.8	−7.2	62.9	−16.6
London	79.1	−14.4	63.9	2.2
South East	80.1	−7.2	63.5	−21.9
South West	80.0	−4.8	63.0	−25.8

Source: ONS (2024a, 2024b)

However, we also see variation within each region, where there are people living in areas of England with lower life expectancy who live far past it and vice versa. Can these differences be explained by our individual actions? Or are these findings about where we live, and what it is about where we live that impacts our choices? As you move down from the macro (England) to the micro (smaller and smaller) geographic regions you will see more differences in life expectancy within each area.

Liverpool in focus

Liverpool is a good example of this. On average, we have one of the lowest life expectancy and healthy life expectancy averages in England. But we can look at this more closely and see how different things are even within Liverpool. We see differences, of up to nine years in life expectancy, just four stops apart on Merseyrail (Liverpool's local train network), between Sandhills (where the average life expectancy is 75 years) and Mossley Hill (where life expectancy is 84 years; well above the North West and England average) (see Figure 3.1; Ashton, 2024). That is a 30 minute train journey or a 26 minute drive (on a bad traffic day) that could cost you nine years of life. This increases to almost 15 years if thinking about life lived in good health. We have presented just one health outcome here, but you will find similar patterns across multiple, if not all, physical and mental health outcomes over one's life course. This includes, for example, infant mortality, obesity, diabetes, cardiovascular diseases and depression (see Bambra, 2016).

Defining health inequalities

Today, our understanding of health inequalities is that they are systematic differences that we see between different groups of people. This is anchored in epidemiology and the social sciences and can be traced back to the Black Report (Townsend and Davidson, 1982). Only 260 copies of this seminal work were printed, it was published over a bank holiday weekend in an attempt to suppress its findings, and it was actively ignored by the UK government (Richmond, 2002). However, the report represented a turning point in our understanding of why there were huge inequalities in health. The authors presented an in-depth analysis of how ill health and mortality are distributed unevenly across the British population. The report highlighted that these inequalities had been growing, rather than shrinking, since the inception of the NHS in 1948. They concluded that the alarming inequalities were not the result of shortcomings in the NHS but associated with broader social factors – social inequalities, such as inequalities in income, education, housing, nutrition, employment and working conditions. At the time, they proposed a comprehensive social policy strategy to reduce the alarming health gap.

Figure 3.1: Life expectancy and deprivation (in quintiles) in Liverpool wards 2022–24, following the Merseyrail train stops

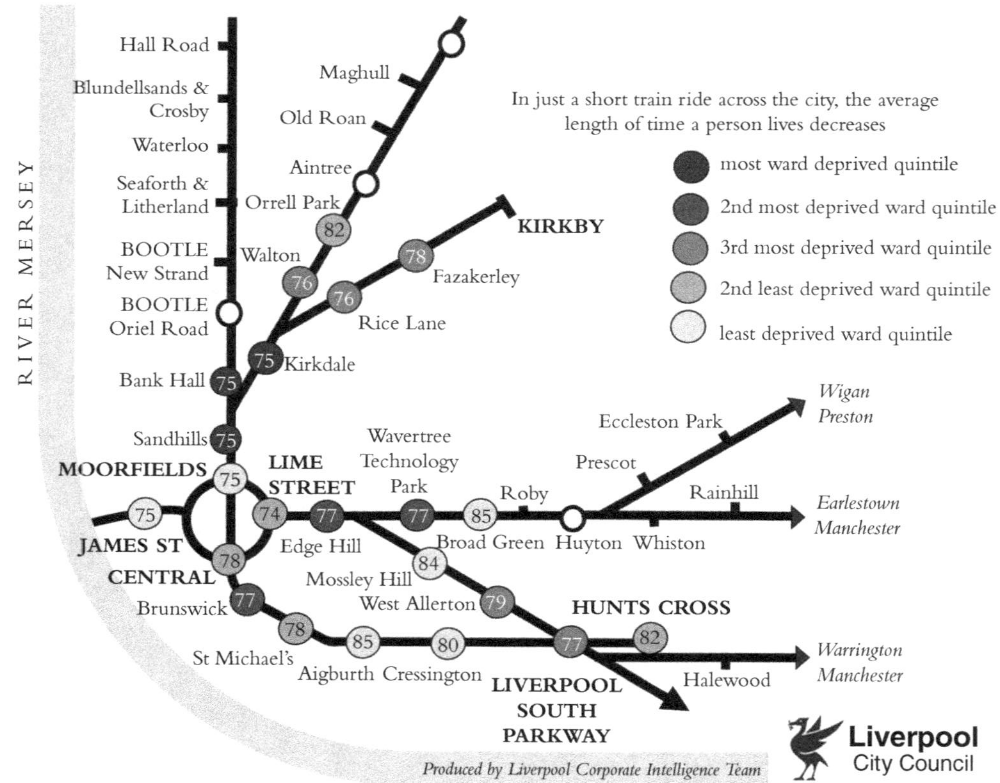

Source: Updated and produced by Liverpool Corporate Intelligence Team in relation to Liverpool City Council, *State of Health 2040 Report* (Ashton, 2024)

Many reports have come after this, for example the Acheson Report (Acheson, 2000), the Marmot Review (Marmot et al, 2010) and the Marmot Review: 10 Years On (Marmot et al, 2020) and the Child of the North report (Pickett et al, 2021) to name a few. All come to the same conclusions, to varying degrees: health inequalities are born out of differences in *access to resources* that are needed for good health. Our health is not solely dependent on our biology, genetics or behavioural characteristics – what we eat and how we choose to exercise – but also depends on something systematic and structural – how, as a *society*, we have chosen to distribute power, money and resources (with access to justice being one resource) to shape people's lives. This has a large role to play in deciding who lives, who dies and when.

This leads to the argument that health inequalities are unfair, they are unjust and perhaps most importantly for our discussion, they are avoidable. Any action to reduce health inequalities is not the sole responsibility of healthcare provision and health policy but relies on a wider provision of policy intervention and action. This means thinking about the potential for unintended consequences, like widening health inequalities as a result of changes to policy and at all levels of government.

This is not an easy task. Some inescapable global events and some local policy responses have impacted the extent to which we are able to take action. For example, over the last 15 years we have lived through the global financial economic crisis of 2008, through more than a decade of austerity-driven policies, the COVID-19 pandemic and, recently, continual, very sharp rises in the cost of living (described in Chapter 1). These affect us all, but they do not impact us all equally. Combined, they have had a catastrophic impact on health and health inequalities (Barr et al, 2015; Barr and Taylor-Robinson, 2016; Taylor-Robinson et al, 2019; Whitehead et al, 2020). The mechanisms that have led to these health declines and inequalities lie in the rises in poverty, inadequate education, insufficient housing and a dramatic increase in food insecurity, precarious work, unemployment and homelessness.

If we do not address these social, cultural, environmental and political factors that promote and support healthy living then we will *all* suffer. To improve health outcomes, it is recognized that action is needed across all the *social* determinants of health (Marmot et al, 2010), but improving these alone will not always reduce health inequalities. There is a need to distribute resources to all socio-economic groups, but with more resources going to those with greatest need (Wilkinson and Pickett, 2009).

But what are the social determinants of health?

Picture where you are right now reading this chapter. Are you warm, fed, safe and do you feel like you have time to carry on reading? Is your house warm enough for you? Is it safe for you? Do you just pay bills as soon as they come in? Do you have to travel far to do your weekly food shop? Are you able to budget easily and can you manage any debts you have? Do you have good employment opportunities when you are out of work or looking for different work? Are you able to access good healthcare when you need to? Are you able to take paid time off work? Is public transport accessible, and will it get you to where you need to go in time? If you are in education, or have children in education, does provision meet your need? If you have been pregnant, did you receive adequate maternity pay? Have you managed to get the welfare benefits you have applied for, maybe for a disability? Do you feel safe in your environment, in your country? Does your area facilitate social connections, for example, through libraries and creative spaces? Do you have access to green (parks, gardens, playing fields) and blue (rivers, lakes, oceans) spaces for pleasure and exercise?

If the answer to any of those questions is 'no', then there is a potential impact on your health. It is the answers to these questions that make up the experience of social determinants (for example, your income, education, employment, working conditions, housing and so on) of health. Problems in any of these experiences can lead to increases in stress and anxiety. They may lead to visits to the GP about a new or worsening mental health condition or cause or exacerbate a physical health condition. As Lawton et al (2011: 73) said:

> An elderly person continues to be at risk for a fall if he or she is not in a safe housing arrangement. A child living with asthma will continue to experience respiratory problems, no matter how much medicine is administered, if she or he returns to a mold-infested [sic] home. Repeated trips to the doctor will not help a cancer patient return to full health if he or she does not have access to adequate nutrition. For these patients and thousands of others, healthcare is necessary but insufficient. The key to better health is improving the social and environment conditions in which they live, work and play.

This is not all about what we choose to do as individuals (behavioural characteristics) but rather how our world is set up. Area-level characteristics – household, community, local authority, region and country – interact to give us, potentially, the best possible start in life, and to some extent determine our social positions in life, what we 'choose to do', and our health.

The WHO describes the social determinants of health as the 'conditions that people are born into, grow, work, live and age, and the wider set of forces and systems shaping the conditions of daily life' (WHO, 2013). They suggest that the social determinants can be more important than healthcare or lifestyle choices in influencing health. 'For example, numerous studies suggest that social determinants of health account for between 30–55% of health outcomes' (WHO, nd).

Evidence from the *European Health Equity Status Report* attributed five key social factors that drive health inequalities between regions (WHO, 2019):

1. income security and social protection (that is, affordability of goods and services essential to living a dignified, decent and independent life);
2. living conditions (including housing deprivation, fuel deprivation, access to green space, crime, overcrowding, air quality and food deprivation);
3. social and human capital (differences in educational outcomes, lack of trust and political voice);
4. health services (that is, quality of services, affordability and unmet need);
5. employment and working conditions (employment status and excessive hours).

Dahlgren and Whitehead (1991) introduced the influential conceptual 'social determinants of health rainbow model' to describe these broad categories of established social, cultural, environmental and political factors (as opposed to the biological or genetic ones) that influence population health (see Figure 3.2).

At the centre of the rainbow model sit individuals, with a set of defined and somewhat 'fixed' characteristics (for example, biological and genetic factors). Surrounding them are layers that describe examples of individual and lifestyle factors (for example, our physical activity, eating habits, alcohol use), social and community networks (who is in our social circle, family and beyond), living and working conditions (for example, access to and opportunities for jobs, housing, education and welfare services) and general socio-economic, cultural and environmental (and political) conditions (how our world is structurally set up) that have an influence on health. The layers in the model denote a simplified and well understood visual representation of *what* influences can impact health beyond those that are fixed. Each component (or social determinant) is interconnected with and between other components across layers and can influence each other. For example, many individual lifestyle factors are structurally determined by wider social determinants of health. The determinants in the model can be health-promoting, protective or health-damaging and can be utilized in multiple ways to understand the core drivers of both good and bad health outcomes.

Contextualized adaptations

Since the model's introduction over 30 years ago it has seen several adaptations. One recent example focuses specifically on the social determinants of child health (Pearce et al, 2019). This model adds layers at the centre that account for the additional social environments that are important for understanding child health. This includes parental and child health behaviours (for example, the interactions between parent and

Figure 3.2: Illustration of the social determinants of health rainbow model, identifying the key social determinants of population health, adapted in 2007 to reflect the interconnectivity between layers

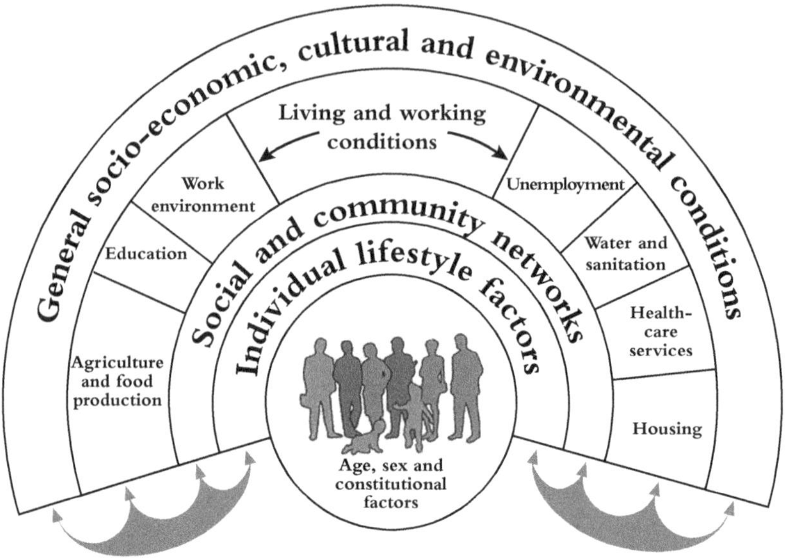

Source: Dahlgren and Whitehead (2021)

child – parenting or caring). This is followed by the parents' and carers' own mental and physical health, which is likely to impact their children's health. Next are layers more closely related to the original Dahlgren and Whitehead model (1991) that describe resources within the household, such as housing quality and income, and then there are layers that are more external determinants, such as community (local crime, services, social connections and walkability), living and working conditions (welfare, housing, schools, childcare) and finally the socio-economic, cultural, commercial, political and physical climate.

Over these 30 plus years there have also been debates about potential determinants and influences omitted from the model's original design that may be important in today's context. For example, some have considered the importance of commercial determinants of health (Maani et al, 2020), digital determinants of health (Rice and Sara, 2019), and racism as an important determinant of health (Paradies et al, 2015). Rather than reworking the model, Dahlgren and Whitehead (2021) have described each of these as 'driving forces' that extend into all aspects of the rainbow model and conceptualize the individual experiences with the institutional and structural processes that underpin all determinants described in the original model. The social determinants of health models help us understand *what* impacts population health and that differences in access to resources can lead to inequalities in health across different groups of people in our society.

Access to justice and the social determinants of health

In the somewhat limited literature addressing law and the social determinants of health, there have been varying approaches to how the impact of law should be considered. Parmet et al discussed 'Law' as a social determinant of health:

> Law is one of the most important determinants of health. It helps establish the framework in which individuals and populations live, face disease and injury and eventually die. By so doing, Law influences myriad of other social determinants, including education, income, housing, racial and ethnic disparities, nutrition and access to health care. In short, Law is one factor that helps determine other social determinants. (2011: 21)

Genn focused on the bidirectional relationship between law and ill health and how social needs become unmet legal needs that can be ameliorated through legal advice. Somewhat like the rainbow model, she described 'macro', 'meso or local' and 'individual' levels of the effect of law on health (2019). Lawton et al (2011) conceived of meeting unmet legal need as a social determinant of health. Teitelbaum and Lawton identified that legal issues are 'embedded' in most of the social determinants (2017).

We consider that Dahlgren and Whitehead would likely identify law as a driving force, in line with their discussion of how commercial, digital and racism determinants should be appropriately accounted for in the rainbow model (2021). This framing feels most intuitive to us and seems in line with most of the earlier approaches, which describe how access to justice and law interact across the social determinants. Law, specifically a 'thick' or substantive concept of justice, as we discussed in the last chapter, has the potential to affect whether social determinants have positive, neutral or negative effects on population health at multiple layers of the model. Think back to the questions we asked at the beginning of this section: about living in a warm and secure house, having a job with secure hours in safe working conditions that provides paid time off, having enough money to manage bills and debts or accessing education that meets your child's needs, and so on. It is evident that law has a role in creating, exacerbating, ameliorating or improving those conditions. We have demonstrated this in Figure 3.3, which explores how access to justice interacts with social determinants of health throughout the rainbow model. In the left-hand column, we have conceptualized how access to justice broadly impacts each layer of social determinants. In the right, we have illustrated this using an example from employment law.

Figure 3.3: Illustration of the role of access to justice in the social determinants of health rainbow model, with concrete examples from employment

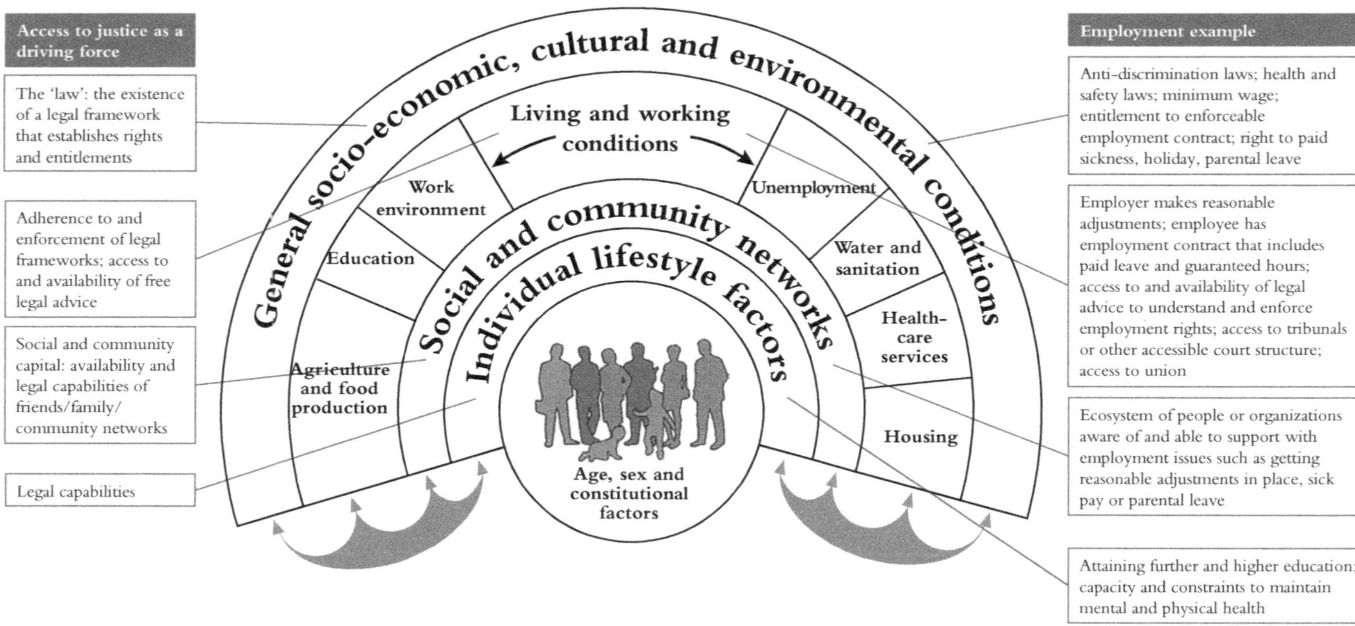

Source: Adapted from Dahlgren and Whitehead (2021)

At the outer layer of the rainbow – general socio-economic, cultural and environmental conditions – law creates the frameworks that establish rights and obligations that govern those conditions. For example, in the UK the Equality Act 2010 prohibits landlord discrimination against potential renters due to a protected characteristic. Landlords also have an obligation to maintain rented properties in good repair and to ensure essential service provision under the Landlord and Tenant Act 1985. Employment rights established through the law ensure better working conditions and safety at work, while children's rights ensure that special educational needs and disabilities (SEND) provision is supported at school.

Central policies, which can help to challenge power differentials in society, can affect whether or not there are paths and resources available for access to justice at the other layers of the model. The Legal Aid, Sentencing and Punishment of Offenders Act 2012 (LASPO) offers a clear example of this, showing how reducing resources for legal aid shifts power towards those that can afford legal representation.

The role of law and access to justice is perhaps most intuitively understood in terms of the 'living and working conditions' layer of the model. Access to legal advice at this level can affect our societal conditions through enabling claims based on central policies that embed rights or employer duties, such as those identified in the previous paragraph. Advice can help to ensure that any welfare benefits claim has a fair resolution and to challenge it in a social security tribunal if it does not. These can all help reduce the potential toxic effect social determinants can have on us.

At the 'social and community networks' layer of the rainbow model, access to justice can ensure that local systems exist to connect individuals to the advice they need. These networks can help individuals understand the legal dimensions of their problems. The landmark Civil Litigation Research Project in the United States characterized these networks as 'agents of transformation', responsible for helping individuals with 'naming', 'blaming' and claiming' – identifying that they had a legal problem, framing a solution and seeking redress (Felstiner et al, 1981: 635–7, 639–49; Albiston and Sandefur, 2013). These networks can fill in where individuals' legal capability falls short. We might think of this as 'community legal capital', an extension of the conceptualization of social capital by Putnam (2000). LATAN is an example of a project that seeks to increase community legal capital.

Finally, at the innermost circle, access to justice can increase individuals' legal capability. Galanter argued that an individual's personal capability is the biggest barrier to accessing justice (1976). Legal capability has been linked to Nobel Laureate Amartya Sen's capability approach (CA) (Pleasence and Balmer, 2019; Watkins, 2022). To Sen, an individual's capability was the 'the substantive freedom to achieve alternative functioning combinations (or less formally put, the freedom to achieve various lifestyles)' (1999: 75).

According to the CA, we need to consider not just access to resources but the contexts in which individuals live and their different needs. Martha Nussbaum has further developed the CA to define a set of 'central human capabilities': life; bodily health; bodily integrity; senses, imagination and thought; emotions; practical reason; affiliation; other species; play; and control over one's environment (Nussbaum, 2007). In terms of legal capability, Coulamares et al considered this to be the personal characteristics that are needed for an individual to be able to resolve legal problems effectively (2012). An Organisation for Economic Co-operation and Development (OECD) report arrived at an agreed definition of legal capability: 'the ability to recognise legal issues; awareness of law, services and processes; the ability to research law, services and processes; and the ability to deal with law-related problems (involving, for example, confidence, communication skills and resilience)' (OECD, 2019: 86). The people that LATAN member organizations support are likely to have low levels of legal capability. The Legal Services Board, following a survey based on the OECD criteria, found that: 'Low legal capability affects a significant minority of the population and extends beyond obviously vulnerable groups. Over a third of all participants had low levels of self-efficacy and legal confidence, and nearly one in five perceived the justice system as inaccessible' (Legal Services Board, 2020).

To fully understand how best to intervene to reduce health inequalities caused by social determinants we need to move from the rainbow model, which illustrates *what* are key determinants of population health. We next move towards another model, the Diderichsen et al (2001) model, which helps us understand *how* we can embed access to justice to conceptualize pathways and mechanisms to benefit health and reduce health inequalities within our societies.

Box 3.1: What is the life course framework?

Life course epidemiology aims to explore the effects of social determinants of health as exposures or risk factors for health outcomes across the lifespan (that is preconception, early, mid to late life), to help identify the most effective preventative approaches for intervention.

Life course approaches bring together complex causal inference methodology to explore the effects of differential exposures, how they may function, interact and vary over time on health outcomes. Wagner et al (2024) present four approaches that researchers use to explore life course epidemiology:

Understanding **sensitive periods**: exploring specific sensitive periods (for example, experiences of early childhood poverty and the effect this has on child, adolescent and adult mental health outcomes.

Understanding **accumulative effects**: exploring the effect of persistent exposures on health outcomes, for example, the experiences of persistent poverty at multiple points in time and over different stages of life. This could also include additional persistent exposures. For example, the experience of persistent poverty and persistent poor housing on health.

Understanding **pathways**: focusing on the sequential link between multiple different exposures, in that one exposure places someone at an increased risk for another exposure and so on, also known as 'chain of risk'.

Understanding **social mobility**: commonly used in understanding socio-economic exposures and exploring the effect of moving in and out of exposures or risk factors. For example, exploring the effect on mental health of moving in and out of employment or in and out of poverty, or in and out of the benefit system.

Policy intervention points

The work of Diderichsen et al (2001) helps conceptualize the pathways to health inequalities *within a population*. It offers potential policy intervention points: this describes the *how*. The model uses a life course approach (see Box 3.1) to describe four mechanisms that lead to health inequalities and the wider social consequences, and depicts four potential policy intervention points. This has been helpful in understanding how some groups of people are more or less impacted by specific toxic exposures like poverty. For example, Whitehead et al (2020, 2021) use the model to describe the mechanisms by which both COVID-19 (the virus) and the mitigation strategies designed to stop the spread of infection (lockdown, social distancing, isolation, working from home) did not impact us all equally. Our social position, employment roles, health status and capacity to isolate, all contributed to the large inequalities we saw in deaths due to COVID-19 (Whitehead et al, 2020, 2021).

We have replicated Diderichsen et al's (2001) model, for our purposes, to describe how access to free legal advice has the capacity to intervene and change both the individual and wider social consequences of health inequalities (see Figure 3.4). Access to free legal advice offers one potential solution to change the face of health outcomes and to reduce health inequalities for all of us, particularly when large national policy changes are limited. The mechanisms of inequality outlined in Diderichsen et al's (2001) model are:

- Social stratification – this can be defined as someone's starting point, the social context and the distribution of power in society that influences one's social position. For example, people with characteristics that are discriminated against may have a 'lower social position' relative to power.
- Differential exposure – this is how a person's social position affects their exposure to health harms. For example, people who are born to parents who did not finish school are more likely to be exposed to poverty than those born to university-educated parents.

- Differential vulnerability – this is how your social position affects your vulnerability to an exposure. For example, for the same level of poverty, a person born to parents who did not finish school is more likely to struggle with their mental health than a person born to university-educated parents. This is often related to the way harmful experiences cluster and interact.
- Differential consequences – this is how your social position affects the consequences of ill health. For example, for the same level of poverty and poor mental health, a person born to parents without school education may be less likely to access specialist mental health services or receive high-quality care than a person born to university-educated parents.

The model describes four policy entry points (labelled A–D in Figure 3.4) that specifically target each mechanism of inequality and have the potential

Figure 3.4: Conceptual model of mechanisms of health inequalities, including access to justice intervention points with examples in grey boxes

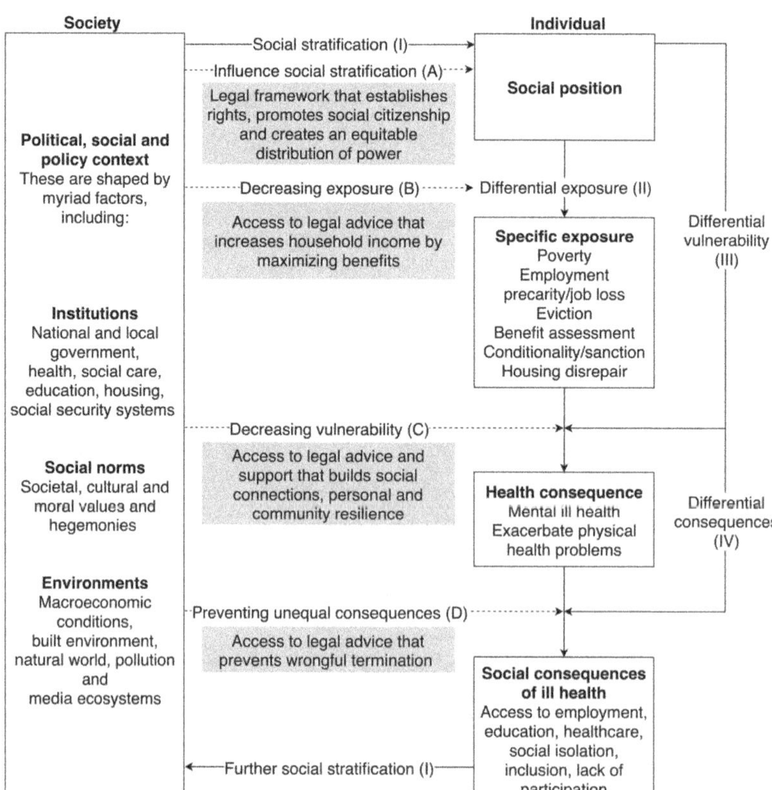

Source: Adapted from Diderichsen et al (2001)

to interrupt those pathways to inequalities. Policy entry point A describes policies that have the capacity to directly change the way we, as a society, stratify people, to change a person's social position, ideally leading to more equal access to (social) justice. This is our legal framework – examples of this in our model may include reducing the wage gap between the highest and lowest earners within organizations, or enforcing equal pay laws between genders, as well as a more generous welfare system and greater funding for free legal advice. This has the potential to reduce inequalities between people's socio-economic status.

Policy entry point B describes policies that directly impact the specific exposure and are an obvious entry point for legal advice intervention. In social welfare law, legal advice related to (but not limited to) evictions, access to welfare benefits or challenging decisions on sanctions or advice that helps resolve workplace issues offer the potential to maximize income and avoid the most serious everyday legal problems, thereby protecting against potential health harms. Alcock et al have a logic model for the potential health benefits of advice interventions (2013). LATAN and similar partnerships have an important role to play here through improving access to (often limited) free legal advice by developing a community of practice and a referral system.

Policy entry point C describes policies that intervene to minimize the health consequences after an exposure, such as an eviction, has occurred. In the example presented in Figure 3.4 we describe how legal advice can build social connections and resilience, enhance perceptions of legal capabilities, or simply embody the idea that a problem shared is a problem halved. This can help alleviate the weight of the problem so that a person does not feel alone when dealing with such an overwhelming issue, and it can help the person connect with other support services. At this point, policies connected to the delivery of free legal advice are important, but perhaps traditionally less obvious. Relatively recent approaches to minimize health consequences after an exposure are health–justice partnerships or other forms of co-located advice services. Co-location of advice services is discussed further in Chapter 6. These policies recognize the connection between free legal advice and the work and living conditions that are social determinants of health – as highlighted in the 'rainbow' diagram shown in Figure 3.2 – and the role of the different gateway and advice organizations in the free legal advice ecosystem.

Finally, policy entry point D offers a possible intervention point for those experiencing the negative health consequences of an exposure and their vulnerability to it. Free legal advice offers options to mitigate against someone in this position experiencing worse outcomes because of their socio-economic position. This may be supporting someone to access reasonable adjustments at work after they have already experienced ill health arising from an eviction or an accident. It may be advice for someone that is facing unfair dismissal from their employment. Or it may be to stop further discrimination that might follow on from their health problem, accident or subsequent disability. This brings us towards the more traditional approach to access to justice: the approach to access to justice that focuses on courts and tribunals and advice from a legal professional. In order to avoid the unequal social consequences of health problems at this point, fair access to a court or solicitor is often very important. The imposition of fees in employment tribunals, the decimation of legal aid, the digitalization of legal and court processes are examples of access to justice issues that will impact the ability to prevent unequal consequences at this intervention point.

Our conceptual model (Figure 3.4) demonstrates how access to justice and access to free legal advice can disrupt the pathways to health inequalities. This means it can limit the potentially negative cycle where problems in one social exposure lead to further problems in others. Problems related to welfare benefits and work are often an important part of reducing this negative cycle and the cumulative clustered effect they have. As an example of this negative cycle, timely employment advice might prevent a situation where an employee is forced to accept unsafe or unfair working conditions, or is wrongfully terminated, disrupting the rest of the cycle by helping maintain social position (for example, through continued payment of rent) and reducing health consequences. These problems are often part of the everyday grind of a life that fluctuates towards and away from destitution.

While it is clear that action is needed across all the social determinants of health to readdress one's social position, there are some determinants that can be viewed as distinct (food insecurity, employment), while others *bleed* into or underpin many, if not all, other determinants (poverty, for instance). Some examples of how we have tried to reduce health inequalities by targeting poverty specifically are demonstrated later in the text (see the section 'Why is it important to think about poverty'). But what is less well understood, and where there is potential for further action, are the clear legal dimensions and opportunities to reduce the health-damaging effects of inequality through access to free legal advice that specifically targets poverty. It is to poverty that we turn next.

Poverty: what is it and how do we measure it?

Poverty is a well-established driver (or social determinant) of many of the poor health outcomes we see in the UK today. Moreover, it is clear that poverty can be intertwined with and impact other social determinants, leading to widening social inequalities and worse health outcomes. Poverty is about lacking the resources needed to thrive in society. Peter Townsend (for his biography, see Renwick, 2023), professor of international social policy at the London School of Economics and Political Science (LSE), social policy campaigner and co-founder of the Child Poverty Action Group and the Disability Alliance, outlined in 1979:

> Individuals, families and groups in the population can be said to be in poverty when they lack resources to obtain the type of diet, participate in the activities and have the living conditions and amenities which are customary, or at least widely encouraged and approved, in the societies in which they belong. (Townsend, 1979: 31)

How we think about poverty matters. It is political; understanding how we decide to define and measure poverty as a society determines how we choose to support people facing adversity (Wickham et al, 2016). This includes how we organize ourselves as a society to explore the causes and consequences of poverty – what we decide is important and how and *if* we choose to take action. This is at the core of social citizenship as a concept (described in Chapters 2 and 8).

In the UK, area levels of deprivation can be calculated using the Index of Multiple Deprivation (IMD) (Ministry of Housing, Communities and Local Government, 2019a). This ranks small areas in England from the most deprived to the least deprived, relatively speaking. It is made up of seven domains that are weighted. This combines assessments of the local area that measure: income (22.5 per cent: the proportion of the population in low income); employment (22.5 per cent: the proportion of the population excluded from the labour market); education (13.5 per cent: the educational and skill attainment); health (13.5 per cent: risk of premature death and poor mental and physical health); crime (9.3 per cent: risk of personal and material victimization); barriers to housing and services (9.3 per cent: physical and financial accessibility of housing and local services); and, finally, living environment (9.3 per cent: quality of indoor and outdoor environment). We can look at the whole IMD (see Figure 3.5) or we can take specific domains (for example, Figure 3.6) to explore the geographic patterns of poverty. This is extremely useful to researchers, voluntary and community sector (VCS) organizations, local authorities and central government to understand funding needs or target resources to an area based on deprivation status. It is not recorded every year, so to capture acute experiences and changes in poverty over time we turn to other measures for both research and policy.

A consistent poverty measure (recorded annually since 1995) that is used by quantitative researchers and the government is based on experiences of low income, or 'households below the average income' (HBAI) (Department for Work and Pensions, 2025a; Francis-Devine, 2025). Data provides information on the number of people living below a median income threshold of the

Figure 3.5: Average IMD (2019) scores in England's local authorities

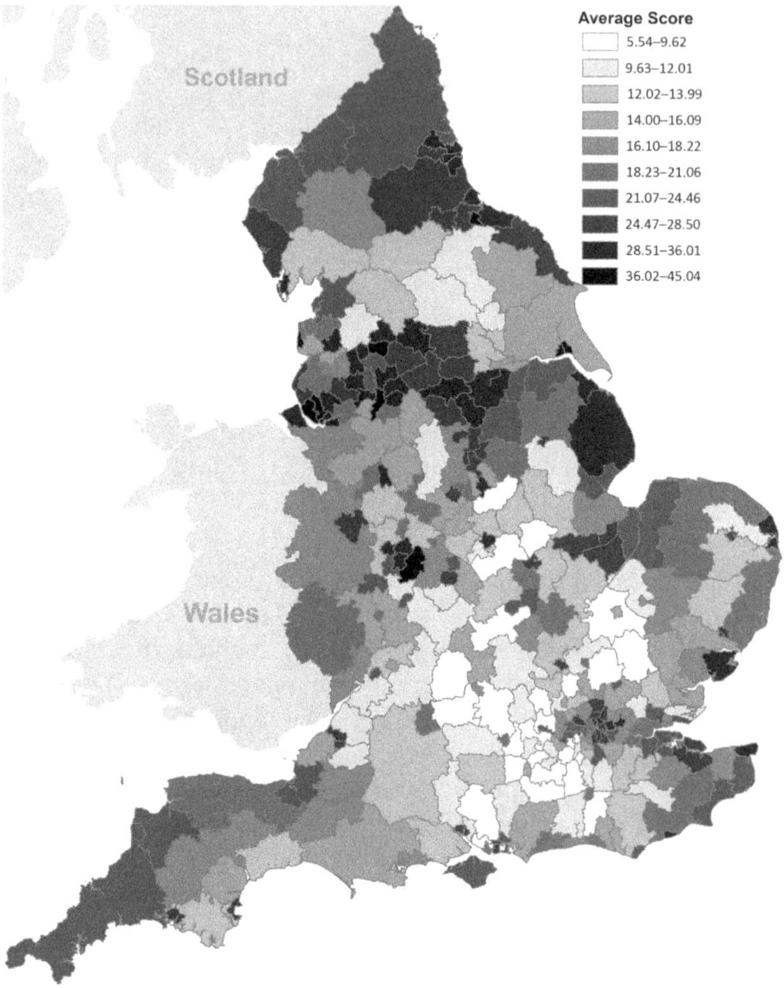

Note: Average levels of deprivation are in greyscale. Darker scores indicate higher levels of deprivation.

Source: Ministry of Housing, Communities and Local Government (2019b)

population, both before housing costs (BHC) and after household costs (AHC). 'Housing costs' refers to the *inescapable* costs of rent payments and mortgage interest payments, as well as other housing specific costs such as water rates, community and council water charges, and also ground rents and services charges for owner-occupied households, and these costs will be reflected in the number of people reported as being in poverty. As AHC adjusts for inescapable costs, the number of people reported in poverty will always be higher than the those reported BHC – you can see this in the next

Figure 3.6: Average IMD (2019) scores for the income specific domain in England

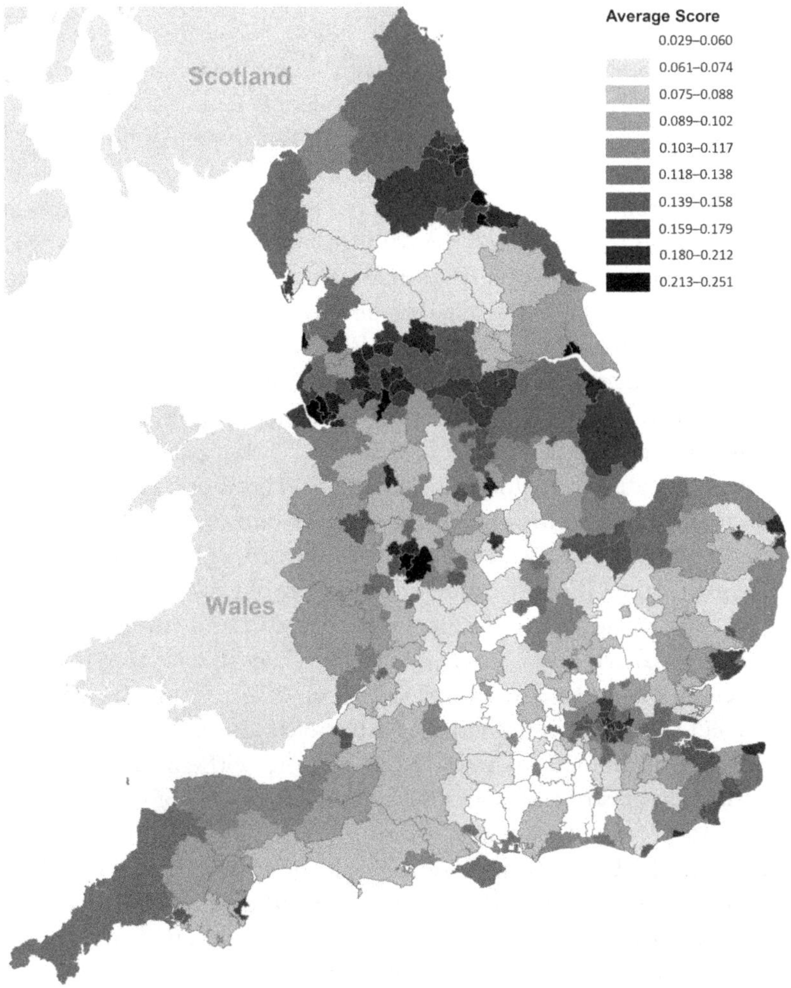

Note: Average levels of income deprivation are in greyscale. Darker scores indicate higher levels of income deprivation.

Source: Ministry of Housing, Communities and Local Government (2019c)

section, 'The scale and depth of poverty in England'. What is not included in AHC data is mortgage capital repayments as these are seen as a form of asset. There are two main indicators that we use – relative poverty and absolute poverty. Relative poverty, which recognizes that standards of living change over time, uses the current year's population median income to classify poverty thresholds. Absolute poverty is measured against a static threshold that only rises with inflation, therefore does not account for society becoming more or less prosperous. This measure indicates individuals living in poverty getting better or worse off in absolute terms. In the UK we tend to classify individuals as living in poverty if their household income falls below 60 per cent of the median income of the population. Individuals are classified as living in deep poverty if their household income falls below 50 per cent of the median income of the population. Finally, individuals and households are measured as living in very deep poverty if household income falls below 40 per cent of the median income of the population (Joseph Rowntree Foundation, 2024).

There are also other measurements of poverty in the UK that have been used for research and policy purposes. For example, the Joseph Rowntree Foundation (JRF) introduced the Minimum Income Standard (MIS) as a benchmark measure in 2008 (Bradshaw et al, 2008). Rather than focusing on poverty specifically, the charity developed an income threshold or benchmark against which to measure households that the general public have agreed is needed to live with dignity. This has been designed using focus group discussions of the income needs for different household set-ups (for example, a single adult who is working age, compared to a lone parent with two children in secondary school or a couple with two children in primary school). The topics for consideration were broken down into broad categories such as amount of income needed for food and drink, clothes, domestic fuel, other household costs, household goods and services, personal goods and services, travel and social and cultural participation (Davis et al, 2024). The JRF updates the measure to keep the MIS 'relevant to today's society' (Davis et al, 2024: 5) and has considered the absolute numbers of individuals living below the MIS, individuals with 75 per cent of the MIS, which describes those with an increased risk of material deprivation, and individuals with 50 per cent of the MIS, which includes those in deeper poverty with increased challenges to meet their essential needs. Using this measure could provide valuable information for policy makers to understand poverty, based on household set-up and what people need to live above a societally agreed consensus. It may be considered as a benchmark for a national living wage and social welfare benefit levels, for example.

An alternative measure used to explore those in extreme poverty is defined as destitution. Fitzpatrick et al (2023: 11) describe destitution as those that 'cannot afford to meet their most basic physical needs to stay warm, dry, clean and fed'. Someone can be said to be experiencing destitution if they meet one of the following criteria: (1) material deprivation, that is, lacking two or more of six essentials in the last month because they were unable to afford them. This includes shelter, food, heating their home, lighting their home, weather-appropriate clothing and footwear, and basic toiletries. Alternatively, they could be (2) in receipt of extremely low income, so are unable to purchase these essential items for themselves and with insufficient savings to make up for the income shortfall.

There are other measures that cover dimensions of poverty, such as material deprivation, this measure describes the number of working-age adults, children and pensioners that do not have the necessary items or access to activities for an acceptable standard of living (Department for Work and Pensions, 2024). There are also measures of fuel poverty (Department for Energy Security and Net Zero, 2025) and food poverty (Francis-Devine et al, 2024).

The Social Metrics Commission (SMC) has developed one of the most recent measures of poverty adopted by the UK government. Its aim was to build a measure that 'better reflects the nature and experiences of poverty that different families in the UK have, and can be used to build a consensus around poverty measurement and action in the UK' (SMC, 2023). The measure combines all household material resources alongside income (for example liquid assets) relative to the population median, and then adjusts for other factors such as inescapable costs that extend beyond housing, for example the cost of childcare and disability, and levels of overcrowding. At the start of 2024 the UK government released its new measure of poverty based on the SMC's proposal entitled 'Below Average Resources' (BAR) (Department for Work and Pensions, 2025b). These have been presented alongside the reported HBAI statistics. The estimates of people living in poverty broadly appear similar between those based on HBAI or BAR. However, where they differ offers important reflections. The new measure shows higher levels of poverty experienced by certain groups of people, such as children, single-parent families and families where someone in the household is living with a disability (Addario et al, 2024; Department for Work and Pensions, 2025c), which is likely to be the result of including liquid assets and high inescapable costs such as childcare. As this is a relatively new measure, there is no research using the BAR to explore its impact on health outcomes and health inequalities (yet).

The scale and depth of poverty in England

For comparison purposes we discuss the scale and depth of poverty using the most recent common year (2022–23). However, for some poverty measurements there has been an additional year of data released, and this can be seen in Figure 3.7. In 2022–23 14.3 million people in the UK were living in relative poverty after housing costs. That is 21.4 per cent of all people. Of these, 8.1 million were working-age adults (19.9 per cent), 4.3 million were children (29.9 per cent of children) and 1.9 million were pensioners (15.9 per cent of pensioners). There were 6.2 million (24.2 per cent) people living in a house where someone has a disability who were living in poverty, including 1.9 million children (34.2 per cent of children in families where someone has a disability) (Department for Work and Pensions, 2025d). According to the MIS, there were 24 million people (35.9 per cent) living

Figure 3.7: Number of people (in millions) living in poverty defined by alternative measurements in the UK between 2003/04 and 2023/24

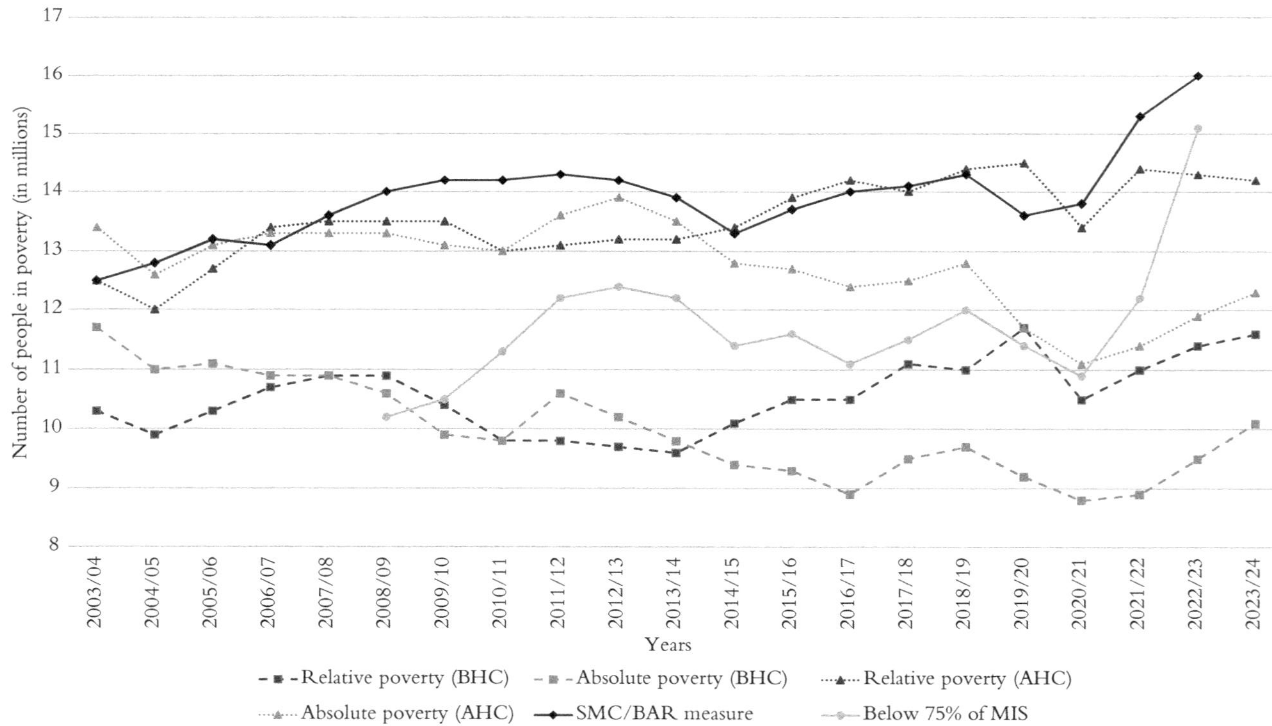

Note: For absolute poverty figures, 2010/11 represents the year that the median income was held constant in real terms.

Source: Department for Work and Pensions (2025d, 2025e) and Robinson et al (2025)

below the MIS in 2022–23: this included 14.2 million working-age adults (35.0 per cent), 7 million children (48.6 per cent) and 2.8 million pensioners (23.6 per cent) (Robinson et al, 2025). These are worryingly higher than those reported by income alone (that is, relative and absolute income) poverty measures. When considering those living below 75 per cent of MIS figures are more comparable to the relative income poverty measures – see Figure 3.7. Within the destitution data, in 2022 there were 3.8 million people affected by experiences of destitution. This includes just over one million children. These figures have more than doubled since 2017–18, when it was estimated that around 1.5 million people were affected by destitution (Fitzpatrick et al, 2023). Without action, poverty levels are predicted to continue to rise and by 2027–28 there will be 4.4 million children living in poverty, as measured by HBAI (AHC), with predictions that this will be largely made up of children in larger families (Hirsch, 2023).

The BAR (Department for Work and Pensions, 2025e) figures are similar, albeit higher, with 24 per cent of people living in poverty, which equates to 16 million people. They also show that 4.5 million people (6.7 per cent of the UK population) are living in deep poverty, estimated as between 25.1 and 50 per cent below the BAR poverty line. They describe higher rates of working-age and child poverty, with 9.2 million working-age adults in poverty (22.8 per cent) and 5.2 million children in poverty (36.4 per cent). Half of the children living in poverty are made up of children living in larger families (with three or more children). They report lower rates of pension poverty with 1.5 million pension age adults in poverty (12.8 per cent), compared with the HBAI statistics. These differences will, in large part, be attributable to how the measure is composed (whether it accounts for the inescapable costs beyond housing costs such as childcare and the inclusion of liquid assets). Figure 3.7 shows the number of people, in millions, living in poverty over time based on the total HBAI and BAR measures. It is clear from this that how we choose to conceptualize poverty has an impact on who is in poverty and how important we think it is, and will consequently influence policy decisions. For example, over time, absolute poverty figures have by and large had a declining trajectory, compared with relative figures that have a rising trajectory. The BAR measure starts at the same point as relative poverty after housing costs in 2003–4 but ends much higher in 2022–23.

Every geographical leap down you will find differences in poverty exposure. If we focus on the HBAI relative child poverty (AHC), for example, in England there are huge differences, with the West Midlands having the highest percentage of children in relative poverty with 39 per cent, followed by the North West (37 per cent), North East, and East Midlands (both at 30 per cent). The lowest percentages of child poverty in England is in the East of England (23 per cent) followed by South East (25 per cent) and

South West (27 per cent) (Loughborough University Centre for Research in Social Policy, 2024).

If you compare parliamentary constituencies within each region, research shows that the North West has the highest rate of constituencies (90 per cent) with 25 per cent or more children living in poverty. This is followed by both the North East and West Midlands with 89 per cent. At the other end of the scale is the East of England, with 31 per cent followed by the South East (44 per cent) and South West (64 per cent). In all cases the North fares worse than the South (Loughborough University Centre for Research in Social Policy, 2024). All these numbers have been rising and rising fast. Indeed, it has been 20 years since there have been any prolonged periods of falling poverty (Joseph Rowntree Foundation, 2024).

Liverpool in focus

Drawing on the latest available data to us, across the 64 wards that make up Liverpool, 40 have at least 25 per cent of children living in relative poverty. The highest rates of child poverty, where almost 8 in 10 children (79.5 per cent) are living in poverty, is found in Arundel (where James lived until recently). This is followed by Princes Park, Smithdown and Waterfront North, where almost 6 in 10 children (57.9 per cent, 57.8 per cent and 57.7 per cent respectively) live in poverty. At the other end of the scale, Mossley Hill, Aigburth (where Sophie lives now), Allerton and Calderstones, all have under 7 per cent of children living in poverty (see Figure 3.8).

Understanding poverty trends over time and between different places is not the only focus. Understanding who is living in poverty is also of paramount importance. We have touched on child poverty here but significant amounts of research and reports have highlighted the inadequate and rising levels of poverty, including 'in-work poverty', that are particularly affecting vulnerable groups such as single parents, larger families and people living with a disability (Social Metrics Commission, 2023; Department for Work and Pensions, 2025b). This tells us something important about how the wider social, political and economic environment affects these trends. How we choose to define and capture poverty can elucidate the multifaceted impact it has on health outcomes (Inquiry Panel on Health Equity for the North of England, 2014). Poverty data show policy makers where resources are needed.

The poverty measure we use can have an impact on how we understand and respond to poverty. Each of the measures we have described in detail extends the reach of the population captured. Much of the research that explores the health impact of poverty (see the next section, 'Why is it important to think about poverty') in the UK (ours included) uses the relative income

Figure 3.8: Child poverty rates (%) in Liverpool wards

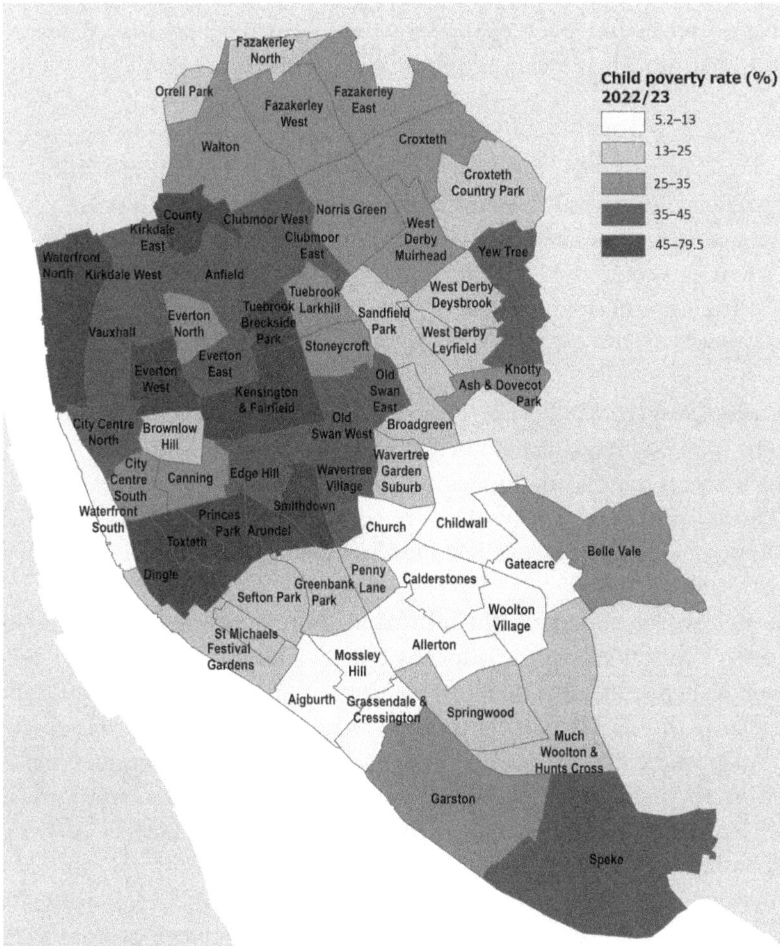

Note: Darker colours indicate high levels of child poverty.

Source: DWP, 'Children in low income households (0–15-year-olds)', LCC Corporate Intelligence Team analysis, September 2024

measures of poverty (using HBAI (AHC) statistics) as it reflects the changing standards of living over time, considers the disposable income available to households and has been consistently reported for many years, allowing for between and within country comparisons.

Why is it important to think about poverty?

LATAN members reflected on the experiences of poverty and the distressing impact it is likely to have:

> I can't imagine what it is like for our service users when you've got a woman calling up and saying, I have got three kids to feed and I only live on what, just over £70.00 a week, what do I do, do I feed my kids first, do I buy cleaning products second? (Interview Q1)

Of course, any level of poverty is bad. It is so clear that not having enough income leads to a lack of resources across a wide spectrum of individual and societal factors that it seems inevitable that it can lead to poorer health outcomes. That has been established, hopefully here, but in greater detail elsewhere (Cooper and Stewart, 2013, 2017; Alston, 2018; Marmot et al, 2010). It is important to think about the following three findings researchers have set out:

1. Rising poverty will lead to poorer health outcomes.
2. The massive inequalities in health and societal inequalities will continue to widen if we do not address poverty.
3. This will affect us all as with every social gradient increase (or decrease) in income (or lack of) we see a difference in health status.

Although we have used clearly defined measurements to enable some kind of categorization of people experiencing poverty and to indicate where resources are needed, that does not mean that those of us floating just outside that relative threshold of 60 per cent below the median income are somehow 'out' of poverty and in good spirits. It is also important conceptually: if we were to wave our magic wand and remove all children from poverty, then, by our definition, health inequalities would still remain. Why, you might ask. It is a mathematical problem. We would have simply shifted the goal posts – our primary measure of poverty is relative and there will still be people at the lower end of the income scale. The work of Kate Pickett and Richard Wilkinson speaks specifically about income inequality and highlights that the greater the level of income inequality in a country, the worse outcomes are across multiple dimensions, including but not limited to health. For example, trust, social cohesion, crime and even pollution and the climate crisis – things that you would not necessarily associate with income inequality (Wilkinson and Pickett, 2009; Pickett et al, 2024). This argument highlights the need to be aware of the depth and scale of poverty alongside the depth and scale of wealth, and to strive to narrow the gap between the rich and the poor in the interests of all of us – because the consequences affect us all.

Children growing up in poverty in the UK experience a wide range of adverse child health and developmental outcomes and are more likely to develop chronic conditions in childhood in comparison to their more affluent counterparts. Even for children with genetic conditions that have no socio-economic basis, like cystic fibrosis, we find that poorer children experience poorer outcomes. This includes worse growth, poorer lung function, higher risk of *Pseudomonas* infection and poorer educational outcomes. Children experiencing poverty are more likely to die in the first year of life (Taylor-Robinson et al, 2019), more likely to experience physical and mental health difficulties in childhood (Cooper and Stewart, 2017), and are also at an increased risk of entering care (Bennett et al, 2022). Experiences of poverty in childhood track forward into adulthood, and can lead to worse employment opportunities, poor adult mental and physical health and ultimately poorer survival. In turn, there is a growing body of literature that is considering the intergenerational transmission of health inequalities as a result of experiences of poverty (Houweling and Grünberger, 2024).

Poverty duration

Up to now, we have only talked about experiences of poverty without considering the impact of duration. A single transition into poverty has been associated with a rise in child and maternal mental ill health (Wickham et al, 2017). It is not revolutionary to say that the longer someone is 'exposed' to poverty the more damaging the effects can be. Living in persistent poverty substantially decreases cognitive development (Dickerson and Popli, 2016), and increases the risk of mental health difficulties as well as physical health issues such as asthma and obesity when compared to children who have never experienced poverty (Lai et al, 2019; Adjei et al, 2021).

Liverpool in focus

Matthew Ashton, Liverpool Director of Public Health, describes the state of health in the city (2024) and, based on current health trends and levels of poverty, predicts the health consequences up to the year 2040. Based on the latest available data from 2022 to 2023, the report highlights that, currently, infant mortality is higher than the national average, with 26 infants dying before their first birthday. Those living in the poorest areas are living with two or more long-term health conditions 10–15 years sooner than those in the most affluent. He finds that the impact of the COVID-19 pandemic has increased inequalities in life expectancy between Liverpool and England, with men living 3.5 years less and women 3.9 years less in Liverpool, and finds that two thirds of those inequalities were caused by higher mortality rates from COVID-19, cancer, cardiovascular and respiratory diseases.

Looking towards 2040, if current health and poverty trends continue without intervention the individual and societal cost is large. The report suggests there will be further reductions in life expectancy, and large inequalities in healthy life expectancy, with women projected to live 53.8 years (a decrease of 4.1 years) in good health and men projected to live 60.1 years (an increase of 1.8 years) in good health. The overall number of health conditions is projected to rise by an average of 54 per cent, with the largest increases seen in the most deprived GP surgeries, which are predicted to increase by 86 per cent compared to an increase of 46 per cent among the least deprived GP practices. The report forecasts the biggest increase in major illnesses will be to mental ill health (such as depression), which is also expected to more than double (Ashton, 2024).

The societal and economic cost of poverty

So far, we have presented the impact of child poverty on the health of children and their families. But the wider societal and economic costs are of paramount importance, particularly when considering why we need to focus our attention on addressing it. In 2008, the total cost of the fallout from child poverty was estimated to be at least £25 billion a year. In 2013 it was £29 billion. In 2023 it has risen to over £39 billion a year, due to both higher prices and higher rates of child poverty (see Table 3.3). These are cautious estimates, and the true cost could be substantially higher (Hirsch, 2023).

Forecasts of a continued rise in child poverty mean that the cost is set to increase to more than £40 billion in today's prices by 2027. These forecasts are based on current policies (as of 2023) such as the benefit cap and two-child

Table 3.3: Breakdown of economic and societal estimated costs of child poverty in 2008, 2023 and predicted costs for 2027 should child poverty continue to rise

Cost category	2008	2023	2027 predictions
Future lost earnings by individuals	8	12.3	12.8
Cost to Treasury in lost income from individuals	3.3	5	5.3
Cost to Treasury in additional future unemployment benefits	2	1.6	1.7
Universal public services (school education, children's social services and healthcare)	12.3	17.4	17.4
Targeted public spending (pupil premium and the Early Year Entitlement for two-year olds)	0*	3.1	3.1
Total	25	39.5	40.4

Note: * This program did not exist before 2011; costs are provided in billions of pounds sterling.

Source: Hirsch (2023)

limit (that is limiting child-related financial support to the first two children for those in receipt of Universal Credit and child tax credit) (Hirsch, 2023). He concludes:

> The alternative to society bearing the costs of the fallout of child poverty is to invest sufficient resources to prevent children from growing up in poverty in the first place. The very high costs identified here demonstrate that even a large investment in an effective anti-child poverty strategy is likely to pay for itself. (Hirsch, 2023: 8)

Now we have read about poverty, how we choose to define it, and how we support those of us that experience hardship. We also now understand the extreme consequences of poverty, for the individual, society and the economy. It should be undeniable that our highest collective priority must be eliminating the experience of poverty, particularly child poverty, to protect against health harms (and wider societal costs). Indeed, poverty is recognized as one of the most important social determinants of child health (and consequently adult health) across high-income countries (Petrou et al, 2014; Sidebotham et al, 2014).

So how do we solve poverty in the interests of our health?

Prevention is key. We are so reactive to the growing need it is hard to look beyond it to the possibilities of prevention. This will always be a multifaceted task, involving multiple players from local communities, businesses, VCS organizations, local government, the NHS and central government. Fundamentally, for prevention to gain any kind of traction (and be prioritized) enough buy in is needed from everyone (you and me included) for it to become universally politically appealing.

In the past, governments have primarily tackled rising poverty through welfare policy and mechanisms to increase employment. New Labour's introduction of their commitment to 'end child poverty' in 1999 involved halving levels of child poverty by 2010 and eradicating it by 2020. Primarily, their focus used principles of proportionate universalism. Key actions to reduce child poverty included (1) incentivizing employment through improving wages; (2) a more progressive tax and benefit system that specifically supported children through child benefit and child tax credit; (3) improved access to childcare; and (4) investment in services such as 'Sure Start'. These were a network of service provisions aimed at providing local support to families with children under five years of age and included health, parenting, early learning and childcare and parental employment support. In a press release, Gordon Brown, the Chancellor of the Exchequer at the time, said:

> Tackling child poverty and disadvantage is not about providing either more money or better public services; it is about the necessity of both. As Government supports parents, in turn it is right that parents fulfil their responsibilities too. We cannot tackle poverty from the centre of Government alone, but must do so with our valued partners in the voluntary, community and faith sectors. These sectors have a unique role in reaching local communities and needs on the ground. I am delighted to meet with our partners today and look forward to taking this partnership even further forward. Together we can ensure that no child is left behind. (Brown, 2001)

While this multidimensional approach did make a dent, and we saw a decline in relative child poverty during this period, the target to halve child poverty in 2010 was missed. The subsequent government scrapped this strategy in 2015 as part of the Welfare Reform and Work Bill and deprioritized child poverty to focus instead on unemployment and family breakdown. This was criticized for obfuscating the causes and consequences of poverty and did not address the increasing levels of in-work poverty that we are still seeing, as work no longer guarantees a life lived out of poverty. It also refocused discussion back towards the individualization of poverty and away from a universal, more societal approach.

At the same time as the launch of the child poverty target in England, there was a cross-department commitment to address health inequalities through the 'English health inequality strategy' (Department of Health, 1999). This focused on reducing health inequalities through supporting families, engaging communities in tackling deprivation, improving prevention, treatment and care, and tackling the underlying social determinants of health. This united the investment of resources into the areas with the greatest need (level of deprivation) with high levels of commitment from across government departments. The English health inequality strategy ended in 2010 with the Coalition government. There was mixed evidence of the effect of this policy. However, when assessing geographic health inequalities, it seems that the life expectancy gap between the most deprived local authorities in England and the rest of the country was increasing prior to the strategy's introduction and then declined during the strategy period before increasing following its end (Barr et al, 2017).

Welfare benefit changes

A key way that we could tackle poverty and health inequalities in the UK is through more generous welfare benefits provision. Recent government policies have not been going in this direction, however. Under the Welfare Reform Acts 2012 and 2016, many of the headline changes have targeted health and disability, and child-related and out-of-work benefits. These include the introduction of reassessment of out-of-work disability benefits (working capabilities assessment), the transition from Disability Living Allowance to Personal Independence Payments, the introduction of Universal Credit, which consolidated six previous 'legacy benefits' into one payment, increases in punitive benefits sanctions under an intensified welfare conditionality regime and other cuts such as the so-called 'bedroom tax', which was imposed on renters of social homes who are deemed to have more bedrooms than they require, the benefit freeze, and more recently the introduction of the two-child limit, which limits welfare support relating to children to the first two children in a family (Hobson, 2020). The recently elected Labour government seems to be continuing a similar approach to the welfare benefits system and a focus on cutting the headline spending figure. See, for example, the Pathways to Work: Reforming Benefits and Support to Get Britain Working Green Paper (DWP, 2025f).

Many of these changes have been criticized for causing harm. Doctors have reported an increased burden to their workload, with a third of doctors reportingly spending between 11 and 30 per cent of their time on social factors that are impacting their patients' health, such as housing, disability status and benefits (Howard, 2024; discussed further in Chapter 6). Estimates suggest that between 2013 and 2018 there were over 60,000 additional people experiencing psychological distress as a result of moving onto Universal Credit (Wickham et al, 2020), and evidence now shows the policy is having a negative impact on child mental health (Song et al, 2024). Rich qualitative analysis elucidates the potential pathways through which we are seeing these negative effects on health. For many, the welfare system is inaccessible and overly complex. For others, the changes have increased financial insecurity, driving people into poverty, increasing levels of debt, exacerbating long-term health conditions and worsening mental health (Cheetham et al, 2019). The recent Green Paper on benefit reform (DWP, 2025f) faces similar criticisms in terms of causing the harms we have seen from welfare reforms over the last 15 years (Bambra et al, 2025). It has been the subject of significant parliamentary revolt and a subsequent Government (partial) U-turn, the outcome of which is yet to be seen.

As a result, there have been multiple calls for action, not least because the social welfare provision in England is often inadequate to meet even the basic standard of living. As Fitzpatrick et al (2023) note, the basic rate of Universal Credit is below destitution thresholds. The rising health harms projected across the life course and long into future generations also urge action. So there are calls, and the calls have been relatively consistent, for central government to remove the benefit cap, cancel the two-child limit, reduce eligibility thresholds, reduce or remove sanctions, and remove or limit welfare benefits conditionality (Tominey et al, 2024).

The welfare system is also inadequate in terms of accessibility, and this is a potential intervention point from an access to justice perspective. There are a huge number of people not claiming the social welfare support they are entitled to. This was costed at £23 billion going unclaimed in 2024 (Ghelani et al, 2024). Ghelani and colleagues at Policy in Practice, a social policy software and analytics business, describe three core reasons benefits are going unclaimed:

1. Awareness: People are not aware that welfare provision exists, or that they are entitled to it.
2. Complexity: The system is too complicated, with many barriers to claiming.
3. Stigma: Personal and societal negative perceptions of the welfare benefit systems stop people from engaging with it.

In the absence of central government making significant steps toward effective change, we have seen increasing local responses to mitigate against the health effects of rising poverty and the inadequacy of welfare support. These have taken the form of capitalizing on shared resources of organizations across a local authority, advocating for and implementing a real living wage, and increased use of 'in crisis' financial support such as the increased use of discretionary payments and the provision of advice (for example, that of Liverpool's anti-poverty approach outlined in Chapter 1, Box 1.1).

Access to free legal advice can both directly and indirectly improve population health and reduce health inequalities by improving individual legal capabilities and improve access to resources that are needed to maintain good health (Reese et al, 2022). As Nobleman noted, 'access to justice can ultimately determine health outcomes in a wide range of settings' (2014: 74). 'Health–justice partnerships' (called 'medical–legal partnerships' in the US and Canada) are an important policy response to this. These partnerships comprise a range of projects around the country that have placed advice services into medical settings. They have gained popularity alongside social prescribing services, which help connect people to non-medical support. Sometimes this support includes advice services. These integrated services are often part of an overall strategy for the local NHS Clinical Commissioning Group (CCG; prior to 2022) or Integrated Care Board (which replaced CCGs in 2022) to implement the NHS strategic goal of universal personalized care for 2.5 million people in the UK by 2024 (NHS England, 2019).

Integrating advice services in health settings reduces demand on the NHS, leads to fewer repeat appointments and fewer prescriptions, and promotes better physical and mental health (Advice Service Alliance and the Low

Commission, 2015). The health benefits also have an important healthcare utilization impact. The NHS estimated in 2019 that if the social prescribing models were implemented appropriately as standard, there would be 14 per cent fewer GP appointments, 12 per cent fewer presentations at Accident and Emergency (A&E), and better health and wellbeing for the individuals referred (NHS England, 2019: 22). This is of utmost importance considering the rising demand for NHS care. This is discussed in greater depth, in the context of co-location, in Chapter 6.

Conclusion

This chapter has taken you through and linked together our core themes: health inequalities, poverty and access to justice. Our intention is to add context for the detailed analysis of LATAN and the policy recommendations we make to improve people's lives across the UK that follow later. At the heart of these recommendations is the need for policy makers to develop strategies and services that recognize the link between poverty, health inequalities and the mitigating role of access to justice.

4

Research in Action

In this chapter, we will explain our research philosophy and participatory approach. We describe the research methods and approaches we have employed during the Liverpool Access to Advice Network (LATAN) project that we believe have given us a deeper understanding of the people in Liverpool trying to get advice and the organizations that service them. We will discuss how we analysed, compiled and reported our research findings.

(Participatory) action research

LATAN is an action research project, with a collaborative philosophical underpinning. The fundamental starting position for action research is said to be questioning how a particular situation can be improved (Bradbury, 2020). Elliott defined it as 'the study of a social situation with a view to improving the quality of action within it' (Elliott, 1991: 69). Action research is about learning about the real world, and building a balance between theory and practice, rather than a particular set of methods (Kemmis and McTaggart, 2005). Reason and Bradbury called this 'an orientation to inquiry', rather than a methodology (2008: 1). The history of action research is commonly traced back to the work of American social psychologist Kurt Lewin (1946; Elliott, 1991; Adelman, 1993; Greenwood and Levin, 2007; Stark, 2014). Lewin's work in industrial democracy valued involving workers in identifying and solving the problems that arose in their work settings and was hugely influential in the development of post-war industrial relations. This movement had a strong democratic and participatory beginning but the initial ideological imperative of democratization was eroded to the woollier 'empowerment', described as a 'step backward' by Greenwood and Levin (2007: 28).

Action research also has a liberationist strand that arose in the Global South, with a strong connection to social movements (Fals Borda, 1979, 2001; Friere, 2005). Sociologist Orlando Fals Borda is considered a founder of participatory action research (PAR) and originated his version of PAR in the 1970s as part of an activist movement that engaged with 'peasant' and Indigenous organizations and other grassroots movements in Latin America. He was a founder of the La Rosca de Investigación y Acción Social (Circle of Research and Social Action) network with Gonzalo Castillo Cárdenas, Víctor Daniel Bonilla and Augusto Libreros (Rappaport, 2020, 2024). In Fals's version of PAR, dialogue-based research would lead to insights that would then be used to inform and inspire political activism (Pereira and Rappaport, 2022). This is one of the strands of participatory and collaborative approaches to social science research that emerged in the Global South and then later spread to the Global North (Rappaport, 2020). This leads to what Greenwood and Levin describe as social scientists in the Global North looking to 'dig where they stand' and confront the structural inequalities of capitalism in their own communities through these same sorts of collaborative and supportive partnerships (2007: 31). As researchers we recognize this motivation in our own approach.

There have been criticisms of the extent to which PAR meets these aspirations. Heron (1996) identified as a potential shortcoming of PAR projects that the privileged researcher going out into the lesser privileged community to effect change often does not bring back a reciprocated effect on the relative privilege of his or her own position. This limits the collaborative nature of the endeavour.

Action research therefore has a strong connection to activism and social movements. It can empower communities and lead to social change (Baum et al, 2006). A discussion of the diverse and numerous approaches to action research is beyond the scope of this chapter and book. Greenwood and Levin have noted that specifics of the various action research approaches bear little resemblance to one another other than in name (2007). More generally, they nevertheless find 'many similarities in values, approaches to the empirical field, and commitments to mutual learning between problem owners and researchers' (Greenwood and Levin, 2007: 14). In their ideal form, these collaborative methods are symbiotic, a dialogue between equal contributors to the research, rather than a more traditional researcher and object of research relationship (Rappaport, 2020). In this book, we will reflect in places about how (im)perfectly we have realized this vision and the potential effects of this on the outcomes of our project.

Action research rejects prior positivist understandings of social science and knowledge creation, although it has variously been attributed with different epistemological underpinnings, depending on the nuance of the strand. Friere articulated a liberatory praxis as an epistemological grounding for PAR, where thought and action are geared toward overturning the structures of oppression (Friere, 2005; Campos and Anderson, 2022).

Our project is informed by a pragmatic epistemology, which holds that 'objects of knowledge are defined by active operations' (Oquist, 1978: 151).

Although there are many interpretations of pragmatism, all pragmatism is informed by the idea that we actively make meaning through interactions with our surroundings (Almeder, 1986; Stark, 2014). Through a pragmatic stance, knowledge is generated by actions taken to understand or resolve a practical problem. Therefore, there is no 'pure' antecedent or essential being to knowledge that exists prior to human understanding and observation, such as is posited in various schools of classical philosophy (Stark, 2014). Knowledge is instead eventual and created through human action (Oquist, 1978). Greenwood and Levin explicitly frame their action research within a pragmatic philosophy (2007). Stark argues for a pragmatic framing informed by the philosophy of John Dewey, with a commitment to radical ideas of democracy as a 'social phenomenon grounded in communication' (2014: 92). This could be realized through opening new spaces for collaborative democratic discussion, informed and accepting of a diversity of views, and with a realization that the process is ongoing and not a fixed position or something to be achieved in some future ideal state (Greenwood and Levin, 2007: 60; Stark, 2014: 92).

Another essential element of the cycle of action research is to reflect on the action and what has been achieved or not achieved in order to assess and plan for the next steps of action. It is this cycle of knowledge production and future action that characterizes the approach. The ongoing development of a cross-sector directory and referral system in Liverpool is perhaps the clearest example from our research. This approach also further explodes the traditional paradigm of the researcher and those researched. 'Action researchers must engage in a continuous process of reflection, thereby simultaneously occupying the roles of subject and object' (Rappaport, 2020: 10). In Fals Borda's conception, and that of the movement he founded, this must also be coupled with political action and activism to inform and develop the research agenda (Rappaport, 2020). Our project was a political project from the beginning, with the idea of changing policy to create a better solution to a pressing social issue.

There are challenges when conducting action research. It is time-consuming (Kemmis and McTaggart, 2005) and involves navigating issues of power and adequate representation of sometimes differing perspectives of participants (McIntyre, 2008). These issues of power and representativeness presented themselves again and again in our project and will be discussed in greater depth in Chapter 7. On the other hand, action research is also seen as more relevant and applicable because this participatory approach improves reliability at various stages of the project, from problem identification through to implementation of solutions and reflection on their success (Kindon et al, 2007).

At the time we began the LATAN project, we had been engaged with this community for more than five years. We were building LATAN upon the findings from several previous research projects in the area (for example, Organ and Sigafoos, 2017). We had been involved with participant organizations in various roles, notably on James's part as a trustee of Citizens Advice Liverpool (CAL). Over the years we have assisted with funding bids and helped with research and delivery of projects for various organizations. We conducted focus groups with staff of the (then) several Citizens Advice Bureau organizations in the city in order to present grassroots views on what was needed to the various trustee boards discussing a potential merger, which eventually created the organization that is now CAL. We have contributed research findings and analysis to various Liverpool City Council (Council or LCC) consultations about funding the sector. Recently, we have coordinated the drafting of the Liverpool access to advice strategy and assisted with LATAN's ongoing transition to a new legal entity.

This 'quid pro quo' approach along with a common vision developed through engagement and discussion with LATAN participants has been very valuable in the research. It has meant, for example, that members of organizations and people that use their services are generally willing to support the research: interviews are easy to set up, surveys are responded to, and plans can be adapted when situations change. It also means that where policy impact is sought, people with relevant experience in the sector and academic experts can be brought together to complement each other's knowledge.

Our role as lecturers is also an important element in our participation in the advice sector. We have worked for nearly a decade in partnership with various participant organizations to identify where students could help with their advice services, and we now train and place approximately 100 students annually to give free legal advice to people at advice agencies, community settings and health centres. During the COVID-19 pandemic we ran the service remotely from the University of Liverpool Law Clinic, engaging with organizations through Refernet, LATAN's online referral platform, to take client referrals, which introduced another element of insider participation in LATAN.

We feel that we are members of the community, loosely defined. Of course, this is as untrue as it is true. We are relatively privileged to some, being white and (over) educated. We are academics, subject to pressures to research and teach and administrate, but nevertheless employed by a university whose financial stability (even in these parlous times for UK universities) far exceeds that of the other LATAN organizations. On James's and Jen's parts, we are mid-career academics in the Law department, which never suffers for a lack of students, with the attendant relative job security that provides. Despite repeated rounds of industrial action on the part of our union, our own days as members of the academic precariat feel historical. Throughout the course of the project, Sophie has somewhat transitioned from early-career researcher, a position that is rife with precarity (short-term contracts, bridge funding), to a personal three-year fellowship that – due to enjoying (or enduring) two rounds of maternity leave, and the COVID-19 pandemic – was extended. She is now starting to accept the idea she is mid-career, having secured a more stable academic role. So as much as we are aware of the extreme financial pressures affecting the advice sector, we inevitably do not feel them as viscerally as those we are working with, who are scrambling for grants and contracts to keep the lights on and to provide another year's contract to their numerous staff who are precariously employed through no fault of their own or of the organization.

LATAN is certainly an action research project, but we do caveat our claim to PAR somewhat. As researchers we are continuously engaged in a process of trying to improve a situation in our community. We have invited and solicited and encouraged participation from stakeholders and organizations across Liverpool, and we have benefited greatly from that participation. We refined the project in partnership with our project partner, CAL, and other stakeholders in the project steering group, but this was done within the broad parameters of the project brief set by ourselves and with a proposed activity in mind (using a new referral system), developed from our experience in this area. We believe that the participatory element to our action research is strong, but we recognize that the extent to which we guided LATAN during this process and the degree to which we are and are not members of this community may qualify this claim.

Mixed or multi-methods research

Over the course of our action research, we have engaged in mixed and multi-method approaches to investigate the problems we were trying to solve. Bryman also called these approaches multi-strategy (2004, 2006). Mixed or multi-methods are a natural fit with action research because action research is trying to understand a social phenomenon, with all its complexity, and one approach often does not give enough traction on the research question. A mixed or multi-methods approach aims to utilize the relative strengths of various research techniques to increase reliability (Teddlie and Tashakkori, 2003; Creswell and Plano Clark, 2018). This complementarity allows for a fuller understanding of complex phenomena (Bryman, 1988; Teddlie and Tashakkori, 2003 O'Caithain et al, 2007; Hesse-Biber, 2010; Tashakkori and Teddlie, 2010; Clark et al, 2021).

While using these mixed or multi-methods, the research team has tried to be transparent and reflexive, and to recognize that our own experiences are shaping the research, from research questions to distilling findings (Creswell and Poth, 2018). Malterud calls reflexivity 'the knower's mirror' (2001: 484). Researchers must critically reflect on their own place in the research, including positionality, biases and assumptions (Malterud, 2001; Watt, 2007; Hesse-Biber, 2015; Creswell and Plano Clark, 2018). Malterud notes that preconceptions are different from biases, unless the researchers fail to mention them and confuse knowledge in advance with knowledge generated from the study (2001). In an action research project such as this one, this line is difficult to draw clearly, as the prior knowledge is built into the perception of the problem that motivates the research. We have grappled with this and tried to be aware that we came into the project with some already formed ideas about how to address identified issues through an interconnected network of advice services and a referral system. We then explored how to implement these ideas with partners. We grappled with this entry into the project in participatory terms, as we did not want to be too directive and lose the sense of participation. We wanted as much alteration and guidance from relevant organizations as possible. On the other hand, we also wanted to ensure that the project had some clear action points early on around which the project could coalesce and quickly gain momentum. This was a hard balance to strike. We were more successful at striking the balance with LATAN as a community of practice than we were with the referral system.

Reflexivity also involves acknowledging and interrogating the power dynamics that shape the researcher–participant relationship (Mertens, 2015). It requires researchers to think about their positionality concerning factors such as race, gender, class and culture, and to consider how these aspects of their identity may affect the research process and the co-construction of knowledge with participants (Malterud, 2001). As discussed earlier, we have attempted to bring to light the boundary between where we are as insiders and outsiders of this community, and to understand how this boundary affects our power dynamics and the success of the project.

As we are participants in the community, we have 'blurr[ed] the boundary between the researcher and the researched' (Chang, 2021: 53), and so the study also includes a strong element of autoethnography. We have endeavoured to observe the ethnographic axiom of 'looking particularly but seeing generally' (Lane Scheppele, 2004: 402) – identifying the theory-building aspects amid the day-to-day immersive observations. Autoethnographic observations as a participant provide more in-depth context than is possible from qualitative interviews, especially as the qualitative interviewer must have sufficient awareness of the detail of a system in order to know to ask questions about it (Kritzer, 2002; Lane Scheppele, 2004). As a research team, we have maintained notes about our experiences and have had regular team meetings, where we have attempted to make clear how our lived experiences within the community inform the research.

This mixed methods design has given the research team a unique perspective on a complex ecosystem of advice. We are embedded in the

LATAN project, both as designers and users of the system. This account therefore brings to bear both the results of our extensive mixed methods research but also our experiences within the system. We have striven for reflexivity, being aware of our position and positioning within the system as both participants and observers. We have also acknowledged from the beginning our activism – our desire to improve the system and for this project to result in meaningful social change.

General project procedural background

As was discussed in Chapter 1, the LATAN project idea was developed in 2018–19 in collaboration with the LCC and the research team based at the University of Liverpool to understand and increase access to legal advice in the city as part of the LCC's anti-poverty strategy. The project was funded by the Council and the University of Liverpool. The university researchers had been in dialogue with the Council and were active participants in various Council committees and taskforces around addressing poverty and social justice. Previous research findings, including studies of local access to justice and from a project for the Equality and Human Rights Commission, had been presented in the city.

After the project funding was agreed between the Council and the University of Liverpool in mid-2019, we recruited a project steering group. The aim of having a steering group was to provide external oversight and accountability, as well as strategic direction for the project. We were very fortunate that a senior and committed group agreed to take part. The steering group was chaired by Chris Topping, Director at Broudie Jackson Canter and the President of the Liverpool Law Society in 2018–19. Other initial members included Councillor Jane Corbett, the Deputy Mayor, Debra Morris, the Dean of the University of Liverpool School of Law and Social Justice, Timothy Nichol, Pro Vice Chancellor, Faculty of Business and Law Liverpool John Moores University, Martin Jungnitz, Head of Revenue and Benefits for the LCC, and Sarah Poblete, CEO of Liverpool Law Society. Over the period of the steering group's role as an external governance body there was some change in its membership, but it nevertheless remained essentially stable.

The project team recruited a postdoctoral research assistant in November 2019 for a one-year period and this position was filled by Gordon Schenwi-Dim.

Tender for third sector partner

The LATAN project was delivered in collaboration with a voluntary and community sector (VCS) partner, which was to take the lead on developing networking and referrals throughout the city. The partner was selected via a competitive tendering process, administered by the University of Liverpool. As mentioned previously, James is a trustee of CAL and so recused himself from any involvement in the tendering process, to avoid a conflict of interest. After a call and an open meeting at the Liverpool Law Society to discuss the project and its aims, 'expressions of interest' were submitted at the beginning of October 2019. In addition to a detailed budget, expressions of interest were required to cover:

- staffing resources available or the process and timeline to recruit other resources needed to support the project;
- any relevant connections that would enable the project to be delivered;
- the timeline to initiate the project;
- technological resources available or proposed for networking.

The technical mechanism for hosting the online referral system was therefore determined by the partner agency.

Because the project was part-funded by the Council, the partner agency was required to agree to abide by the Council's 'Fair City' agenda, to promote the creation of more and better-quality jobs with fair pay and employment practices across the City of Liverpool and use its best endeavours to achieve the following:

- to have fair employment policies and procedures in place at all times, which you will comply with;
- to pay all members of staff at a rate no less than the 'Real Living Wage' as determined and amended from time to time by the Living Wage Foundation (2024);
- not to use zero-hours contracts (for the purposes of these terms and conditions, that term refers to contracts under which there is no guarantee of work being offered to the member of staff and under which the member of staff is restricted from taking on other employment or work).

Several expressions of interest were received and ranked by the steering group. The project delivery team were deliberately excluded from the tendering process to ensure transparency. Jen was the secretary to this process but had no deliberative role. The steering group placed the expression of interest submitted by CAL as the top ranked candidate.

After further discussion, CAL agreed to the terms and was awarded the role of partner agency. Before the project launched, we refined the idea through co-development with LCC and CAL. CAL had experience of and a licence for using the online referral platform Refernet, so that was the technical referral mechanism put into place for the project. CAL advertised and hired Iqra Mazir for the network coordinator role.

2020–2021 research phase

This phase of the research aimed to (1) map the delivery of free legal advice services across Liverpool and the existing connections between the different organizations, and (2) to explore the meaning of free legal advice to the staff in the different organizations. The project was approved by the University of Liverpool Research Ethics Committee in 2019.

Mapping

Mapping is a visual research method that involves creating graphical representations of spatial relationships, connections and patterns (Wheeldon et al, 2019). In this study, mapping was used to explore the spatial dimensions of the research topic, capturing the physical and social landscapes for the advice ecosystem in Liverpool. It was envisioned that this mapping would integrate qualitative and quantitative data (Knigge and Cope, 2006) to explore how the provision or lack thereof of legal advice is experienced differently across the city. The mapping was intended to capture both the geographic distribution of legal advice resource throughout the city and the geography of the connections and partnerships between various organizations. It was planned that the research team would hold an open coffee morning in every Council ward in the city and use councillors' connections to invite all community organizations to attend in order to understand advice needs that were presenting to community groups, and whether and where those groups were able to refer these people with everyday legal problems. By orientating our inquiry geographically, we would be able to understand the spatial dimensions of everyday legal problems and the advice available to address them.

Having begun fieldwork in early 2020, the COVID-19 pandemic almost immediately forced project reorganization. This meant that we were in an excellent position to understand the impact of the pandemic on people's everyday lives and their advice needs, and the provision of advice during that period. We adapted the semi-structured interviews to explore this. We published an article on this topic in 2021 (Organ et al, 2021) (for more information on this, see Chapter 6). Councillors' resources were used to invite participation from all organizations known to provide free legal information or advice, and further organizations were identified using local services directories. The meetings became online interviews, but there was some inevitable loss of participation as the smaller community groups were difficult to find, and many ceased operating at all during the early stages of the pandemic. Some organizations had been initially contacted prior to the lockdown, and interviews were delayed until after the initial lockdown period when many organizations, like the research team, were transitioning to home working. At that point, some organizations told us that that they had capacity to take part in the study because pauses on mechanisms that drive clients to them, such as evictions, meant that they had a lull in client demand. They therefore had a window of time when it was convenient to participate in the research. This experience was common across many of the organizations we interviewed.

Between April and June 2020, we conducted 30 interviews with 40 interviewees. Participants worked for organizations based in Liverpool that signpost or refer people to advice organizations, or give some level of legal information or free legal advice. The organizations work in all areas of social welfare law – housing, welfare benefits, immigration and asylum, debt, employment, family – and vary in size and breadth of work. Some are branches of national organizations, while others are local organizations.

The participants represented 30 of the 89 identified charity and VCS organizations that publicized an offer of free legal information or advice in Liverpool at that time. Due to lockdown restrictions, the majority of interviews were conducted via online platforms such as Zoom or Microsoft Teams and lasted between 45 minutes and an hour and a half. Interviews were recorded and transcribed verbatim. Interviewees were either managers, supervisors or lead caseworkers. Smaller organizations indicated just one person at that level whereas larger organizations had more than one person who participated in interviews. We use a letter and numbering convention to label interviews, the organization with a letter, and each participant at an organization with a number where there is more than one participant (for example, Interview A2). We used this same convention in each research phase, but differentiate between staff and client interviews (for example, Interview BB, staff 6).

We categorize 12 of the 89 participant organizations as advice organizations – Citizens Advice, law centres, Shelter, other local advice providers and so on. Advice services are the core of their work. Their services are open to everyone in Liverpool, unless there is a specific pathway into the service, such as from a housing association. The other 18 participant organizations self-identified as providing free legal information or advice, but this supplemented their core support services. These usually focused on a specific issue, such as homelessness or domestic abuse, or were targeted at specific groups based, for example, on ethnicity or health condition. The level of information and advice depended largely on available funding streams, and some of them did not deliver advice, but acted mainly as a referral gateway into the advice network.

In the semi-structured interviews, we explored the work of each organization; what they understand by 'information' and 'advice'; the availability and capacity of services; the networks they are part of and what they understand by 'referrals' and 'signposting'. As the project turned out to be a timely opportunity to explore the impact of COVID-19 on the legal advice sector at a time of particular need, we added a section to the semi-structured interviews about how the COVID-19 crisis had affected their services and the ability of clients to access them.

Interview data was analysed collaboratively using a thematic analysis to develop common themes (Braun and Clarke, 2006). NVivo software was used to code and organize the data. Each transcript was coded by at least two members of the research team. Potential emergent themes were discussed in regular team meetings and transcripts re-coded to compare against new themes. These iterative processes of reviewing and re-reviewing the data help to improve reliability and confidence in the resulting themes (Nowell et al, 2017).

In addition, the data from these interviews were re-coded for mapping purposes into a series of binary yes/no questions in terms of: the areas and levels of advice provided; perceived gaps in services across Liverpool; where referrals were sent to and received from; whether the organization had inclusion criteria for people wanting to access their services; the financial situation of the organization; and staff and volunteer numbers. The areas of advice for this part of the research were: asylum, asylum support and housing, community care/support, debt, discrimination, employment, family (children), family (non-children), housing, immigration (non-asylum), public law and welfare benefits. The levels of advice provided were coded as: information, advice, one-off casework, ongoing casework, support with tribunal preparation and representation at tribunal. Organizations were re-contacted and asked to verify the resulting spreadsheet line with their organization's data.

The project team was bolstered for the summer of 2020 by Amee Tyrell and Katherine Magee through the University of Liverpool Graduate Research Intern Scheme. The team searched the websites of every organization listed in the LiveWell Directory for the Liverpool City Region and coded them into the spreadsheet based upon the available information, then contacted the organizations and asked them to verify their resulting data. In total, 128 organizations were included in the resulting dataset. The dataset was then used to generate a series of maps using the Tableau analytics platform. The maps were presented at a meeting with LCC representatives.

The mapping exercise was not without controversies, as the way the data were coded meant that we could not determine which level of support an individual organization provided in the various areas of advice, and led to some organizations that might provide higher levels of support in some areas but not others appearing as if they provided higher level support in all areas they worked in. An organization that works in a niche area of advice objected to the resultant map giving the impression that the advice in that area was less scarce across the city than is indeed the case. This proved to be a limitation of this element of the project. The maps and their limitations are discussed in more depth in Chapter 5.

Focus groups

In November and December 2020, the project team conducted six focus groups with 47 participants to investigate themes identified in the qualitative interviews during the initial phase of mapping. The focus groups were centred around advice areas: welfare benefits, debt, asylum and immigration, family, housing and employment. The focus groups were recorded and transcribed verbatim. This phase of the research was focused on client experience and understanding referrals in each area of law. In each group we discussed the typical clients pre- and post-COVID-19, and the best and worst service delivery and referral scenarios. The focus groups brought the total number of participant organizations for this phase of the project to 37.

Focus groups were recorded and transcribed verbatim and NVivo software was used for coding. The project team worked together to code and analyse them using a thematic analysis, similar to the approach used for the qualitative interviews (Braun and Clarke, 2006). We also considered the group dynamics and interactions to find points of consensus across the groups, as well as disagreement (Liamputtong, 2011).

2021–2023 project phase

After the initial research phase, and with the renewal of the Council funding for a second and subsequently third year, we shifted into a phase of running the project and a period of autoethnographic observation primarily. In this phase, Iqra Mazir left LATAN and CAL hired Cosima Doerfel Hill to the Network Coordinator role. Later Liz Reed took over the role, followed by Edward Hodgson in 2024. Over this period, we periodically received the data on Refernet usage, including membership and referrals, from CAL. By the time that the funding for provision of Refernet ended, nearly 6,000 referrals had been sent across the City. For part of this period, James and Jen were also taking referrals for welfare benefits clients via Refernet through the Liverpool Law Clinic, so were participating in the system as users as well. The project team met regularly to discuss the project and issues we perceived were developing. The overall project steering group continued to meet quarterly, convened by the Liverpool Law Society, and provided strategic direction.

In 2022, Martin Jungnitz, who had retired from the LCC, agreed to take up a position as the independent chair of LATAN. This was something of a coup as Martin was head of revenue and benefits at LCC and brought a wealth of knowledge about the subject area and navigating Council procedures. This insider knowledge and experience has proved invaluable. James and Jen began to have weekly meetings with Martin, Liz, Heather Jessop, the CEO of

CAL, and Leanne Campbell-Syers from CAL about project administration, funding and strategic planning. Notes for these focus meetings were taken by the CAL project administrator, and the research team also took notes and regular research memos.

The initial two-year LCC funding was intended to be seed funding for LATAN. A central aim was for the network to be sustainable in the long run in terms of funding and as an independent entity. The plan was for a new funding source to take LATAN forward at the end of two years. Funding for secondary support services, that is, those that do not directly engage with people, is hard to come by. Despite strenuous efforts, we could not find alternative funding. So, to maintain the continuity and momentum of LATAN, we were forced to go back to the Council for an extension of the initial grant funding in 2021, and then again to bid for funds from the Clinically Extremely Vulnerable grant scheme alongside CAL. This second, reduced grant enabled us to pay a network coordinator part-time through to end of March 2023, but there was no longer funding for research activity. Without these two extensions it is likely that LATAN would have ended. In 2022, we made a bid to the Legal Education Foundation for funding to support LATAN. They were very positive about the approach being taken and we were successful with a bid that paid CAL for a network coordinator until the end of 2025 (now extended into 2026), and a referral system coordinator for one year. This funding has been critical for the development of CAL.

2023–2024 research phase

In this second intensive research phase, we wanted to learn about whether and how LATAN had affected the experience of people with everyday legal problems. We also wanted to learn about how LATAN was functioning. We received extended research ethics approval from the University of Liverpool Central Research Ethics Committee.

Our project team was bolstered by an Economic and Social Research Council (ESRC)-funded doctoral researcher, Eve Pennington.

Secondary data analysis

We analysed data collected by our partner organization, CAL. The data included:

- Aggregated data on numbers/types of referrals and outcomes as collected by the Refernet system. Examples are: referral accepted – client advised; referral refused – unsuitable; referral refused – capacity. None of these data had any client identifying data attached.

- Information from previous CAL consultations with LATAN and Refernet service users about their experiences and what improvements could be made. All information were suitably anonymized.

Case studies

We also conducted seven case studies designed to explore the experience of people with everyday legal problems in Liverpool in terms of accessing joined-up services. Each case study focused on an organization where people with everyday legal problems might be seeking help, such as advice agencies, and other community organizations that are not primarily advice organizations. In each setting we conducted three to eight client interviews and two to seven staff interviews. The interviews took place at the organizations and lasted approximately 30–60 minutes. In total, we interviewed 56 individuals across the seven organizations.

We were trying to understand if people knew that they could potentially get advice to help solve their everyday legal problems, if they understood where they could get that advice, or be referred to, and what their experience had been of trying to get advice or a referral (if they have done either). These case studies give us some insight into how those co-located services might function and if there are benefits for the individuals who use them.

We included community organizations to try to find people who had not already sought advice (though many food bank users will have been referred by an advice agency, as they gatekeep by requiring a referral voucher, many of which were administered in Liverpool through the Refernet system). An issue in the many studies in this area is identifying these individuals who have been deterred from seeking advice for some reason. We have previously addressed this by asking current advice seekers about past problems for which they did not seek advice (Organ and Sigafoos, 2018; Sigafoos and Organ, 2021).

The interviews were all recorded and transcribed verbatim. The research team also kept field notes about the interview circumstances and settings. The transcripts were coded for themes using a thematic analysis, similar to the process for the earlier research stage (Braun and Clarke, 2006). The research team met regularly to discuss the themes, and transcripts were reviewed again in light of the emerging themes discussed in these meetings.

Synthesizing data

As discussed earlier, action research approaches often use mixed or multi-methods, as the addition of other ways of understanding the problem can help to bring about the desired change. Our use of mixed or multi-methods is inspired by what Bryman categorized as completeness and enhancement motivations (2006). Throughout this study, we have taken iterative steps to refine and revise our approach as we better understood the phenomenon we were studying. These sort of refinements to research design are recommended as a response to the changes in direction that present themselves over a research project, and as new findings lead to a different understanding of the research problem (Hesse-Biber, 2010). Bryman notes that the multi-strategy research is not always predictable, with the result that it 'frequently brings more to researchers' understanding than they anticipate at the outset' (2006: 111).

In this study, the data were analysed sequentially, as there were two distinct research-intensive phases. However, as we have been immersed in the participatory study for a period of years, our own understanding has changed, which has affected our interpretation of the data. We have continuously re-examined and revisited our earlier findings over time. The data are integrated here by our reporting, through narrative weaving, where we connect the findings from the various approaches thematically and group the discussion of the various elements to provide a more complete and enhanced understanding of the situation (Fetters et al, 2013).

The concept of intellectual bricolage, and 'making do with what is at hand (Lévi-Strauss, 1967: 17), has considerable traction for our approach to this action research project. We were making do with what little resource remained in the community for advice services and trying to make something new by linking up the community through LATAN and the referral mechanism of Refernet. We have also made do all along by linking together our research and inquiry in a way that was not evident a priori, but rather by taking forward new opportunities and directions that presented themselves through the emerging bricolage as the project progressed (Di Domenico et al, 2010). In their study of bricolage in social entrepreneurship, Di Domenico et al propose a framework for social bricolage as 'a process that involves making do, the refusal to be constrained by limitations, improvisation, social value creation, stakeholder participation, and persuasion' (2010: 698). Our own social bricolage is an attempt to add social value and positively impact policy to improve access to good quality legal advice to help people resolve issues to fundamentally improve health.

Kurt Lewin coined the popular social science maxim: 'The best way to understand something is to try to change it' (Greenwood and Levin, 2007). The LATAN story is the story of our venture through this process *as we try to understand and change the way advice is delivered in Liverpool.*

5

Liverpool's Advice Ecosystem

> Demand is always gonna outweigh capacity. We deal with as many people as we can, but we're heavily reliant on volunteers. We have a number of paid staff, but there's always people calling in … We get bits and pieces of funding, someone will fund us for an outreach, which could pay for an advisor one day a week. Or it's little bits and pieces of funding we receive here and there that collect together that allow us to employ people. But the majority of people come from the volunteering side. But I think even if I had a room full of 100 volunteers working all day, that phone would still be ringing at the end of it. (Interview BB Staff 6)

Liverpool's advice ecosystem is complex, fragmented and over-burdened. This is a sector that has been in a state of flux for many years as funding comes and goes, projects start and stop, and employment is often short-term and precarious. The Liverpool Access to Advice Network (LATAN) has a very diverse range of organizations providing services in different ways, underpinned by differing overarching objectives, often with differing target client groups. We wanted to fully understand what services were being provided, to what level of legal service and in which part of the city, and the collaboration between different organizations. In this chapter we present first a comprehensive picture of the ecosystem, developed initially from the mapping exercise and then further refined over the course of the LATAN project. This is integrated with a discussion of the difficulties presented by mapping, and some reflection on what this shows for this and other attempts to understand the need for and access to legal advice. We then conclude the chapter by setting out the steps people take to get advice to resolve everyday legal problems, which is developed from and synthesizing what we have learned about LATAN.

Mapping and understanding the advice ecosystem

As was described in Chapter 4, we began the LATAN project with a research phase to map and visualize the legal advice provision that existed in the city. As far as we are aware there have been no attempts to map free legal advice provision in Liverpool fully.

This work was challenging for a number of reasons. There is no single source of funding that can be used to trace availability of services. Advice services in Liverpool are funded from a diverse range of funding streams. Some services are provided by central Ministry of Justice funding streams, such as legal aid and the recent Improving Outcomes Through Legal Support funding for housing advice, which in Liverpool is a collaborative project run by Support Through Court, Merseyside Law Centre and Citizens Advice Liverpool (CAL). There are myriad other funding streams. The biggest project for CAL, for example, is funded by the National Health Service (NHS), followed by a Department for Work and Pensions (DWP) project called 'Help to Claim'. Other funders for advice across the city include social housing associations, foundations – such as the Steve Morgan Foundation, Wolfson Foundation, Access to Justice Foundation and PH Holt Foundation – utilities companies, banks, Liverpool City Council (Council or LCC), the European Social Fund, Macmillan, the Big Lottery, private donors and so on. This huge range of funders is indicative of the fragmented, uncoordinated funding of free legal advice in Liverpool, and everywhere else in the country.

Funders also finance and measure the delivery and outcomes of free legal advice in different ways. Organizations therefore measure activity and outcomes in a multiplicity of ways. This meant that asking for client numbers was not possible. Organizations count client numbers and issues in different ways. An organization might count just individual clients, or the number of issues presented (at various different levels of detail), or the number of interventions on behalf of the client and so on. Some organizations – mainly smaller ones – do not count clients at all. There is also no single understanding of what constitutes legal advice for service funders or providers or of the different levels of advice that are delivered. There is no common quality mark applicable, which might be used to identify and sort organizations. Instead, there are multiple quality marks that organizations might adhere to: the Advice Quality Standard, Debt Advice Quality Framework, Legal Aid Agency's Specialist Quality Mark, Office of the Immigration Services Commissioner's (OISC's) regulation of immigration advice and so on.

As was discussed in more detail in Chapter 4, we gathered the data for this mapping through two main approaches:

1. Qualitative interviews: We conducted interviews with 31 of the organizations in Liverpool that provide access to legal information or

advice. For some of these organizations we spoke with more than one individual, so we interviewed 40 people in total. The interviewees were primarily chief executives, managers or supervisors. We analysed these interviews qualitatively and then re-coded to identify quantitatively main issue areas.

2. Interviewer administered survey: We identified every organization in the LiveWell Directory for the Liverpool City Region (a larger geographic area than Liverpool itself) that advertised an offer of advice. We then coded the data from the directory to see what services were offered at each level and then contacted the organizations to confirm that the information was correct. We reached 89 organizations through this approach.

We will discuss these two sets of data in an intertwined way to show identified areas of priority and need from the qualitative interviews, comparing them with the advertised offer of services from the survey data. We will also use the qualitative information from the interviews to contextualize the survey data.

In both of these data gathering approaches, we asked organizations to classify the areas of law they provide advice for, and the level to which they work. The levels of advice offered were categorized: information, advice, one-off casework, ongoing casework, tribunal support and tribunal representation. We included information in our categories to try to make clear the distinction between advice and information as far as possible.

In our interviews, when we tried to explore what participants considered to be the distinction between information and advice (a discussion introduced in Chapter 2) we found that understanding varied among many participants about where the line was between information and the different levels of advice. It was not possible to draw a common definition across participants, but the distinction was well recognized. This participant, a manager at an advice agency, very clearly explained the different levels of advice that generally exist across the advice ecosystem, and the distinction between information and advice:

> I love this debate. I have had this debate through my whole career. So information: fact sheet, it's generic. It's not tailored to a specific person's requirements or needs. It's for everybody. Read it and take of it what you will. That's information. Um, generalist advice is: 'I will take your situation and I will give you advice in relation to it and give you options about what you need to do or what you could do.' Um, you will then go away and do it … Then casework is: 'I'm gonna work with you, but I'm pretty much going to do things for you. And then I will contact you at every stage.' And then obviously you get to specialist advice. So you can have generalist casework and then you can have specialist casework. So your generalist casework is I might fill

> out this PIP form for you. But your specialist is: 'Well, I'm now gonna help you appeal', and you need somebody that actually understands … to help you appeal a decision, or to go to a tribunal. (Interview A2)

Our questions about the nature of advice delivered in Liverpool's advice ecosystem showed that the same voluntary and community sector (VCS) organizations often offered both legal and non-legal advice to support their clients. Again, it is difficult to draw a clear picture of where the distinction is and many organizations do not really draw this themselves. This non-legal advice is often still related to those exposures and risk factors that are rooted in the social determinants of health. It generally involves supporting people to engage more positively with these issues, for example, advice on how to write a curriculum vitae (CV). The overlap between employability advice and free employment law advice is one example where the distinction between legal and non-legal advice can be blurred, such as when someone is getting support to be able to apply for jobs and at the same time advice on what they can expect in terms of reasonable adjustments in the workplace.

What is out there nationwide?

There has been no comprehensive description of organizations that offer free legal advice nationwide in terms of mapping what exists and how it functions. The Law Society (2024) has created a series of insightful maps of legal aid provision in welfare benefits, education, community care, housing and immigration. The Law Society mapping clearly shows the failure to provide a geographically comprehensive legal aid funding scheme in multiple areas of social welfare law. Ninety per cent of people in the country do not have a local legal aid funded advice provider for education. This is also true for 85 per cent of people in terms of welfare benefits provision, 71 per cent for community care, 44 per cent for housing and 63 per cent for immigration and asylum. This is unsurprising when we see the civil legal aid provider income data. In the two areas of law that are most closely associated with raising people's income – employment and welfare benefits law – the income for legal aid providers nationally in the second quarter of 2023 was £10,000 and £90,000 respectively. These are the two lowest figures on the table (Ministry of Justice, 2023).

This means that the majority of people in England and Wales who cannot afford to pay for legal advice rely on sources other than the traditional legal aid route. It is highly problematic that this important source of funding – the highest profile and principal source of funding for free legal advice for many years – has been so severely diminished. The mapping of the crisis in legal aid is therefore an important part of the picture in relation to access to justice. It is, though, only a small part of the free legal advice ecosystem today.

We recognize that legal aid funding is generally targeted towards more legally complex cases and so client numbers will be lower, but nonetheless services funded by other means dominate the free legal advice landscape in terms of meeting demand for free legal advice overall.

What advice provision exists in Liverpool?

In our administered survey data, it was identified that the whole range of social welfare issues was covered by different organizations in the Liverpool City Region. The area of law that the most organizations (49 out of 89) reported providing advice for was related to housing. Housing is often mentioned in interviews and LATAN meetings as an area of priority need in Liverpool. Welfare benefits and debt are the next most common areas of law with 45 and 34 organizations, respectively, reporting that they provide advice in these areas of law (see Figure 5.1 which shows the provision of advice distribution across the city, in percentages). This is also unsurprising in a city like Liverpool with high levels of deprivation and correspondingly high levels of benefit uptake. As of October 2024, there were 75,400 Universal Credit (UC) claimants in Liverpool with a claimant rate of 17.8 per cent, which is 4.9 per cent above the national average. This is unevenly spread across the city. Eight wards have over 25 per cent of working-age people claiming UC, with Tuebrook the highest at 40 per cent.

Figure 5.1: The provision of advice offered across the 89 organizations in Liverpool, in percentages (%)

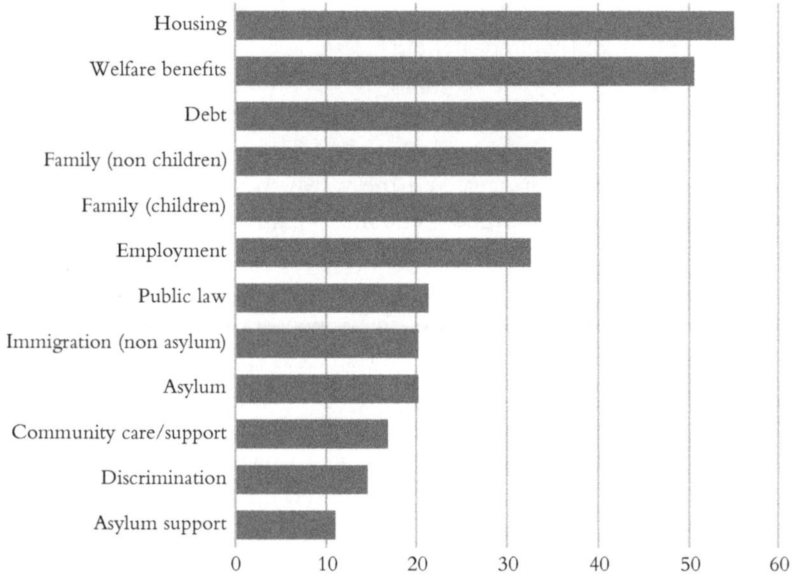

The sort of numbers reported in the mapping exercise give the impression that people are well-served in terms of social welfare law advice in Liverpool. There are lots of organizations trying to help people. When you drill down into the numbers and cross reference with the services on offer, however, it becomes clear that the capacity to provide legal advice in these areas is far less that it appears. Community care is a good example of this. It is the lowest reported area of advice with only 12 organizations saying they could provide advice in this area of law (see Figure 5.2, which shows the Liverpool City Region map for organizations that provide community care advice). Of these 12 organizations, only one, Merseyside Law Centre, could actually be said to provide the full range of community care advice. Of the remaining organizations, three are MP offices that will help by advocating and/or signposting people; five are refugee and immigration support services helping people integrate into the community, but do not employ specialists in community care law; one is a local support service for people with mental health issues; and another a housing association, which will advise people on how to get community care and which assists mainly through advocacy, but does not have a formal legal advice role; and, finally, CAL provides advice on all issues but does not have a specialist in this area.

This type of spread is true across all areas of law, with a handful of specialists available in the city, but the remainder of legal advice being provided by volunteers or non-specialist staff using their experience to do so alongside their other roles. Given the funding environment and the high levels of excess demand, this is an inevitable, informal blurring of advice and information provision, and between projects and funding streams. In some places the role that people play at this boundary between information and advice, and between legal and non-legal advice is called a trusted intermediary (see Chapter 8). Debt and welfare benefits stand apart to some degree as they have a higher number of paid members of staff funded specifically to provide advice than in other areas of law, but demand still far outstrips supply.

Organizations tend to be located around the city centre, which people can easily access to receive services, and the wards to the north of the centre, where poverty tends to be higher. The initial plan at the start of the project was to explore the physicality of service provision and to see connections to other indicators of poverty and health inequalities. The onset of the COVID-19 pandemic a month after the project started meant that this was no longer possible as offices closed and services shifted online. Figure 5.3 shows the spread of housing providers in the Liverpool City Region.

The maps of the distribution of the advice providers are of the wider Liverpool City Region geographic area. As a reminder to reorient you to the distribution of poverty geographically within Liverpool (as discussed in Chapter 3), Figure 5.4 is a map of the percentage of children living in poverty by ward in Liverpool.

Figure 5.2: Liverpool City Region map for community care advice

Note: The size of the bubble indicates the level of advice provided: 1 information; 2 advice; 3 one-off casework; 4 ongoing casework; 5 tribunal support; 6 tribunal representation.

Figure 5.3: Liverpool City Region map for housing advice

Note: The size of the bubble indicates the level of advice provided: 1 information; 2 advice; 3 one-off casework; 4 ongoing casework; 5 tribunal support; 6 tribunal representation.

Figure 5.4: Child poverty rates (%) in Liverpool wards

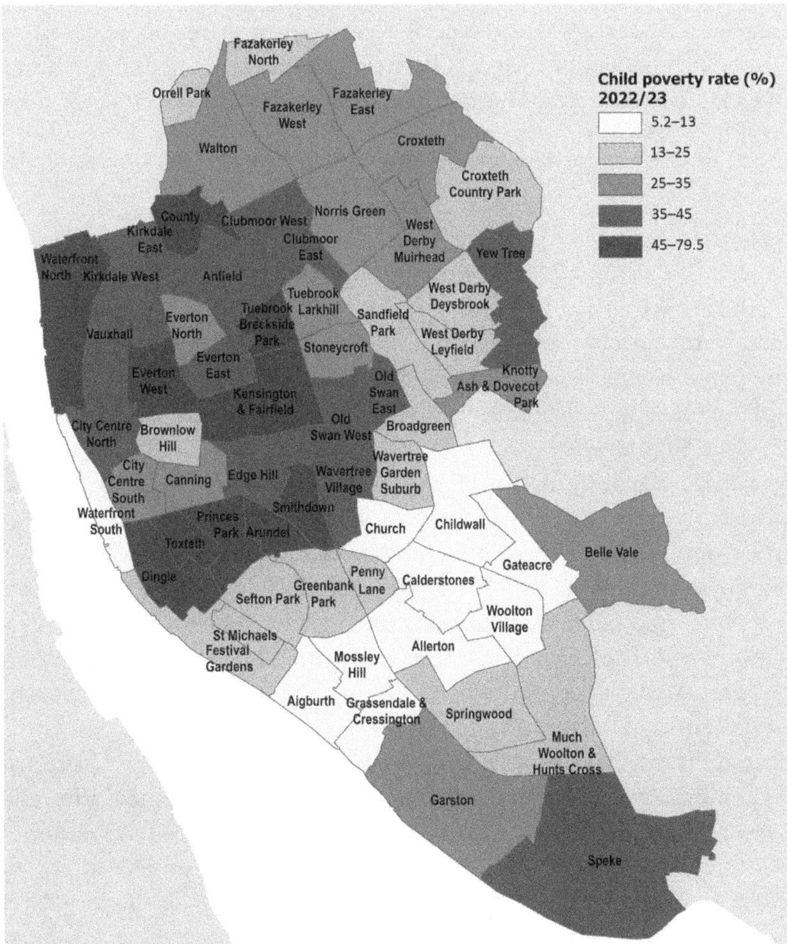

Note: Darker colours indicate high levels of child poverty.

Source: LCC Corporate Intelligence Team, September 2024

The mapping shows that Liverpool's advice ecosystem has a widespread, but fragile organizational infrastructure containing dozens of VCS organizations. The number of organizations in the free legal advice sector must be set in context. Many are relatively small organizations and many have shrunk during the period of austerity politics because of the severe funding cuts the advice sector has suffered. This has significantly reduced the number of people whom organizations can help, and reduced the level of advice that people can get.

Liverpool has high levels of deprivation and high levels of demand for social welfare law advice. Austerity-driven policies increased this demand and this was exacerbated by the COVID-19 crisis. Both have disproportionately affected Liverpool. There are hundreds of charities and volunteer-led services in Liverpool trying to mitigate the worst impacts on people, but demand for legal advice far outstrips demand, which in turn exacerbates poverty and negatively impacts other social determinants of health.

Gaps in provision

The research also sought to explore gaps in provision of social welfare law advice. We asked organizations to identify the main areas of legal advice that their clients needed but could not get. The organizations that participated in the research spoke about numerous gaps in services that people need. They also commonly stated that they expected this to get worse (see Figure 5.5).

The main takeaway is that all the organizations we spoke to identified gaps in the services that their clients needed, and that these gaps were wide ranging, applied to all areas of law and were increasing.

Employment advice was the most commonly identified gap. Nineteen per cent of respondents cited employment advice as a significant gap in advice provision in Liverpool. Employment advice is particularly limited in Liverpool. At the time of the mapping there were no employment advice specialists, except for those employed by the Equality and Employment Law Centre and a single caseworker employed by the Brain Charity. The Equality and Employment Law Centre provides a free employment law advice line, but casework is then usually provided on a no win, no fee basis rather than being free at the point of delivery, and their biggest project at the time was the national discrimination advice line. The CEO of the Law Centre

Figure 5.5: Bar chart of gaps in provision identified during interviews with organizations, in percentages (%)

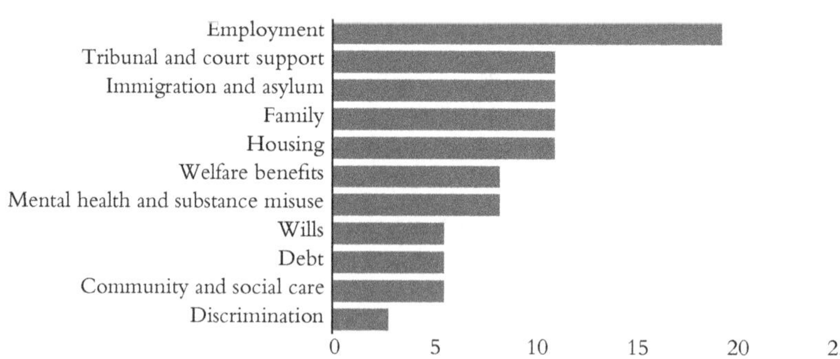

stated: 'there is a real lack of free employment advice within the city region. But not just within the city region, we are getting enquiries from Wales, we get enquiries from Essex … there is a real crisis in terms of employment law provision' (Employment Law Focus Group). Within this context of very limited specialist advice being available, 29 out of the 89 respondents stated that they gave employment advice, and 12 that they would represent people at a tribunal (Figure 5.6 shows the map of employment law provision in the Liverpool City Region.)

Given the response in the organizational interviews and our knowledge of the sector through working with LATAN, this map gives the appearance of more free legal advice being available and to a higher level than we believe is offered. The numbers of people accessing free employment law advice is limited. As was discussed earlier, and in Chapter 2, there may be some overlap between employment advice and employability advice. It is also likely that the advice being given is legal in nature but relatively straightforward with little casework, such as helping write grievance letters and checking wage levels and holiday pay expectations. The reported tribunal representation support is likely limited to information about how the process works, rather than drafting ET1 forms – the main Employment Tribunal form – or preparing court bundles. This is likely to be the case for the MPs' offices, housing associations, training centres and others that responded affirmatively when asked if they give employment advice. The exceptions in terms of casework and tribunal representation are the Equality and Employment Law Centre and the Brain Charity and the solicitor firms on the list; although it is unclear on what basis they provide free legal advice and/or tribunal representation in employment law. Legal aid funding is limited to discrimination cases in employment law, so it is possible that it was this narrower area of law to which they were referring.

Lessons learned from mapping Liverpool's advice ecosystem

Mapping is an imperfect exercise. There are a number of ways that the mapping might lead to a false impression that more advice capacity exists in Liverpool than is the case. In this section we will critically analyse some areas of the mapping to better understand what provision actually exists. This section will also illustrate some of the difficulties of that process when trying to build a comprehensive picture of a complex system.

Snapshot in time

Any mapping exercise like the one that we undertook will be a snapshot in time. The map needs to be updated regularly. This is particularly true for the type of advice ecosystem described and analysed in this chapter,

Figure 5.6: Liverpool City Region map for employment advice

Note: The size of the bubble indicates the level of advice provided: 1 information; 2 advice; 3 one-off casework; 4 ongoing casework; 5 tribunal support; 6 tribunal representation.

where funding is piecemeal, variable, often short-term and can lead to organizational mission creep away from the services where their expertise typically lies:

> More money [is needed] … more long-term funding, more funding of services that they know work already instead of always looking for new services … often our services are led by what people are paying for rather than what we want to deliver and what's the sort of flavour of the month, if you like, and people will start funding those services. So we start changing our services, if you like, in order to access the funding that's available rather than people giving us money to do things we do really well and that we've been doing really well for a very long time. (Interview V1)

This short-term and fluctuating funding means that advice services provided by an organization will vary over time quite considerably. For example, the Chinese Wellbeing Centre had funding for two welfare benefits advisers when the mapping took place, but the funding ended and the posts ceased two months after the mapping information was gathered. Some organizations, such as Liverpool Community Advice, have ceased to operate since we completed the mapping exercise.

Issues of self-identification

Another issue is that mapping data is based on self-identification of the areas of law and the level of advice provided. The area of law with the lowest level of provision identified was community care at 10 per cent and the highest area of law was housing at 48 per cent. We illustrated the resulting distribution of these advice services earlier in this chapter in Figures 5.2 and 5.3. It was surprising that a higher percentage of organizations said that they could provide advice in the area of housing than welfare benefits. In interviews and focus groups, housing issues were raised a number of times as an increasing area of demand. It is possible that the higher-than-expected level of housing advice reported is due to organizations switching focus and resources to that area of law to try to meet demand that reflects the ongoing housing crisis.

The most surprising response was the percentage of organizations that indicated they helped with tribunal representation. This was not supported by the interviews about gaps in provision. Tribunal representation was the second most frequently identified gap in available provision (13 per cent). We are not aware of any projects that are funded to provide tribunal representation. There is some funding for tribunal support in the sector, and perhaps there was some reporting of tribunal representation provision where, in fact, they provide advice and preparation for tribunals where people represent themselves. Even when legal aid funding paid for specialist casework in welfare rights law in the early 2000s, it did not cover the costs of tribunal representation. However, organizations used to represent clients where there was a particular need. That activity was funded through other sources or provided pro bono. It is possible that this approach has continued, and so staff have reported in the survey that their organization provides (or provided) tribunal representation as a service. In terms of pro bono, since many of the organizations surveyed were law firms, it is also possible that they were reporting some pro bono activity in this area.

We think that many of the organizations identifying that tribunal representation is supported will be referring to a very small number of people that are helped, perhaps as few as just one or two in a year. A final explanation on this point is that staff may have identified providing tribunal representation where they accompany someone to tribunal to support them but are not actually providing legal advice or representing that person. In the family court this sort of role is often referred to as a 'Mackenzie friend'. As well as accompanying someone, a Mackenzie friend offers information about how the court process works and helps them to understand outcomes but does not provide legal advice.

It is also important to note that the numbers reported in the mapping are by organization and not the number of clients being helped. CAL, which deals with over 8,000 issues a month, has the same weighting as any other organization in the mapping, but this total number is a disproportionate percentage of people helped. The number of clients helped in each area of law is also not evenly spread. CAL provides a holistic advice service, but the majority of clients receive welfare benefits advice (40 per cent) and debt advice (36 per cent). At the time of writing, in mid-2025, there were no specialists in housing or employment law at CAL. In these areas, the advice given will be general advice from a non-specialist adviser. We did not try to map the number of issues or clients being provided with free legal advice because, as explained earlier, there is no settled way to measure this across the sector.

Providing a gateway, not the advice itself

Another way that the mapping exercise overstates the provision of advice is by not clarifying where advice delivery is through collaboration between organizations. (This collaboration will be discussed more extensively in Chapters 6 and 7.) Some organizations have accurately stated that they provide free legal advice in a particular area of law from their offices, but the advice is often, in fact, provided by another organization through co-located services. This reporting will then lead to duplication in the mapping, as both the host organization and the service provider will indicate they provide advice in this area. The MPs' local constituency offices are a good example of this. They indicated that they provide advice in almost all areas of law. For the majority of this work, it is visiting specialists from other agencies that provide that advice, or it is provided through a direct referral. The MPs' constituency offices are providing an extra access point to existing free legal advice services, rather than building greater capacity in the system and providing advice themselves. Nevertheless, they are acting as an important gateway into the advice ecosystem, while mainly sending people on to other places to get advice. The role of these offices is discussed further in Chapter 6.

Unmet need for advice services

The LATAN project shows that there is considerable unmet need for advice in every area of social welfare law. Organizations are running at full capacity and experiencing long waiting times for triage and advice. Clients are presenting with multiple complex issues. CAL alone deals with almost 4,000 issues over the phone each month, but regularly in interviews we heard complaints from other organizations that tried to arrange client referrals to CAL that neither they nor their clients could get through to CAL. Despite the high number of people helped by CAL, their telephone service data indicates that there are another 1,500–2,000 calls each month that are not answered. We heard similar reports from smaller organizations of long queues forming outside their doors before opening times. One organization reported response times of several weeks just to reply to initial email enquiries because of the high level of demand and even though they had significant staff resources dedicated just to this point of triage for their services. Waiting times for help can often be longer than the time available to people. One participant organization stated: 'We're at complete capacity, someone's got four weeks to send a form back even with an extension, we can look at two, three month waiting lists on that' (Interview GG Staff 5).

The Council's Benefit Maximisation Service team, which is one of the most important sources of benefits advice in Liverpool, are also at capacity. As an advice seeker at a local community centre said: 'I normally go to the Benefit Maximisation team at Liverpool City Council but there is a waiting list as long as your arm, and that's for them just to get in touch with you' (Interview DD Client 2). In fact, Refernet data indicate that the Benefits Maximisation team is one of the biggest senders of referrals – mainly to CAL – for services that they cannot provide. Some of these will have been referrals for clients to obtain vouchers for emergency food parcels from the food banks, as these referrals are provided by CAL and commonly sent through Refernet. Nevertheless, there are clearly high levels of unmet demand and a need for much higher capacity in the advice ecosystem.

These organizations are all working to capacity and maximizing their funding – often cross-subsidizing between projects and running on low margins – to minimize waiting times and meet targets. Between 85 and 90 per cent of project funding going on salaries is not uncommon. This leaves very little to fund back office and support costs, to fund access to services, or to cross-fund other projects such as volunteer-led services. We saw effective innovation during the COVID-19 pandemic to reduce the impact of closing face-to-face services, though this was a struggle for smaller organizations. We also saw through our own online advice provision during the pandemic that there is still a significant digital divide for many clients, and there were some who were effectively excluded from our services despite our best efforts. This is an issue, as many government and local authority services provide information primarily online. LATAN organizations appear to be working in an environment where there is a very high level of demand beyond the services that they are able to supply. Funder-led commissioning of organizations to fill this unmet demand is having limited success.

We are seeking to provide policy makers with an alternative starting point when making decisions about advice service provision. We want to tie free legal advice to the social welfare, health and anti-poverty policies and strategies of central government and local authorities. This has the most potential to affect the social determinants of health for the population positively, by making easily accessible the means of ensuring that these programmes and strategies are actually able to reach the intended populations, whatever their level of legal capability. This approach should be underpinned by an understanding of how different types of organizations are contributing to a person's attempts to resolve everyday legal problems in different ways. At a fundamental level, this of course means there is a pressing need to increase the funding for advice provision to reduce the thousands of people that are unable to get the advice that they are seeking every month in Liverpool alone. At the same time, it is also important to understand how issues relating to issue identification and legal capability can be improved. In the next section of this chapter we will present the findings about the types of organizations that exist in Liverpool's advice ecosystem and then synthesize this into a description of the stages of a typical client journey, identifying the opportunities for better targeting of advice.

What the advice ecosystem structure means for the client journey to solve an everyday legal problem

Types of organization

We found from the mapping exercise that organizations broadly fall into two categories in relation to a person's efforts to resolve everyday legal problems: advice providers and gateway organizations. We are referring to the primary activity of the organization, and for most there is some degree of overlap between advice and gateway. Even within the category of advice providers, there are a relatively small number of organizations whose principal objective is to provide legal advice. In Liverpool these are:

- Citizens Advice Liverpool – debt and welfare rights specialists, but also comprehensive general advice provision;
- Merseyside Law Centre – immigration, welfare benefits, housing and debt specialists;
- Vauxhall Community Law and Information Centre – welfare benefits, debt, housing specialists with a bereavement support and advice service;
- Equality and Employment Law Centre – discrimination and employment law specialists;
- Shelter – housing and welfare benefits specialists;
- Raise – debt and welfare benefits specialists;
- The University of Liverpool Law Clinic – immigration, special educational needs and disabilities (SEND) and family specialists;
- The Liverpool John Moores University Law Clinic – family, civil litigation/ small claims, wills and community economic development specialists;
- Liverpool Hope University Law Clinic – employment, discrimination, contracts, consumer, family, landlord and tenant, and administrative law; mainly targeted at staff and students but some public advice;
- Private law firms that have legal aid contracts and those that do social welfare pro bono work.

The gateway organizations are those that help people in relation to social issues/rights – health, education, employability, anti-poverty, food security and so on. Their role in the advice ecosystem is to help people identify that they have a legal issue and to help them overcome some of the legal capability barriers to getting advice. They might, for example, help clients with understanding processes so people feel that they can cope with trying to resolve everyday legal problems and that they have a chance of a fair outcome. The organizations also help make the advice ecosystem more accessible through referrals. They are a starting point and a facilitator in the advice ecosystem – helping people recognize that an issue could be helped by getting free legal advice and helping them find that advice. The reality, however, is that all too frequently this is a gateway to nowhere as there is simply no available advice capacity.

The gateway organizations' focus is not legal advice. They may be housing associations, food banks or pantries, organizations providing community care, organizations supporting a specific demographic by background (for example, the Polish Community Centre, Refugee Women Connect and

Chinese Wellbeing) or their personal circumstances, often related to health (for example, Sahir House and the Brain Charity). All these organizations exist to serve a specific purpose or group, but not specifically to give legal advice. However, a large number of these organizations have recognized the close connection between social rights and access to free legal advice and have obtained funding to provide advice services, most commonly relating to welfare benefits and debt to raise incomes and combat poverty. St Andrew's, for example, a religious organization that runs community food banks and food pantries as its main activity, also employs welfare benefit and debt advice caseworkers.

These organizations, often charities, have stepped in as the state has withdrawn funding from free legal advice provision at the national and local level. Some of them will just provide information. Others will provide information and some ad hoc advice that is dependent on the knowledge and experience of the people working or volunteering in that organization. The extent to which these organizations provide advice services varies according to funding and priorities. These co-located services will be discussed in more depth in Chapter 6.

The advice organizations have also adjusted in response to the barriers to people getting the advice needed. This is often a reflection of where money is available. As with the gaps in advice provision in areas of law, this is driven by the decisions of policy makers. Law centres now provide a wider range of advice services, where traditionally they focused on solicitor-led activity at the more complex end of legal casework. They now provide more general advice and one-off casework, such as Vauxhall Law Centre's (VLC's) bereavement advice service. The funding of law centres was hit particularly hard by the ending of most legal aid funding for free legal advice casework in social welfare law. Today less than 20 per cent of funding for the Merseyside Law Centre and VLC is from legal aid. It has been a severe financial challenge and they have had to make significant changes, and are now much smaller organizations than they were before the Legal Aid, Sentencing and Punishment of Offenders Act 2012 (LASPO). Merseyside Law Centre alone lost 16 caseworkers as a result of LASPO and local authority funding cuts.

Citizens Advice Liverpool, which is the largest advice organization in Liverpool with a turnover of over £4 million and over 100 employees, is an enabler of the advice process as well as a destination for referrals from elsewhere. An important element of its biggest project, the NHS-funded Citizens Advice on Prescription project (CAP), is to facilitate the connection between health and free legal advice, and thus overcome barriers in terms of referrals between these areas of people's needs. The rise of social prescribing services recognizes the need to connect medical and non-medical support services better. Importantly, CAP is not just a referring social prescribing service, it also employs people that give free legal advice alongside people that work specifically to make the links between health and legal advice. These types of health–justice partnership, which we discuss more extensively in Chapter 6, reflect an understanding that public legal education and legal capability barriers need to be addressed, and that legal advice is good for your health (Genn, 2019).

The membership of LATAN has been organized to reflect these two broad groupings of organizations. There is a level of membership for advice providers and an associate membership for those that provide other support services, often to reduce the impacts of poverty and health-related problems, and to act as a gateway for their users who need free legal advice.

Organizations are aware that people go to several places when trying to resolve issues and that there are several steps for those needing legal advice. This process is often an ongoing one in people's lives, with issues overlapping and recurring. Organizations recognize that, as things stand, the ecosystem needs all of its current components. Small organizations recognize the importance of the larger ones to be able to provide the range of services people need. Large organizations recognize the need for smaller organizations that can be responsive to local needs and centred strongly in their communities as starting points for people to try to resolve issues. This systems level cooperation is discussed in Chapter 7.

The three stages of an individual's journey to resolve an 'everyday legal problem'

Our framing of the contemporary free legal advice ecosystem is focused on the communities of people and the advice they need in relation to the problems they are trying to resolve. The importance of this 'bottom-up' approach has been emphasized for many years in the legal needs and paths to justice literature (Genn, 1999; Pleasence and Balmer, 2014). We explain the environment in which people try to get free legal advice, which is, of course, a central component of access to (social) justice. This means that a person's 'path' to justice is in the context of their social rights, wider governmental policies and the realities of life they are facing, framed for example as the 'cost-of-living crisis'. The majority of people do not go to a solicitor to resolve legal issues. It was as few as one in ten prior to 2014 (Pleasence and Balmer, 2014: 1). Free legal advice policy in social welfare law is about people resolving the bundle of everyday legal problems alongside issues that do not have a specific need for legal advice. As a result, the policy focus on access to free legal advice is a specific topic that needs particular attention, but it is also a policy area that overlaps with multiple other policy areas: anti-poverty strategies, housing, immigration, employment and so on.

In other words, with the social determinants of health. The key question in policy-making terms is: what advice is likely to be needed to achieve our social policy goals, and where on the journey to get this advice are the barriers for people to access it?

Three elements must be present for a person to receive free legal advice when needed:

1. Issue identification – the person is aware that there is a legal element to the problem and that legal advice would be of benefit to them. This is exacerbated by low levels of public legal education in England and Wales.
2. Legal capability – there are specific issues related to legal capability that can act as a barrier to a person getting advice, both from an individual and organizational perspective. The Legal Services Board in their 2020 report *Reshaping Legal Services to Meet People's Needs: An Analysis of Legal Capability* framed these barriers as relating to *legal confidence* in a fair outcome; *legal self-efficacy*, in other words a person's ability to handle the stress and complexity of the process; and *accessibility of justice* (Legal Services Board, 2020).
3. Service capacity – that there is capacity in the system to get advice in the relevant area of social welfare law and to the appropriate level.

The complexity, seriousness, inter-connectedness and high prevalence of issues in social welfare law mean that people may need assistance in relation to each of these elements in their efforts to resolve everyday legal problems. It is essential, of course, to build capacity in the sector to reduce the excess demand for free legal advice, but it is also important for policy makers to consider issues relating to identifying when and what legal advice is most beneficial, and how public legal education could be provided. Success in addressing these issues, though, is dependent on an individual's legal capability and collaboration between free legal advice providers.

We recognize that some people (for some issues) will be able to identify that there is a legal element to the issue(s) at hand and be able to self-refer themselves to an advice provider. In fact, the self-referral tool on Refernet had to be turned off because it generated such high demand. Some people may also be able to manage everyday legal problems and find a solution for themselves just by using relevant information sources and without needing free legal advice, or who have the social or financial resources to pay for legal advice. There are, however, as our research suggests, a very large number of people that need support with one or all three elements involved in getting free legal advice. It is these people – often the same people that anti-poverty strategies are targeting – that this book intends policy makers to focus on.

The complexity of the welfare system, the levels of debt in society, insecure employment and housing, poverty and poor public administration are just some of the policy-related reasons for the high demand for free legal advice. In subsequent chapters we focus on the value of collaboration, co-location and effective referral systems in the advice sector. The importance of building capacity in the system so that more people can get free legal advice must not be forgotten though. We still need policy makers to address issues with the way services are commissioned, the recruitment issues in the sector (Rathbone et al, 2022) and the amount of funding for free legal advice. The final section of this chapter looks at how the advice ecosystem in Liverpool is used by people in relation to each of the three elements outlined previously – identification, legal capability and advice capacity – that are present when addressing everyday legal problems.

Steps to resolving everyday legal problems through free legal advice

We have framed the strategic aim of LATAN as 'No wrong door; advice for all'. This aspirational aim is explained in more detail later, but in essence it means that anyone can initiate their journey to resolving legal issues by walking through the door of any VCS organization, and this will lead directly to getting the free legal advice that they need. As indicated in Chapter 2, this strategic aim of LATAN and our research and policy proposals sit within the broad ideas of paths to justice. However, it is important to be clear that the idea of a path or a journey to justice is not a linear or sequential process (Boyle, 2022). There are a number of elements to a person's attempts to get free legal advice and to try to resolve everyday legal problems and a range of differing barriers. The significance of each of these varies according to the type of problem, the extent to which it is a legal or non-legal issue, the access to informal social capital, the demographics and characteristics of the person trying to resolve the problem, its severity and relevant governmental policies.

Our research has indicated three roles for LATAN organizations when trying to help people resolve their everyday legal problems: *gateway*, *referral* and *advice provision*. These three steps or activities broadly map on to the identification, legal capability and service capacity trilogy of issues outlined previously.

Gateway

The first step in a person's journey to get advice is to recognize that their problem has a legal element (housing disrepair, job loss, welfare rights claim and so on). 'No wrong door' means that any organization in this network, or the public or private sector, can help people with this and then act as a gateway to Liverpool's advice providers. This recognizes the value of organizations that do not give advice, or where it is only part of their remit, in the free legal advice ecosystem. Helping people identify that their problem may have a legal element is an important role.

Low levels of public legal education mean that people are often unaware that their issue has a legal component and could be helped by legal advice. Developing close collaboration across a trusted network of VCS organizations to raise levels of public legal education for their staff and volunteers, as well as their clients, can help people take this first step towards resolving their problem. This is one of the aims of LATAN's community of practice.

Multiple access points and a diversity of gateway organizations mean that different forms of advice-seeking behaviour can be provided for. Access to advice can be facilitated for people with particular needs and from particularly vulnerable groups in a fully inclusive advice ecosystem. As we have discussed, the breadth of the advice network is a particular strength in terms of accessibility and in terms of its ability to overcome all forms of exclusion, breaking down barriers such as those relating to digital access, language or disability.

A staff member of a gateway organization made this point clearly in relation to people from Black and minority ethnic (BME) backgrounds and employment:

> I work only with BME people, and they do have other barriers, language and cultural, low self-esteem and lack of confidence, lack of awareness. So that's why, like, most of them, majority of them, actually don't know about the local services which they can access. So, it's like a big issue of lack of awareness actually, at first, people don't even know if they get discriminated against. (Employment Law Focus Group)

This makes clear that for marginalized groups in particular, the ability even to recognize that that there is unlawful discriminatory behaviour is limited – this is before they consider whether to challenge this behaviour – and on top of this they are unaware of the services that might help them with this sort of employment issue.

Beyond identifying the issue, 'No wrong door' should also mean that a person can use any organization as a starting point to overcome any barriers associated with legal capability, and to effectively access free legal advice at the right level at an appropriate time and through an appropriate channel. Ultimately, the aspiration is an appropriate and timely level of 'advice for all' after taking the first step into a gateway organization.

Referral

A referral is often an important next step in a person's journey to resolve everyday legal problems. The aim is that whenever an organization, be it VCS, a health setting or any other, determines that advice could help someone, they know how to refer the advice seeker to an appropriate place that can provide the advice needed. This should not just be signposting, which can lead to referral fatigue, but instead an active, managed referral using a single referral system. Self-referral by members of the public could be available to assist with this. We analyse LATAN's introduction of Refernet, which was our chosen electronic referral system, and the importance of associated collaboration in Chapter 7.

The possibility of improved referral processes was generally welcomed by the VCS organizations we interviewed. They clearly understood that signposting is limited and that it can lead to referral fatigue and trauma for the client. This phase of the research was before we had launched and implemented Refernet. When asked about referrals, a number of organizations said that they get regular signposting from other VCS organizations in Liverpool, often other advice providers, but that they cannot cope with the extra demand this adds to the service:

> What we get through the wider advice service is very much signposting, and people getting told to see us by CAB or by Raise or by Liverpool Community Advice. But our partners will direct people to us but very rarely follow up. (Interview W1)

> Part of the whole problem with access to justice [is] people finding the right services. That they get bounced round and round the houses … We are having to phone around trying to find somebody to take [them]. It's, you know a lot of work ends up being done … For the client, they are just more and more frustrated, because they've told you and they are telling the same story to the next person, the next person, the next person. (Family Law Focus Group)

Trauma was mentioned in several interviews in relation to signposting and referrals. As the member of staff made clear, the clients are having to repeat a story, often a traumatic one, again and again in an attempt to get advice, without being certain each time that it will lead to support. Consequently, if an organization wants to avoid this negative element of signposting, it may have to spend a considerable amount of time contacting other organizations one by one by phone to see if a referral is appropriate and possible.

When we mapped the advice ecosystem, we found a range of ad hoc referral methods that inconsistently overcame the challenge that advice seekers face of moving from recognizing and accepting the need to get advice to finding a place that could provide that advice. Part of the referral process is understanding the services that are provided by others. There is limited time or opportunity to access information about the services currently available in the myriad organizations across the city. We found in the focus group workshops we ran on particular areas of law that staff from different organizations were exchanging contact details so that they could make referrals after the workshop. Referrals are being made in numerous different ways:

> We do warm hand offs … I think is the appropriate terminology … but rather than just send someone round to someone else, generally we would do it via a phone call, so we would ring them up and say we've got someone here that's experiencing this issue, is that something you could support with? So we already know the capacity situation of the people we're trying to refer on to, before we send the client round to try and stop that wasted journey for the client. (Interview W1)

The referrals being made by advice organizations are for a range of advice needs. The referral system is ad hoc for both legal and non-legal issues within the set of organizations working in relation to everyday legal problems. As one manager of an advice organization said:

> We've got to make referrals to social services. We've got to make referrals to carers support, to mental health support, to learning disabilities support. You know, we've got to connect those people to organizations that are gonna support them to ultimately make their lives better, improve their lives … We're just welfare rights and money advice. (Interview A2)

It is not uncommon for small groups of organizations to have set up a referral or 'signposting plus' engagement between themselves where they have common interests. For example, this organization, whose focus was on health, maintained:

> We can only refer to four or five organizations. But we might, we obviously sign-post people to many more. The organizations that we can refer to that we have referral rights into are Advocacy Works, VoiceAbility, the Advice on Prescription Service that's managed by Citizens Advice and we can refer into Careline and adult services in order to signal the need that people have for needs assessment. (Interview H1)

Then outside these established processes there is little that can be done other than to give someone details of a service so that they can make contact themselves. Organizations recognize that this is a poor alternative for many people, especially those who have low legal capability.

We recommend that a directory of services that is kept up to date by a member of staff be integrated with any referral system. Organizations can then inform possible service users and other organizations what services they provide, which will increase the effectiveness and accuracy of referrals so that clients are more quickly accessing the services they need (where they are available). It will also help some people self-refer to the service that they need and save time for themselves and the organizations involved. This collaboration is discussed in more detail in the following chapters.

Advice provision

The third element in someone's advice journey is to receive independent generalist and specialist advice at the appropriate level of legal complexity that enables them to address their everyday legal problems as early as possible.

It is recognized that particular populations may need more, or targeted, support to make this happen. It is also recognized that areas of law have fluctuating demands depending on social and policy circumstances. The key areas of social welfare law identified are: welfare rights, debt/money advice, housing, employment, SEND, immigration and family. Deciding where to allocate scarce resources will depend to a large degree on the social rights-related priorities of the relevant funding authorities. The organizations in the advice ecosystem should participate in the decision-making processes. LATAN has had some success in increasing the participation of its members in LCC decision making, and giving a stronger joined-up voice to its members.

Conclusion

The mapping of Liverpool's advice ecosystem highlighted the fragmentation of the advice sector, which has largely been driven by the patchwork commissioning of services based on competitive principles, scarce funding for advice and reduced and changed provision of social rights. There are hundreds of charitable organizations in Liverpool, often very small and hyper-local, trying to provide the support that was previously provided by the state. This wide range of organizations has become part of the free legal advice journey for people. This is not just a story of underfunded and limited service provision that only partially mitigates the disproportionate cuts that the LCC has suffered during the era of austerity policies, but of a sector that is continually buffeted by the vagaries of funders with poorly informed decision making.

The mapping research showed that it is challenging for policy makers and funders to measure precisely the availability of free legal advice in a local area. A national conversation is needed about how to measure the availability of free legal advice, and how to manage the close connection between access to free legal advice and social rights policy, particularly the alleviation of poverty and the social determinants of health. There is guidance on how to carry out legal needs surveys (OECD/Open Society Foundations, 2019) and significant experience of assessing the need for legal advice, which goes some way to measuring existing demand. Our experience in Liverpool suggests that given the resources needed to do a comprehensive legal needs survey of this sort, the temporary nature of the results and the continued flux in people's needs (driven by policy changes and world events such as COVID 19) and in the services that organizations are able to deliver, an alternative approach is needed that includes interviews to build a clearer picture of advice seekers needs and the barriers they face.

The delivery of what remains of free social welfare law advice is in a precarious state and it is a challenge for people to start to resolve their everyday legal problems or to connect with the residual services that remain. It is important to have as clear a picture as possible of the advice ecosystem. However, our experience of trying to map Liverpool's advice ecosystem – one that we are strongly embedded in – has indicated how challenging it is to map what free legal advice exists. At the same time, it has highlighted how important it is to try to understand where gaps in provision exist and how organizations interact so that scarce resources can be effectively targeted. The manifesto in the final chapter of this book is, in part, a suggestion to policy makers of how to provide greater support for people trying to resolve everyday legal problems: to tie policy making and the funding of services to strategies and initiatives that address the social determinants of health.

Having explained Liverpool's advice ecosystem, we now turn to further discussion in the next two chapters of the benefits of the co-location of advice services and about the advice ecosystem from a systems level perspective. These chapters will further draw the connection between legal advice and its integral part in breaking the cycle of health inequalities.

6

Legal Advice and the Co-location of Services

> Okay, well, before lockdown, there was a very, very successful service that was in St. John's precinct on the first floor, it had the One Stop Shop, it had the Job Centre, it had Housing Options for people who present as homeless, it had someone from Citizens Advice doing similar to what I'm doing, we had a debt worker and we had the Help to Claim. So people could turn up and there was six organizations. I think everyone recognized that that was successful, but obviously 'cause of [the] pandemic, organizations moved out. But the sort of recognition of working in partnership with the Council assists both ... So it does work, the partnership working does work. (Interview H2)

Co-location of advice services is an increasingly important aspect of Liverpool's advice ecosystem. Our research highlighted a variety of these types of partnerships in the Liverpool Access to Advice Network (LATAN), including the comparatively well-known health–justice partnerships that have dominated the limited literature in this area up until now (Beardon and Genn, 2018). Here, we present evidence for and develop discussions about the co-location of advice services more broadly. Co-location of services often occurs because many organizations whose primary focus is on services other than advice, such as support for homeless people, general practitioner (GP) surgeries (the first point of contact to the National Health Service (NHS)) and food spaces, recognize that their clients are likely also to have a need for legal advice.

People often do not identify that their problem has a legal dimension (Pleasence et al, 2017). As we discussed in Chapter 5, voluntary and community sector (VCS) organizations play an important role in a client's journey toward advice by helping them to identify and understand that their problem has a legal component and could benefit from advice (Organ et al, 2020; Organ et al, 2021). In our model of the stages in the journey toward effective advice for a legal problem, also in Chapter 5, we call this the gateway stage. Some organizations then take a step further, to either host or link up directly with an external advice-giving organization to provide advice services at their location or to seek funding to deliver advice services themselves, most commonly welfare rights or debt advice. In this chapter we will discuss four models of co-location that we see:

1. social prescribing through GP surgeries;
2. access to advice in food or community spaces;
3. the provision of advice and generalist support in organizations that cater to groups with a particular vulnerability, such as a health condition or being a member of a particular population sub-group; and
4. access to advice in or through the offices of a member of parliament (MP).

In some of these cases, the organizations have partnered with other services, such as Citizens Advice Liverpool (CAL) or a law centre, but also with specialist organizations, such as Shelter for housing advice. What seems of equal importance to some clients are the advocacy and generalist support services that can be a part of casework, such as calling a public utility on the client's behalf to negotiate a payment plan for debt related to energy usage. These services are often provided with in-house funding, rather than through contracting with an outside agency.

The provision of links to legal advice in these settings builds upon relationships of trust between the client and the organization and can reduce stigma and trauma around advice seeking. As one LATAN participant from a VCS organization put it, 'You know, people trust this place, you will get much better value if you were here, providing advice in this context' (Interview B1). Other participants also discussed the value of the built-up trust they have from their clients. It also presents difficulties for clients if they have to explain their situation anew to a different service provider, which goes against the trauma-informed care approach adopted by many organizations:

> When you hit a certain stage where you may not be able to support [service users], it is very difficult because that service user has got so much trust and so much security in you … also if they move to anyone else, it means that they are constantly having to repeat their story meaning that they are reliving that story and potentially re-traumatizing. (Interview Q1)

Co-location of services also builds upon the VCS organization's knowledge of the client's potential needs, to help to identify and address problems early, before they spiral out of control. In the examples that we describe here, it is easy to see how these interventions – whether one-off advice or casework – can have (and have had, in the cases of the clients to whom we spoke) positive impacts on clients' lives. These are powerful anti-poverty interventions. Clients described directly positive effects for their health, as well as improvements to their social determinants of health.

This chapter, therefore, introduces, analyses and provides support for one of our primary recommendations to policy makers – that they support the embedding of advice services within other settings where people with everyday legal problems might access related services. We will first discuss three of the more common models of co-location outlined earlier: health–justice partnerships, community and food spaces, and specialist organizations. We will then close the chapter by discussing a fourth option that is less well recognized – the provision of or connection to advice in an MP's local office, commonly taking place in regular support hours called 'surgeries'. We were not sure where this fitted into our story, but on reflection we decided its similarities merited discussion here, rather than elsewhere, because of the evolving role that we see for these locations to act as a gateway for MPs' constituents to access the advice and support they need.

Health–justice partnerships

When we are discussing the impact of legal advice on population health the obvious starting place for this discussion of co-location of advice services is health–justice partnerships. As we indicated in Chapter 3, integrating advice services in health settings helps to reduce demand on the NHS through fewer repeat appointments and fewer prescriptions, and they promote better physical and mental health (Advice Service Alliance and the Low Commission, 2015). To date, though, there has been no overarching strategic approach to commissioning, delivering and evaluating the delivery of health justice services (Genn, 2019).

There are a range of organizations and projects around the country that have delivered social welfare advice services into medical settings in various ways (Moffat et al, 2004; Abbot et al, 2006; Woodhead et al, 2017; Beardon and Genn, 2018). The recently recommissioned Citizens Advice on Prescription (CAP) Liverpool project is one of the longest running services of this type. These services have established their value in terms of reducing socio-economic problems and improving health outcomes. As the report following the Low Commission on the Future of Advice and Legal Support stated: 'There is demonstrable evidence that when advice and health sectors work more closely and strategically to meet advice needs this contributes to reducing health inequalities. Direct commissioning …

targets the most vulnerable within settings which they trust and where their specific health needs are understood' (Advice Service Alliance and the Low Commission, 2015).

The 2024 legal needs survey by the Legal Services Board and Law Society identified that a doctor was the second most commonly used adviser for people who had assistance to try to resolve a legal issue (The Legal Services Board and the Law Society, 2024). Ten per cent of survey respondents said that a doctor was their main adviser for their legal issue, compared to 19 per cent of respondents who identified a solicitor (the most common response), 8 per cent another organization or person, 6 per cent family or friends, and for 5 per cent Citizens Advice would be their main adviser (The Legal Services Board and the Law Society, 2024: 17). The impact of social welfare problems on medical professionals' time spent dealing with non-medical issues has been well documented (Popay et al, 2007; Blane and Watt, 2012; Advice Services Alliance and the Low Commission, 2015). As we indicated in Chapter 3, linking health and advice services leads to fewer GP appointments and fewer presentations at Accident and Emergency (A&E), as well as better health and wellbeing for the individuals referred (NHS England, 2019: 22). Further evidence on the benefits of social prescribing advice services is provided later.

Providing access to advice allows medical staff to focus on their area of expertise, that is, medical issues. The patient's overall health picture is also improved by support that recognizes that there *is* a legal element in their everyday legal problems. Many people do not appreciate that their issues have a legal dimension. Advice and support can then help clients address these issues and improve their circumstances for the social determinants of health. LATAN participants were clear that the link between advice and health can offer advantages to both the health setting and the clients whose needs are served. 'One of the reasons we [the advice organization] were called in by the CCG [Clinical Commissioning Group] was to reduce the number of nonclinical presentations … a widely spread view is that up to 20 per cent of presentations to GPs often are for non-medical purposes' (Interview 03). Provision of the advice services in health settings also allows for timely advice in moments when it is needed: 'Because we are in [a health setting] … which we've been for 20 odd years … we are able to meet people in the [health setting] as they are coming out of clinics. So we're there at their point of need' (Interview C1).

Integrated health and legal advice services are an important part of Liverpool's advice network. The CAP project at Citizens Advice Liverpool receives significant NHS funding to provide a social prescribing service to health professionals in Liverpool. This service is described by Citizens Advice Liverpool (2024) as 'a treatment option that helps patients work towards debt reduction, financial stability, better housing and employment conditions, and reduced social isolation. It also provides a wellbeing service that aims to combat loneliness and isolation in our community' (Citizens Advice Liverpool, 2024). GPs in Liverpool can directly refer patients to the CAP project once they identify that a patient has a non-medical issue that may have a legal dimension. This makes it more likely that the client will receive prompt, free legal advice, which minimizes the impact of issues on people's lives, and frees up the medical services to focus on health outcomes. Participants beyond the CAP project discussed the benefit of these co-located projects for client groups with particular needs:

> I only work with BME [Black and ethnic minority] community. So, sometimes we have to help with clients out of our job remit, so we often work around benefit issues a lot. But I am not, like, expert or I don't have that much expertise on that matter. So, for me the best-case service I always refer them to is Advice on Prescription, and it's the best service so far. Have had no complaints – my clients – whatsoever, when they use the service, they are always happy as well. So, that was like best scenario. (Welfare Benefits Focus Group)

A recent evaluation of the CAP project, exploring its physical and mental health effects, was conducted by Aregawi et al (2025). The authors estimate that 75,000 people were living in households supported by CAP between 2017 and 2023. People accessing CAP were characterized by intersectional inequalities, including 70 per cent living in poverty, 90 per cent with long-term health conditions and 60 per cent with multiple health conditions (Aregawi et al, 2025). Findings, using causal, instrumental, variable methodological approaches, suggest that people in receipt of CAP had lower anti-depressant prescribing, lower mental health-related GP attendances and lower mental health-related A&E attendance compared with the rest of the population in Liverpool. They also estimate a £2.7 million saving to the NHS during this period, while acknowledging this only reflects healthcare utilization and not the costs/benefits to other services. The evaluation summarized that the most important aspects of the service were: 'a simple rapid referral process without complex eligibility criteria, with case managers pro-actively contacting clients. In other words, clinicians just needed to make one phone call to make the referral, and the patient was then contacted within two working days' (Aregawi et al, 2025: 7).

The vagaries of funding can have distorting effects for the usage of even these services, however. The story of this client, let us call her Sarah, shows us some of the issues when services are not connected, and why co-located services are so important for people's health. We spoke to Sarah in a Citizens Advice Liverpool weekly advice session, at the Cunard Building on the docks, home to Liverpool City Council (Council or LCC). She was nearly

30, was disabled, was in receipt of Universal Credit (the main UK income-based benefit) and had two children. Sarah wanted advice about Personal Independence Payment (PIP), the UK working-age benefit for people who are disabled. She had been awarded PIP already but over the previous three months had been underpaid by more than £100 each time, and this month had received nothing, with no letters to explain why things might be different. The loss of this income from PIP was making it difficult to make ends meet, so Sarah was borrowing money from her mother, who could not really afford it either: 'I don't really want to ask my mum, but when it's – when it's your child you need to make sure that they've got the nappies or new clothes or food and we haven't always got that amount of money to do that' (Interview BA Client 5). Nobody in her family had any extra money. She described even being reluctant to eat her grandmother's food when she went to her house: 'She's, like, make yourself a cup of tea, make yourself a butty [sandwich], do this, do that. I'm like, Nan, I'm not taking your food' (Interview BA Client 5). The family's poverty had been affecting her older daughter, as well: 'And she gets upset and she cries, like, "I wanna go out", like, [and I say] "We can't baby, Mummy's got no money, let's play with your toys instead"' (Interview BA Client 5).

Most months, even when Sarah's benefits were paid correctly, she and her partner, who was in work, struggled. They needed to ask Sarah's partner's father, with whom they lived, to buy the food shopping some of the time. Like salaries, UK benefits are paid on a monthly basis, so towards the end of the month money gets tight for many:

> We've been struggling. We've had to ask people to lend us, like, our family, to lend us money. We've had to ask his Dad to get the baby's nappies. And I know they're only like, four pound something, but sometimes when you've got no money, you can't even do that.' (Interview BA Client 5)

Sarah seemed to have a good level of legal capability. She had tried to sort her problem by ringing the government helpline:

> I rang the number, and it said press one for the inquiry line, so you press one, and it says to speak to somebody about overpayments or debt – and I'm thinking it's not overpayments or debt, it's underpayment by significant – press five, so I press five. Please visit the Gov website (the UK government hosts many information services at the www.gov.uk site) And then the phone call cut off and I was, like, are you actually joking me? So I went on the Gov website and there's nothing there to tell you about how to contact them with underpayments. So, I contacted my friend [who works for Universal Credit] and that's

> when she said, yeah, she said the day I told her, she said she had a lot of clients ring her with the same thing, and there's nothing you can do 'cause she's only got the number that I've rang as well. She said there's nothing on the Gov website. She said they need to step up and put the proper contact details on, the proper things on the website so that people know how to get in touch for things like this because it's not fair on anybody. (Interview BA Client 5)

She also described a previous DIY attempt to appeal a denial of PIP at a First-tier Tribunal (Social Security and Child Support) without assistance. Her PIP had been denied unjustly, in her view, without consideration of enough evidence to show the effect of her condition on her life:

> They don't know any of my health problems. They don't know how it affects me, why it affects me, how many times I've been in and out of hospital with it. They didn't even know why I was on crutches. So, they don't know anything. They just know what's on paper and they've just gone off that and gone 'yeah she's fit for work'. (Interview BA Client 5)

Sarah appealed to the tribunal: 'I took it to tribunal and they were like, yeah, they've [the Department for Work and Pensions (DWP)] made the right decision, so we're not giving you it back.' She was then able to access some specialist support from Citizens Advice Liverpool. Sarah told us:

> She came with us to the tribunal and then I think she helped us do the letter [of appeal] again, and then I got everything back again, I got what I would normally get and then what I was owed. So it was like £1,500-something, because it took a couple of months as well. (Interview BA Client 5)

Even for this client with relatively high levels of legal capability the tribunal process did not reach the right outcome without support. She described an *Erin Brockovich*-like moment where she spoke truth to power in the tribunal:

> I was like, they've taken the mick, and I said, they've taken it off people who genuinely need it and given it people who don't need it. You've got people who have got health problems, longstanding ones like me, who can't work, and you've got people who've got nothing wrong with them, can work but choose not to. And you're giving it to them and taking off the people, even the elderly people you're doing the same thing to, and it's not very fair. And the man didn't like it and I went, well, I'm only speaking the truth. And I'm not probably the

> only one, probably a lot of people who think the same. It's just the system's a joke, 'cause it's not helping the way it should be – in the way they say they are. (Interview BA Client 5)

We can see here the lack of trust in the fairness of the system, which is endemic in our participants, and the level of determination needed to battle through. We may also be able to see how the 'othering' strategy of previous governments to stigmatize benefits has been absorbed, even by those in receipt of them.

In order to resolve her problem, and after her unsuccessful attempts via the phone and the www.gov.uk website, Sarah sought further help. She went to a different Citizens Advice Liverpool office, but they were only able to help with debt issues that day so told her to go to the drop-in service at the Cunard Building. But when she got to the Cunard Building, they could not really help her either:

> [The Citizens Advice advisor] asked me what number I rang, so I told her and she only had that, the only one that they'd been given. So, she told me to try that number again and if it doesn't work, go to my GP surgery and ask the receptionist if I can see somebody from Citizens Advice, she said, and they'll help me sort it out. (Interview BA Client 5)

Essentially, Citizens Advice Liverpool told her to go to her GP's surgery and ask to be referred back into their services through the CAP project. Her issue appeared to require support that was not available outside of the CAP project, perhaps due to capacity issues or the level of support needed

The grinding poverty of this family's lives was affecting them all. Sarah had a long-term health condition. She described how the situation was creating anxiety for her partner, who was in work: 'He's worrying in case I don't get it back and what are we gonna do?' (Interview BA Client 5). If they were unable to solve the PIP issue, the client would have to take her older daughter out of preschool/nursery for the extra afternoon a week they currently could afford, beyond the 15 free hours to which the daughter was entitled. As Sarah was disabled and not working, her daughter was not entitled to the 30 free hours of childcare for working parents. Since nurseries and preschools are an important part of the early childhood education system in the UK, any reduction in her daughter's hours there was also a blow to her daughter's education and future prospects for good health.

If we think about this family's situation using a life course approach, introduced in Chapter 3, we can see how the social determinants of health – poverty, education, access to food, housing – both within Sarah's life and those of other generations she described – her Nan, mother, partner and children – are all entwined. The prospects of the past and the future generations are interacting in a negatively reinforcing cycle of ill health. A number of these issues are structural issues within the social determinants, because they are directly attributable to government policies – such as the decision in England to limit the extra 15 free hours of childcare to those where both parents are in work.

The CAP project, like other health–justice partnerships, makes apparent the connection between health and advice.

Community and food spaces

Food banks, food pantries and other community spaces are also a very common setting for the co-location of services. Community spaces can vary quite widely from informal (and sometimes infrequent) groupings of a few people to regular meetings with a large supporting cast of characters. Part of what makes these groups so interesting to us, both as people and as researchers, is how they are the real grassroots of VCS organizations. They are generally run on a shoestring and often do not have a formal legal entity. They rise above this as a true expression of a democratic ideal of participation at a very local level. Matthew Harding has praised the value of the charitable sector as a site for the altruistic and voluntary production of plural public goods (Harding, 2021). The community spaces are tightly tied to their local communities and offer services that are tailored to these communities' needs. The community spaces that we have visited over the course of the LATAN project have offered an incredible range of activities to their participants, from gardening to language groups. They very commonly offer free coffee and tea and a place to gather for a chat. Many act as food banks or food pantries and some offer a free hot meal at regularly scheduled times. Moreover, quite a few of them offer a chance for people to get help with their everyday legal problems. As discussed earlier, and in Chapter 5, this can be either by providing an invaluable gateway to advice or sometimes by providing advice themselves.

Food banks and food pantries are distinct services that serve different but overlapping populations. Food banks generally are spaces where clients can receive a pre-determined bag of free food per week. They are meant to be three-day food parcels, but clients are often only able to come once per week. Food banks usually require a referral (often from Citizens Advice Liverpool) to access the food bank and have a limit as to how many times a client can come, though various food banks have explained that they can be flexible if a family presents with extreme need. At one food bank in Liverpool, where we have volunteered and placed students for several years, clients receive one bag per family member with a set amount of vegetables and fruit, which is then supplemented with a per-family allocation of cupboard staples such as cereal, pasta, tinned meat or fish, tinned soup, tea or coffee and biscuits.

Jen has had multiple shifts with the other volunteers filling the fruit and veg bags and a common allowance would be two carrots, two onions, two potatoes, an apple or two or an orange per family member for the week. Food banks also have nappies, toilet paper and toiletries. Again, we have spent multiple shifts splitting up multipacks of toothbrushes and razors so that each client can get one.

Food banks, at least in Liverpool, often serve a temporary (or not yet permanent) migrant population. Liverpool is a major dispersal site for asylum seekers in the UK, so many live here in long-term temporary housing while they await the decision on their asylum claim. Most asylum seekers have 'no recourse to public funds' (NRPF) immigration status (Home Office, nd). NRPF status has been a standard condition for several decades for all people in the country on temporary immigration status, such as those seeking family visas for partners and spouses of UK nationals or for parents of UK national children. A ban on accessing benefits has been in place for temporary migrants, those without legal status and asylum seekers since the Immigration and Asylum Act 1999. Although the ban is discretionary and can be removed for several exceptions, such as to avoid destitution or when there are concerns about child wellbeing, it is nevertheless the default position for those with temporary status (Home Office, 2024). Consequently, the client population at food banks often has little scope for accessing welfare support to improve their financial condition. They are usually entitled to £49.18 in cash asylum support per family member per week, in addition to housing. Families with babies and small children also get a small additional weekly amount of money (£5.25–£9.50) to enable them to buy fresh food. If their accommodation provides meals, they are entitled to £9.95 per family member per week in asylum cash support (Home Office, nd). Liverpool is a lower cost city, but it is easy to see why asylum seekers sometimes need to seek support from food banks.

Advice about whether an asylum seeker's circumstances meet the exceptions in the Home Office guidance that lead to some extra support from the state, despite having NRPF status, and whether it would affect their application for leave to remain, is very hard to come by. Understandably, asylum seekers are focused on their immigration status application, for which it is also very hard to get advice. These are long and complex processes. Asylum seekers are unlikely to want or have time to do anything that further complicates or delays their status application. Language and cultural barriers also make accessing advice in relation to welfare benefits challenging. At one community centre in Kensington we co-locate a pop-up advice service alongside the food bank, specifically placing students who can speak Arabic to try to reduce these barriers. Word quickly spread that advice was available and demand to speak to the students was high. The advice they can provide is quite limited though. Immigration advice in the

UK is a regulated specialization and is not an area where students can assist without close supervision by a regulated individual. And the benefits advice needed is often complex and requires referral to a specialist. Students can still help people gain some basic understanding of the situation they are in. They answer a range of questions, for example, about children's access to schools, about whether there is any further local support available, about NRPF and so on. At the time of writing in mid-2025, though, we have heard that this food bank is closing due to funding cuts.

Interview participants also reported to us that it had become increasingly difficult to get food donations since the pandemic. This reflects the uncertainty that pervades the food bank sector. Reduced access to food spaces will increase poverty and destitution and make it even more difficult to access advice in Liverpool, especially for the most vulnerable. Food pantries are a bit different. Most food pantries have a regular population that accesses their services. These people pay a low, fixed weekly amount and then are entitled to choose a certain number of food items from the available stock. One client of the weekly food pantry at the Liverpool Lighthouse, just down the road from Liverpool FC's Anfield Stadium, explained the advantage of the food pantry:

> But [Universal Credit] doesn't help very much because I only get £350 a month Universal Credit pay. Yeah, which is not much when you think about it, it works out to about £80, £90 a week, which you're expected to live on. You know, and at the moment with the cost of living, you know, I'm really struggling … but like the price of electric, the price of gas, to pay for shopping has just gone sky high. So you just have to just try and get by on that. That's why I'm here [at a community food pantry] today. Because, you know, what you spend today helps you out over the week shopping wise … Last week I came here, it's £3.50 and then when I got home, I always count up if I would have gone to Asda or [another] supermarket, how much it all would have come to and it would have come to about £18 … What I got here last week for £3.50 … you're saving a lot. And there's the free lunch first. You get your free lunch, and you can have a little chat and you need to get out [of the house]. (Interview CC Client 2)

Food pantries generally do not require a referral from another agency and tend to serve the immediately surrounding population. They might have more clients who have British nationality and a legal status that allows them to receive public funds than is typical at a foodbank. When we started placing students in food spaces to offer welfare benefits checks, we found that in food banks there was less opportunity to do this due to the high number of people with NRPF status. We have therefore started placing students in food pantries instead (including at Liverpool Lighthouse), as more often they can find people who would like some assistance with a benefits check or benefits form-filling. However, it is a sad fact about the UK welfare benefits system that the levels of payments are set so low that people even in receipt of their full entitlement, like the client just quoted, often need to make use of these food spaces to make ends meet (Hayes and Maynard, 2024a, 2024b). As the client also explained, these spaces generally have a free lunch or coffee morning associated with them, so clients get a hot meal and also have 'a little chat' and build some community with their neighbours. These spaces help to combat loneliness and social isolation, and reduce vulnerability to negative health consequences.

It was quite common at the food spaces we have visited – both food banks and food pantries – to have a community closet or similar. This would have some donated clothes that clients can look through. Lack of clothing is a less commonly acknowledged, but important, part of poverty and destitution in people's lives (Graham, 2023). One of the food banks we work with has found this aspect challenging, however, as there can be a lot of stock to maintain and store alongside the food, and since the food bank operates inside a church, everything needs to be cleared away between sessions so parishioners can access the space too.

Food spaces, in general, recognize the role of legal advice in helping reduce other problems, such as food poverty and debt. One participant from a food bank explained that they trained volunteers to open conversations with service users with the aim of identifying where other services, including advice services, could be beneficial to resolving the life issues that had brought them there. They reported that, regrettably, the steady rise in demand for food parcels prior to COVID-19 had already meant a reduction in the time available to train volunteers and to carry out this role (for more on this, Loopstra, 2018). The training of volunteers was temporarily halted at the time of interview. COVID-19 further increased demand for the food bank, reducing the time available to identify and support wider issues even more, and the contact restrictions made it harder to engage with service users. The food bank, which already delivers debt advice, decided to apply for, and was awarded, funding to deliver welfare rights advice.

Co-location of advice services and generalist support in specialist settings

The next type of co-location that we will discuss in this chapter is the provision of advice alongside generalist support and advocacy in VCS organizations that serve populations with vulnerabilities. As we discussed in Chapter 1, the intersectionality of disadvantage can mean that the multiple layers of identity that the clients of these services have, such as being

LGBTQ+, or disabled, or living with HIV, or being an asylum seeker, or living in poverty, or some or all of those things at the same time, interact together to create a particular set of vulnerabilities or abilities for a particular individual at a particular point in time. This amounts to a need to think about people and the services they need in a holistic way. The timeliness of the social welfare legal advice that is needed, particularly welfare rights advice, can be crucial for the populations served in these settings. For example, PIP, the UK working-age benefit for people who are disabled, is a 'passporting' benefit to other state services. A successful claim for PIP can open up other sources of state support, including top-up premiums on other state benefits, such as housing benefit, a blue badge (disabled parking permit), rail pass discounts, or free bus travel or exemption from the benefit cap (limit on the monthly amount that an individual can receive in state-funded support), and in some cases the 'bedroom tax'. So, making good and timely claims is very important. What we can see in the following case study is the real value that clients place on the more general support provided alongside specialist support and advice.

The Brain Charity

The Brain Charity provides a range of services, from social activities such as art, knitting and music therapy to legal, employment and counselling support to clients with neurological conditions, including brain injuries. This includes advice and updates on welfare benefits. For this case study we interviewed three members of staff and four clients (In order to prevent the staff members from being identifiable, we have not attributed quotes to a particular member of staff but instead left them all at the generic 'staff'.)

The Brain Charity often gets clients at the point of crisis or dramatic change in their lives, such as when they have had a difficult diagnosis or a brain injury. This advice is then very timely for this period that is likely to be advice need-intensive. The charity aims to provide well-rounded support to clients, referring them to various services within the charity based on their need. Participant staff discussed the increasing need for legal advice concerning welfare benefits due to the complexity of the welfare system. There is also greater need for advice on housing and employment law issues. The Brain Charity offers support through various means such as phone calls, online forms and an inbox clients use to access advice via their website and can refer clients to legal partners or other organizations when necessary. They also offer a drop-in service at various hospitals in Merseyside. Clients often come to the charity as a last resort after being let down by other service providers. Staff members also highlighted the impact of not receiving legal advice to solve everyday legal problems, especially for neurodivergent clients (The Brain Charity, 2024).

One member of staff reflected on the barriers that their clients face when seeking advice to solve their problems in a more traditional legal setting:

> There's always a legal aspect to most issues people are faced with and I think … because a lot of the times our client base are already quite vulnerable, and I think the idea of letting people with these neurological conditions, physical or hidden distress, go and speak to solicitors in their scary suits, or that's how [the client] may see it … Sometimes our clients are too vulnerable, they don't know where to get the legal support from … So it puts them at ease that they don't need to go into a big, scary office to speak to someone who speaks 'gibberish' to them, because they're speaking in 'law language'. (Brain Charity staff)

The member of staff was clear that they were not implying that lawyers actually spoke 'gibberish', but rather that the relationship built up between the charity and the clients could act as a bridge across what many clients perceived to be a frightening divide. Receiving that advice in a familiar setting was also helpful to bridge this divide. Each member of staff interviewed highlighted that the charity's broader services helped clients feel more comfortable with the setting. This can help to build trust and confidence so that the issues that are making clients' lives difficult can be tackled:

> Some of our clients are so isolated that the first step to get into employment might be attending an activity in the charity like Chess Club, so that they get used to communicating with others before we get them into work. We're led by the client, so we don't ask them to do anything they don't want to do. We don't force them to do anything and we work with them to kind of help what would make their lives better. (Brain Charity staff)

Clients also discussed how the wider services had drawn them to the organizations and built the connections needed to eventually tackle their everyday legal problems: 'Initially I came for wellbeing and those kind of things. [The client had mentioned aromatherapy.] But then in the middle somewhere, I needed some of the advice and help to start my employment … And then they start helping me with certain things' (Interview D2).

Participant staff members were guided by the level of need for an individual client. Some clients, who were relatively independent, might only need some guidance to use the website where individuals can bid for particular social housing units in Liverpool. Other clients, who were homeless, might need to have the staff ring the Council's housing options team to get them assessed and accommodated in a hotel for a while.

Staff members, while providing an enviably holistic service, also expressed the pressure brought by performance targets in government service provision contracts. One staff member helped a homeless client who had come in for services by allowing him a shower and some donated clothes. But these kindnesses are in addition to the services the charity is funded to provide, creating pressure between the approach clients need and the limitations of funding:

> He walked out the shower and he had his fresh clothes on, and he just says, 'I feel like I've won the lottery'. And I just thought, that's why I do it. And then sometimes I worry that when I do things like that, like, that's not your job … We've got targets to meet … funds to get. I've got KPIs [key performance indicators]. The charity only gets money to pay our salaries if I meet my target. (Brain Charity staff)

This staff member's concerns are reflections of the wider pressures on the sector, which is often required to be target-driven by the contracts with funders. This also reflects the broader shift across the whole charitable sector from grant to contract and results-based funding.

Another client discussed how instrumental the Brain Charity staff had been in referring them to other organizations for housing advice and then pushing those organizations to do more to intervene on their behalf:

> Until things got pushed from [the Brain Charity] and 'Michaela' [an anonymized staff member from another LATAN organization] pushed my domestic violence organizations and then all of them gave them a bit of more backup. Then I got moved to a temporary house. You know with children it's not easy to live in the hotel during school days for months and months with no cooking facility and with no laundry in there … [I]f that help was available before, then I think I wouldn't be having such tough time being homeless with a child. (Interview D2)

This quote also shows the value of the right advice at the right time. The client could have been spared 'months and months' of being homeless in a hotel with her school-aged child. Timely advice can be an advantage of co-location, where the client does not need to go to another location to have the required advice. Here, we can see that the right advice at the right time can also be provided through a timely referral. However, it took follow-up from the Brain Charity to spur the organization referred to into making a greater effort. It also may be an example of the deeper level of trust between the LATAN organizations that gave the staff person a connection at another LATAN organization who they could press to respond more forcefully to this client's need.

Another client described how he had received confidence coaching sessions at the Brain Charity to help with seeking work: 'My confidence, when I'm angry, I can do anything. But when I'm normal now, see I'm sweating, my hands are dead sweaty. But yeah, [the Brain Charity]'s just give me so much, it really has. And other places don't' (Interview D1). He had also had help to deal with a serious debt owed to the Department for Work and Pensions (DWP):

> My brother was getting Carer's Allowance for me and we declared it and it racked up a debt, 20 grand. £20,000. Well, just under. And we got it waivered. But it was just – I was just gonna end it all. Like, I had [the means to commit suicide], I had everything ready to just end it. And then I got the letter the day after, said it'd all been squashed. I had to double take at first, like, really? They done everything, on my behalf they done everything. [A staff member] said that it could've easily just carried it on, but it got squashed in the end, got waivered. They got the MPs involved. They got someone else, I can't remember who it was. It was an MP and someone else, but I can't remember who it was. But honestly, this place is one of the best places I've ever been to. (Interview D1)

We believe this debt to the DWP was an overpayment of Carer's Allowance. It was reported in May 2024 that the DWP was trying to recover more than £250 million in overpayments from 134,000 carers (Whitworth and Smith, 2024). Family carers for disabled people can receive this payment if they provide care for more than 35 hours per week. However, at the time of the interviews, if they received another income of more than £151 a week they were not eligible. This threshold was raised in the 2024 autumn budget by the new Labour government to £196 per week, equivalent to 16 hours per week of employment at the National Living Wage. This means that approximately 60,000 more carers nationally are eligible to claim Carer's Allowance (Carers UK, 2024). However, people whose incomes fluctuate sometimes fail to report their circumstances correctly to the DWP, and thus can be overpaid. Overpayment of just £1 in a week requires that the whole carer's allowance must be repaid. The DWP did not routinely inform claimants of overpayments, so debts of thousands of pounds built up for many people. The support provided to this particular client is an example of the value of advocacy on behalf of a client, in this case from the staff at the Brain Charity but also by their rallying further support including that of an MP. Any strategy for the provision of legal advice needs to consider how the provision can be tailored to meet the requirements of populations with specific and intersectional vulnerabilities.

Advice surgeries in MPs' local offices

In Liverpool, MPs' local constituency offices are becoming a form of community hub for people with everyday legal problems. This is in addition to their perhaps more traditional role of advocating for constituents. Liverpool has five MPs, all of whose offices are connected to LATAN. MP Dan Carden's office hosts a SEND specialist from the University of Liverpool Law Clinic and welfare and housing specialists from Vauxhall Law Centre. MP Ian Byrne's constituency office was opened as part of the West Derby Centre for Social Justice on 21 March 2025. Other MPs provide welfare advice and even provide some funding for local advice agencies. Apart from these (generally small) pots of funding from their office budgets that they direct to local advice services, the MPs' constituency offices are generally providing an extra access point to existing free legal advice services, rather than building greater capacity in the system and providing advice themselves. Nevertheless, they are acting as an important gateway into the advice ecosystem and mainly sending people on to other places to get advice. As this worker in one of the constituency offices stated: 'My background is advice, I can give advice on benefits or housing, right? But in this job you don't have to really because what you're doing is getting in contact with another agency, who then give you back the information, so really it's a lot of signposting' (Interview Z1).

MP office staff numbers are limited, usually one or two caseworkers plus an office manager, but they deal with a high number of constituents. In interviews these staff showed very good knowledge of the wide range of organizations in their local area where they could signpost or refer constituents, which is essential to managing such a high number of people. Being in an MP's office makes a big difference to the ability to access advice services. One member of staff in an MP's office recognized the relatively privileged position they hold in terms of being able to find advice for someone:

> When we are looking around [for casework], and I know we are very fortunate because we are from an MP's office and they [advice providers] all help us. But the average person would find it very difficult to access these services because of the amount of people going through the services. (Interview P1)

This use of MPs' offices as a place to go when people need free legal advice, or are simply desperate, appears to be a growing phenomenon and a sad reflection of the current state of access to justice in England and Wales. This role of MPs needs further research to understand how best to integrate it into the advice ecosystem (Newman and Robins, 2024: 241).

We first interviewed the MPs' offices in 2020, and several of their office teams spoke of 'postcoding' – the need to screen seekers of advice by their postcode to ensure that they were residents of the relevant parliamentary constituency and therefore entitled to call on that particular MP for advice. This reflected the overwhelming need for advice in the city. At that point, during the COVID-19 pandemic, they spoke of the need for employment advice around eligibility for furloughing. They had less demand for welfare benefits and housing advice as many of the normal mechanisms that drive immediate demand, such as medical assessment for PIP or eviction in housing, were paused in the policy response to the pandemic. Some participants did consider that their constituents' needs had changed over the recent past:

> They weren't able to represent themselves, a lot of them have serious issues or they were mentally vulnerable. And a big chunk of the people we represent we think going back 10, 15 years ago, they would have had carers with them, they wouldn't be required to do these things. They are not capable of filling the forms … so they are not capable of representing themselves. They have a massive disadvantage. (Interview P2)

Reflecting on how the resources available in the city had changed since austerity:

> There were only two places in the north of Liverpool that had the ability to do that [representation], which was Vauxhall [Law Centre] or Fazakerley [Information and Advice Resource Centre] [which has since closed] … And it was just … a solicitor who was in his 70s and we had one advice worker who was in his 60s and that's all we had to signpost to … That was … my frustration … You take away 30, 32, caseworkers, you know, representatives that can actually take you through that system. That was such a massive part of what the system involves. So, we've gone now, from that to two. That's quite a massive issue. (Interview P1)

This participant is referring to their estimate of all of the welfare rights workers positions currently available and those that were lost due to cuts to local authority funding under 'austerity' policies. Many agencies across the city had previously been funded to provide this advice but the positions were lost in the wake of cuts to available grants and contracts from the LCC. As this participant pointed out, now there are simply not the resources available to refer to.

As was discussed previously in Chapter 5, MPs' offices also talked about clients shopping around from organization to organization to get needed advice. As one participant from an MP's office said, in many cases the clients that came to them for information and advice were simply getting signposted back to places where they had already been:

> Say immigration advice, I will signpost to AsylumLink because my knowledge of immigration is very limited. A lot of the time, they've already got the case. Say with Citizens Advice. If I ever signpost to Citizens Advice, they mostly know the constituent. They will know the person I'm speaking of and they'll have a case on them. So, it's really about signposting and working together with the other agency to get the best results for the constituent. (Interview Z1)

In addition to the provision of advice and providing a site (and funding) for co-location for other advice services, MPs also have a role as a potential lever of political pressure that organizations might be able to apply, as was seen previously in this chapter. MPs' offices have a privileged position in terms of advocating for people with an acute everyday legal problem. Advocacy is used here not in the legal sense, but as 'action to help people say what they want, secure their rights, represent their interests and obtain services they need' (Advice Services UK, 2011). This is an alternative to a resolution of an everyday legal problem through legal advice. The importance of advocacy by politicians is not limited to MPs. One client we interviewed had spent a month ringing the DWP to try to get sanctions removed after they were unfairly applied to her disabled son. Eventually she went to her local councillor in desperation because she had heard they had helped someone else she knows. The councillor got in touch with the local DWP office and the issue was promptly resolved. MPs' ability in some cases to advocate for their constituents who needed to resolve everyday legal problems came through clearly in interviews, as this example shows:

> One of my old colleagues at Citizens Advice got in touch with me because one of her clients was sitting in the city centre. She had nowhere to go. So, she's contacted Housing Options who deal with all the homelessness in Liverpool and she asked them to house her. They were just referring her back and forth. This lady – it was about half five and this lady is still sitting in the city centre with nowhere to go. So, she contacted me and asked me to contact Housing Options on behalf of the MP. I made a phone call, an hour later the lady was housed. So that's literally the difference. (Interview Z1)

There are limits to the extent to which an MP's office can just pull strings, though. They attribute their success or lack thereof in particular cases to the location at which the pressure and advocacy is needed. As a caseworker explained:

> Some of the cases, you'd be shocked and then they [service providers] think the MP can pull a miracle, but that can't happen … I would say

> the MP, when it comes to Liverpool City Council, the MP's got a good hold there, you know, there's a lot she can do because the City Council work closely with the MP. Anywhere else, it's a bit more difficult and I don't think people understand that. (Interview Z1)

Another spoke about their frustration with the lack of options available to their constituents:

> When people come to the MP's office, they are often absolutely desperate, there is nowhere else to go. They've gone through the system and an MP's office is sort of an afterthought sometimes for a lot of people. But obviously … from an immigration perspective, that's a lot of people's first port of call … But nine times out of ten, what they, what they actually need is representation. You know, they need both legal representation, so having fired off letter after letter, [the MP's office] has had some successes, but I think for them couple of successes we've had, we've fired another 35 letters off which they haven't even been replied to … The MP's office cannot be a solution to the access to justice crisis which we are facing now. What we need is a fully funded advice legal system where people regardless of their circumstances can access justice. That's it. (Interview P1)

Conclusion

In all of these types of settings, we can see how clients value the provision of a holistic service that allows them to meaningfully tackle the range of everyday legal problems they are experiencing. Many of these clients do not have a level of legal capability that will allow them to tackle their problems. This is particularly true for the clients with intersectional vulnerabilities. Previous negative experiences have, in many cases, led clients to have no expectation that they will be able to make change themselves. As a result, they are afraid to even attempt it. This leads to and reinforces avoidant behaviours, like the clients who will not open their mail from the DWP. Their lack of trust in the system undermines what legal capability they do have. Although these clients did need and value information and general support, part of what the support workers provided was the knowledge and ability to make connections to advice, and specialist support for more serious issues, and to rally MP pressures where it might be useful. This support was linked up to connections in the LATAN network and knowledge of how to operate within the city.

Many of the situations these participants describe demonstrate the depth of the poverty into which clients can sink without proper access to help to solve their everyday legal problems. But the co-located services described here have shown how valuable advice can be in intervening to unpick a negative spiral of everyday legal problems. Making the connections between non-legal advice and legal advice can speed up access to the legal advice needed (assuming of course that this advice is available in the under resourced advice ecosystem). This can have positive effects for the social determinants of health and improve their health outcomes across their life course for themselves and their families.

7

A Systems Level Approach

> I just got to the end of my tether and I just said this … We are just fighting each other for clients … there's enough of them and we are fighting each other for money … there's not enough of that. What we've got to do is come together. (Interview A2)

In this chapter we will discuss the Liverpool Access to Advice Network (LATAN) as a system. A primary goal of LATAN was to build up a community of practice and to enhance collaboration within the Liverpool advice ecosystem, endeavouring to improve efficiency. We will relate the LATAN project to insights from systems thinking literature. We will do this by reflecting on boundary issues – both external boundaries and those hierarchies nested within LATAN itself. We will also think about the effects of trust within LATAN. The advice system was characterized by a lack of trust and collaboration at the beginning of the project. This can be attributed to various causes, but a principal cause was that the competition for scarce funding resources had pitted these various organizations against one another in recent decades. The detrimental effects of the shift in government funding at all levels from grants to government contracts for service provision, as well as the effects of long-term austerity will be considered in this light. Some hopeful signs in terms of improved trust within the network and with the research team show the positive impact of the high leverage intervention that we have designed. These effects can be seen in the successful collaboration between LATAN members and the research team to produce the Liverpool access to advice strategy.

A systems approach

Systems theory offers some insight into the LATAN project. Bertalanffy (1968) proposed a general system theory that considered the 'wholeness' of functioning systems, emphasizing the interrelationships between the elements that make up the system. The fundamental idea is that a system functioning together is more than the sum of its parts. In *Thinking in Systems*, Meadows and Wright (2009) considered how the functioning of complex systems can be understood and argued that most societal issues are fundamentally system problems requiring a holistic and interdisciplinary approach. They defined a system as 'an interconnected set of elements that is coherently organised in a way that achieves something' (Meadows and Wright, 2009: 11). The Liverpool advice system can be understood as a system in this sense.

Stroh (2015) identified that a key difference between a conventional and systems thinking approach to solve a problem is to improve the relationships between the elements of the system, rather than focusing on improving the various elements of the system themselves. With the LATAN project, we have attempted to build up the relationships between the organizations that have advice provision as a core mission – such as advice agencies and law centres, but also more traditional law firms that take legal aid clients in some areas. We have also attempted to link these core advice organizations to other community organizations that might have advice as a secondary purpose, or which might simply have people presenting to them with everyday legal problems that need solving.

Stroh also recommends focusing on a few key initiatives to try to restructure the functioning of these relationships, rather than many smaller changes (Stroh, 2015), an approach that we followed. Our project has created 'the community of practice' that is LATAN. It functions as a discussion forum and strategic direction venue for the advice ecosystem in Liverpool. We also focused on developing and supporting a secure online referral pathway to try to create a tangible link for the sharing of client information in a secure way and to reduce the phenomenon of 'referral fatigue', where a would-be advice seeker is signposted from organization to organization, and needs to re-tell their potentially traumatic story once again, only to find that they cannot get advice at this new organization either. By designing this platform with agreed data security procedures and a support worker to answer questions, we tried to bridge this gap for the advice-seeker. In systems thinking these sorts of interventions are called 'high leverage'.

Boundaries

A major concern of systems thinking is the boundaries of the system (Meadows and Wright, 2009). Boundaries delineate what is inside the system and what is outside of it. These can be either conceptual or physical limits that define where a system ends and its environment begins. Our project had a physical boundary imposed upon it from the beginning, as the funding came from the Liverpool City Council (Council or LCC), which limited expenditure to organizations within the city limit. This might seem like a boundary that would be perceptively obvious to those not familiar with Liverpool, but, in fact, this is a fairly porous boundary. Health and other service providers often ask clients who are seeking services 'what colour is your bin?' LCC-provided rubbish bins are purple 'wheelie' bins. It is often the case that houses on one side of a road will have purple bins, and on the other side they will have a different colour, as the Council boundary goes down the middle of the road.

There is some boundary spanning of this physical boundary, as organizations within the boundary often serve clients from beyond this physical boundary. This is especially true for the advice agency participants, who often have clients who travel some distance to receive services, or clients who call in to advice lines. An example is Liverpool's employment advice law centre, which holds the national legal aid contract for remote services for those with potential claims of discrimination in employment or services. We drew this boundary according to the location of the participant organizations, rather than the clients they serve, as no services were directly funded through LATAN itself.

One LATAN participant, with funding that extends beyond the Council limits, described the benefits of not being limited by this physical boundary:

> Yeah. So, it doesn't matter where you live. There is no postcode boundary or anything like that. So, if you are, especially if you are on the border, saying 'Am I in Liverpool, am I in Huyton, you know, where do I live?' It does not matter to us. So we are really saying it doesn't matter what colour your wheelie bin is. (Interview C1)

Boundaries can be conceptual, as well as physical. A conceptual boundary of the project is the limit between the advice network, which is a remover of barriers to justice, and the environment in which it functions – for example, the state-administered welfare benefits system, or LCC's housing policy. This boundary between the voluntary and community sector (VCS) organizations in the LATAN system and the Department for Work and Pensions (DWP) or LCC is an open boundary, permeable to exchange with the state-administered systems beyond the network. Indeed, the biggest referrer across the LATAN network was the Council, which sent referrals to Citizens Advice Liverpool (CAL) for those who presented in need of advice beyond the scope of the Council Benefits Maximization Team.

This was a feature of LATAN from the beginning – we were trying to expand the boundaries of the Liverpool advice system beyond the agencies traditionally at its core, such as Citizens Advice, Raise and the law centres. With LATAN, we tried to include smaller, neighbourhood organizations and other non-advice organizations where people might present and discuss their everyday legal problems. It was our goal to link these local groups, and other settings such as food banks and health organizations, into the core advice network. We hoped via this approach to expand the capabilities of these smaller organizations to identify legal issues when people presented with them. Shared training would improve the capability of these organizations to understand what were legal problems and perhaps provide some basic information about how the problem might be addressed. The organizations would be connected into the wider network, so would know where people might go for advice.

Systems thinking tells us that the location and limits of boundaries is a frequent source of tension and conflict within the system (Bertalanffy, 1968; Meadows and Wright, 2009). Within LATAN we can see this tension between advice agencies and other organizations. The membership of LATAN is two tiered, with advice agency membership for those organizations that provide advice as their core purpose, and associate membership for other organizations. This, in effect, creates a veto power for the advice organizations in decision making within LATAN – a reasonable approach given that it is these organizations' advice resources that the system is trying to distribute.

Another way of thinking about this from the systems thinking approach, considering the boundaries nested within the system, is that there are sub-systems within systems. The advice-providing agencies are a sub-system nested within LATAN, the system.

Trust

Trust plays a crucial role in systems thinking. Trust can function as a resource of the system. Systems with high levels of trust as a resource can then generate further trust both toward and beyond the system. So trust is both an input and an output of the system.

Trust is created by the interactions between the different organizations that make up LATAN; it is more than just the individual relationships between these persons who are most closely related to LATAN. Trust is built up through repeated interactions over time. McEvily et al (2003) noted that the presence of trust in an organization helps to convert the organization's resources into the desired outcomes. This operates through knowledge sharing, their commitment to the overall outcome, willingness to pool resources and also the willingness to forgive errors (McEvily et al, 2003). So, trust can operate by having direct effects, but also by having moderating effects on other relationships within the system. Senge identified that there are trust-based reinforcing loops in systems (1990). The presence or absence of trust within the system can create feedback loops that either improve and reinforce the performance of the system or work to the detriment of the system's performance in a way that is also self-reinforcing (Stroh, 2015).

Trust was a fundamental issue for the network and its functioning. Trust affected relationships in multiple interrelated and connected ways. For example, trust affected the relationship between:

- organizations embedded in LATAN;
- organizations and the research team;
- organizations and the council;
- organizations and LATAN the network;
- clients and the organizations providing services;
- clients and LATAN;
- clients and the state.

In most of these situations it was primarily a lack of trust that was most evident at the beginning of the project. This has been driven and amplified by more than a decade of austerity policies that have hollowed out thicker concepts of justice, as discussed previously. The initial state of the system was that the feedback loops reinforced this lack of trust.

Trust and information flows

We can see the effect of trust in how information flows through the system and how knowledge is shared in the system. This is particularly important in LATAN because we have found over the course of the project that it is often just one or two individuals within an organization that provide most of the connections to the rest of the system. It is often the case that the individuals participating in most of the meetings and discussion in terms of the community of practice and decision making are chief executives or similar. The trust between these individuals is all-important for the successful functioning of the network and for creating feedback loops that reinforce overall trust.

Even within that sub-system made up of the core advice organizations, there was a lack of trust at the outset of the project. The evidence from the beginning of the project was that the advice organizations were not even in very good communication with one another. Participants said that there was no discussion of how to work together to improve outcomes for clients:

> All I know is that … unless everybody else is ignoring me, we don't talk to anybody. So, Liverpool City Council gives six organizations funding for advice … and that's normally where your route for the advice comes from … the local authority-funded advice organizations. [But] there's no meetings. There's no email exchange. There's no updating each other about when we're open, when we're closed … if we were sent a referral that's wrong, if we could sign post to them or not. That's the bare minimum, and that isn't even happening. (Interview A1)

The research team has been part of the Liverpool Law Society's Access to Justice subcommittee for more than a decade. Most of the core advice agencies are also members, as well as a number of law firms with legal aid contracts. The subcommittee meets quarterly and provides a forum for common issues, as well as occasionally a platform for group efforts to raise awareness of particular issues affecting the sector. There is also a bi-annual Access to Justice forum, which extends beyond the subcommittee and includes the local judiciary, as well as elected members of the Council and members of parliament. Although these meetings are a step forward for enhancing communication, they were not having a strong effect for the advice organization chief executives at the outset of the project.

There is evidence that the LATAN project has had a positive effect on helping to build and establish this trust between these organizations. LATAN members made clear in survey responses their support for continued development of the Access to Advice Network:

> The Network is revolutionary, there is nothing else like it, this is just the start and it cannot stop. (LATAN, 2023)

> I have found out about a lot more of the services and organizations in Liverpool and have been able to make more contacts to offer our services and support. (LATAN, 2023)

> These meetings not only help our clients and give access to networks for everyone, but also provide invaluable support for those who attend the meetings. Myself and [my organization] have found the meetings and the group such an amazing way of keeping in contact with other organizations in the city region. We cannot lose this group, it's essential to the people of Liverpool. We desperately do not want this group to come to an end. (LATAN, 2023)

LATAN members expressed their opinion of the benefits of the network for sharing information and making sure that services are provided in an efficient way, without duplication:

> In principle, the project has scope to be very beneficial to all services that can utilize it. No more referrals sent to an agency and not knowing the outcome … and what I like most of all is that you have a direct link to the agency you have referred to … it has also opened up the opportunity for services to know and understand what other services actually do, and can prevent duplicate work and promote partnerships. (LATAN, 2023)

This idea of knowing what areas of service provision were already present elsewhere in the city is important to prevent duplication. Wasting scarce resources was a theme in our interviews and focus groups. This was identified as an area that is fruitful for partnership: 'We would then see that's where our partnership would work. Where we think somebody else does that better, why would we specialize in it? … So, there is plenty [to do] out there, work to do, I do know where we can stop' (Interview R1).

There is another important level of connection to the network for the functioning of the online referral platform, Refernet. Over and over, we saw that organizations would have one individual who was the primary operations connection that our LATAN coordinator had established. This individual was the person who was trained in how to operate Refernet. The notifications of Refernet referrals sent and received would be sent to this individual's email inbox. They might well hold the only organizational login and password for Refernet. In those situations, everyone else in the organization needed to defer to this person who has been trained in order to send referrals or to become aware of referrals being made. One comment from a focus group participant illustrated how this worked in their organization: 'Yeah, we are … myself … my other colleague … she is actually looking after that side. So, what we do if you need to refer somebody, we send her details and she kind of sorts out stuff for us. But we are using Refernet' [Employment Focus Group]. Another organization that is a member of Refernet, but has never used it, responded when asked why not: 'Because [staff member name] set it up and she doesn't work here anymore' (Interview FF Staff 2).

This was not only true of the smaller or non-specialist organizations. For a year during the COVID-19 pandemic, we were running an in-house welfare benefits form-filling service through the university's Liverpool Law Clinic, taking referrals over Refernet for our students to fill the forms for clients under our supervision. This is not our usual practice, but during the pandemic it was impossible to place our students in community organizations to provide this service as usual. Many organizations could not support placements and did not have the technological capability to provide online access for their clients for a number of months, and some were never able to do so. When we were running this form-filling service, we sometimes found that we were short of clients for a particular advice session, so would contact LATAN partners to let them know of open appointments, in case they had clients to refer over to us. We repeatedly found that even in the very largest partner organizations, such as CAL, the advice shift supervisor had no ability to send the referrals themselves. Instead, they would promise us a number of clients, often expressing how urgent these clients' forms were, as appointments were very scarce in the city at that time. Then, however, the process would break down as that shift supervisor would have to contact the member of staff who was responsible for sending the Refernet referral and ask them to upload the client information and send the referral across. This frequently did not happen in a timely way or, sometimes, at all.

This is particularly notable, as CAL is our partner organization and actually employed the LATAN network coordinator and hosted the Refernet platform. Even their staff had not adequately cascaded this knowledge down through the organization (or up, in this case) in order to allow for quick and easy Refernet administration. Since we were ourselves Refernet users, we are aware that it is user friendly and easy to operate, both for sending and receiving referrals. And yet, even in what one would imagine as the best-case scenario for take-up of this system, these structural barriers existed in the path of smooth administration of the referral system.

Trust transfer

The idea of trust transfer is relevant for our project, too. A trust transfer can occur when a member of a group extends trust to another member of the group just based on the shared group membership. The group transfers a trustworthy attribute to the other member (Zucker, 1986). Increasing trust transfer between members of a group increases the organization's social capital density and can lead toward enhanced cooperation toward organizational goals (McEvily et al, 2003). There is also an increased risk of groupthink that needs to be avoided (McEvily et al, 2003). By building the community of practice that is LATAN we have built institutional arrangements that can amplify the trust between its member organizations (Zucker, 1986).

LATAN has been very fortunate to have found dynamic coordinators over the length of the project. The role was at times split between an individual responsible for developing the community of practice aspects of the network and another individual responsible for developing the technical referrals side of the project. At other times, this has been a single role with dual responsibilities. The capable and personable LATAN coordinators have often functioned to build and transfer this interpersonal trust to the network itself. The member organizations' regard for the various coordinators over time, and recognition of their importance to the functioning of the network, was evident in interviews and focus groups, as well as in surveys conducted by LATAN itself: '[The partnership coordinator] is the glue that sticks all of this work together!' (LATAN, 2023). '[The partnership coordinator] has kept us on track and it's great to have her at the helm … there is strength in numbers' (LATAN, 2023).

Trust between organizations and clients

Another way that trust impacts upon the LATAN project is the trust between clients and organizations. It is very common for organizations to have repeat clients even for basic level services like welfare benefits form-filling. For example, clients might return to the organization that assisted them to fill their Personal Independence Payment application (PIP2 form) when faced with a renewal form. We regularly have clients contacting us to whom we have previously provided services. This is true across the spectrum of advice organizations but may be particularly true for those organizations that specialize in particular demographics of the populations, such as women or particular ethnic or national origins. In the latter case, this might be because of a language service being provided, for example. LATAN organizations have reflected on this loyalty among their clients:

> So, although we work great with signposting, I like to think and say that we work great with partners … We do tend to find our women do come back to us, because obviously they've built the trust, they have built sort of security with us. And I think because of that trust, I think, it's not that they don't believe the other partners, in terms of advice and the support they are receiving, but I think because they have got such a long-standing relationship with us, they just look for that confirmation. They look for that sort of security that, yes everything is going how it should be. (Housing Focus Group)

> And there is the trust as well. There is trust, you know, and don't forget, there is 30 years behind the charity. Thirty years and the trustees, at least five of them, have been there for 30 years. They were the founding trustees … So, the organization is known and trusted and that's quite a significant … time. (Interview G1)

Sometimes organizations expressed less trust in their clients. They spoke of clients shopping around for different or repeated advice on the same topic:

> I think there are parts of the referral system that do work … the partnerships and the networking … it's great, it's brilliant. And I think since the COVID-19, it's pulled professionals and projects together even more and partnerships together even more. But the frustration with me sometimes with some clients I have had in the past is when clients have gone to different organizations and have requested the same sort of support. You know … tried to get organizations to kind of go against each other in a way. (Immigration Focus Group)

Trust and competition

Conflicts arise in systems over scarce resources and undermine capacity for trust. This is true of the LATAN system as well. It is our view that the primary source of distrust in the system, with consequences for negatively reinforcing feedback loops, arises from competition for increasingly scarce resources. As was discussed previously in Chapters 1 and 3, more than a decade of austerity politics in the UK has stripped public services down to the bone. Many public services are outsourced to CVS organizations, and this is true for advice services as well.

Even before austerity, the shift from grants to contracts for government funding of CVS organizations had set up a relationship between these organizations and the state that was performance managed. Debra Morris called this shift from grants to contract for voluntary sector funding the rise of the 'contract culture' (Morris, 1999, 2000). Her early work on the subject showed that the way the funding relationships operated in practice bore little resemblance to the underlying contracts in place (Morris, 1999, 2000). The contracts also threatened charitable independence by limiting their ability to speak out against government policies for fear of losing their funding (Morris and Atkinson, 2003).

This shift toward contracts has intensified. The National Council for Voluntary Organisation's (NCVO's) *UK Civil Society Almanac 2023* reported that a quarter of the income of the sector is received from government sources. Three quarters of this income is in the form of contracts, rather than grants (NCVO, 2023). Central government funding has plateaued for the past decade, except for a slight uptake during the COVID-19 pandemic in 2020–21, while local government funding has fallen (NCVO, 2023). Nearly half of this income is in the social services and health sector (NCVO, 2023). We saw an example of the effect of this concern about contract performance management within the LATAN context in Chapter 6 when the staff member worried about their contract targets or key performance indicators (KPIs) when allowing the homeless service user to use the shower. Their contract terms possibly did not match the client's needs for more a more holistic approach.

The contract culture relationship has evolved over the ensuing decades to be more focused on performance management and sees a new expression in terms of payments by results (PbR) contracts and social impact bonds (SIB). PbR contracts condition the receipt of the funding on achieving whatever desirable social result is intended by the project, rather than simply delivering the services themselves. An example would be a contract with the outcome of transitioning a pre-determined number of people into work, rather than delivering a service assisting jobseekers with curriculum vitae (CV) development and career counselling. A community organization that entered into this contract could not ensure the outcome solely through the aspects of its performance that were under its sole control, thereby risking its funding upon uncertain results. This shifts the risks of the contract from the state onto the voluntary sector. A literature review of studies of PbR contracts across a number of jurisdictions has cast doubt on their efficacy (Webster, 2016).

Morris (2020) concluded that PbR contracts were unsuitable for the involvement of charities in the delivery of public services, as they exposed the charity to risks and unnecessary costs, and potentially presented issues in terms of the quality of the services provided to beneficiaries. Another example of a risk of government contracts from within LATAN is funders such as the DWP and NHS failing to keep up with the sharp cost-of-living rises during the lifetime of a contract in recent years. This has even led to some contracts being loss-making for a period of time.

This shift toward contracts has also set up conflicts between organizations, as they increasingly bid against one another for contracts to provide public services. The competitive tendering means that smaller organizations have a hard time competing with larger organizations, who have advantages of scale. NCVO (2023) data confirms this impression: in 2023, larger organizations with incomes above £1 million annually received 86 per cent of central and 87 per cent of local government income. A common complaint of LATAN participant organizations is that contracts are available to provide new services, but very seldom, if ever, available to support the organization's core operating costs. This can additionally mean that an organization's mission can drift from its core charitable purpose to wherever the funding is available.

A LATAN participant describes this focus on targets in government contracts:

> Yeah. And I think, in terms of funding, we've had to learn to write business cases and produce plans and strategic focusing and targeting focusing, you know, it's never the case of can somebody give us some money. You've really got to show what the money is really got to do, the need for it, how it is really going to be spent, how it is going to be accounted for. And I think because the sector is much more target-driven than it has ever been before, the line management of staff who are delivering targets, you've got to invoke performance capability procedure. That sort of thing that 20 years ago was not really heard of. But now it's the norm. (Interview ZZ)

A LATAN participant talked about the negative impact of government contract-imposed targets for services:

> I think in an ideal world I could deal with everything, I could deal with the benefit, I could deal with the debt, but that's unfortunately not how it works because we are funded by the Legal Aid Agency and as such, we really rely on that funding for our organization to exist. Without that funding, we wouldn't be here. So, we are target-driven to such an extent that we have to deal as many cases as we can, and we have to do that within a specific period of time so that we keep that cash flow coming. (Housing Focus Group)

The members of LATAN are often placed in a situation where they are forced to bid against one another for scarce funding resources within the system. At times contracts run by one organization are awarded to another after a re-tendering process. This competitive funding situation erodes and undermines trust. There has been an ongoing tension that surfaces around this transition from grants to contracts. Some of the organizations within the system are better placed to take advantage of this, particularly CAL, largely because of scale. They are better placed to provide advice to a larger number of individuals but at a lower level of complexity. Better placed to play the numbers game that many modern public sector contracts have devolved into. They do have some specialist advice available, and would deliver more if funding were available, but the majority of the advice provided by CAL is at a generalist level, and a significant proportion is provided by volunteers. Specialist organizations such as the law centres, which provide a higher proportion of casework to relatively fewer individuals, can sometimes perceive this competition as unwinnable for their organizations.

There is a recognition on the part of LATAN participants of the need for a diversity of organizations, including smaller ones targeting specific groups, in the information and advice services network. They also recognized the need for the bigger advice organizations in the city, such as CAL and Shelter, which provide holistic or universal services:

> The difficulty for us is, we cannot win in that situation because … no one, least of all us, wants to undercut a CAB [Citizens Advice Bureau] contract that props up the advice sector in Liverpool. Because the CAB is doing the lion's share of the work and if they weren't there we'll be in disaster territory. But we know they are not meeting the demand at every local level. There needs to be CAB plus something here. What they need is an additional contract to do more grassroots, more innovative face to face, more complicated complex support work here. So, it needs … a double tier really. [In addition to the generalist contract held by the CAB] It needs organizations like food banks, learning disability charities, you know, addiction recovery specialist, they need a form of advice worker at that level, which is not a CAB centrally procured money contract. (Interview B1)

> You can't survive without the smaller [organizations] … if they fall over then we fall over. But then that's the other side. You know, if Citizens Advice Liverpool fell over we'd all be screwed. So we can't cope without each other. (Interview A2)

The distinction between the different roles that organizations play during a person's route to resolving an issue can be fluid and does not always hold true over time. This is primarily due to the highly fragmented nature of funding for free legal advice. One participant organization, for example, works out of hospitals to support people with a brain injury in all aspects of their lives. The degree to which the organization can provide advice varies. Their funding for giving employment advice ended in March 2020, just as the demand started to increase due to COVID-19. The regularly changing service provision and the diversity of organizations mean that the information that supports a referral system needs to be continually monitored and updated.

Today, legal aid has become a relatively small part of the funding for the organizations that make up Liverpool's advice network. Funding now comes from local authorities, the NHS, the Big Lottery, charitable foundations, the DWP, legal aid, utility companies and a myriad of other sources (Sommerlad and Sanderson, 2013). Participants perceive this fragmented funding environment as having a negative impact on collaboration and integration. As one advice service manager said:

> We found ourselves in competition with our own colleagues and with organizations that we've previously worked with, and that is really heart breaking … But I think on the top of it, what we then lose sight of is the humanity and we lose sight of the person, and the individual. (Interview Q1)

There have been some positive movements toward building trust in this area, with shared funding bids being a good example. Three organizations successfully bid for funding from the Ministry of Justice's Improving Outcomes Through Legal Advice funding stream to provide various elements of housing advice. One of the lead participant organizations said that this collaboration between the three 'only came about because of LATAN'. Some other bids within the system have happened in a collaborative way. A LATAN participant describes conversations that occur with other organizations that have been successful in winning contested bids for contracts: 'Sometimes you will make an approach to those agencies and say is there any way we can assist you with this? Often, that will not be the case. And those organizations want to just pursue it themselves, which is fair enough' (Interview ZZ).

There were further signs of recent moves toward a more collaborative approach to funding bids:

> So, for example, the bid for the Birkenhead Housing Possession scheme [another organization] and I had a conversation with another party as well. And we kind of said rather than the three of us bid against each other for one contract, would it not make sense to join forces and split it three ways?' (Interview ZZ)

> But for me I want to sit in a room and have a coffee with someone and just work with more people … because it's the partnership work that leads to funding opportunities. (Interview A1)

> I think people want to preserve their own organizations and strengthen their own organizations as much as they can and can sometimes be reluctant perhaps to give away money or share money with other bodies. So, I think it is a balancing act, really, between strengthening your own organization, but then recognizing strategically where it's better to maybe join up with somebody. Because you may provide the better service by having somebody else on board which appeals to the funder more. And that's a judgement call you have to make with each individual funding round really. Difficult conversations. (Interview ZZ)

Referring to a successful local collaboration with which their organization was unable to compete, one participant said:

> They've got this collaboration with The Women's Organisation, which is really smart, because it's a procurement vehicle in which they can deliver commissioned national, international, or at least regional bids … in a way that small providers like ourselves … would never be able to compete against it. We are way down on that infrastructure, we've not got a finance department that monitors our framework or any of that stuff to be able to procure a commission at that level. So, that's … that's a problem. Several times we find ourselves almost in competition with the CAB with no desire to be so. (Interview B1)

Trust in the research team

The research team has also been through a period of developing and building trust with LATAN participants. Our insider/outsider role has hampered us in some ways and helped us in others. One of us, James, is a trustee of CAL, creating a perception of alignment with the behemoth of the Liverpool advice ecosystem. And, of course, charitable trustees have an obligation to act in the best interests of their organization. We have tried to mitigate any actual conflicts by making this connection visible and recusing James from decisions about funding allocation and the tender process for our third sector partner. The perceived conflicts of interest have been more of a challenge to address.

In some ways this negative view was a surprise to the research team at the beginning of the project. We had been training and placing students in advice agencies for more than five years in Liverpool. We participated in the Liverpool Law Society Access to Justice subcommittee and the Access to Justice forum. We thought we had fairly broad acceptance within the sector but at the beginning of the research we encountered resistance. The third sector partner at the start of the project was chosen by an external panel, rather than by the research team, and CAL won the tender fairly. They were an asset to the project and James's close connections created trust with this crucial partner for project delivery. In some ways, however, it may have been easier for us, from a wider network perspective, had the second-place bid been successful. On the other hand, different trust issues might have been created instead. We had, in effect, ourselves placed the organizations in competition with one another for funding, with the attendant loss of trust.

Over the period of the project, we have slowly built up our experience and exposure in the advice system. We have listened to a wide variety of perspectives and tried to be transparent in our research process. Views have shifted toward a more positive perspective on the research team. We have also shifted to less involvement in the day-to-day running of LATAN. We held a position on the LATAN steering committee in its initial iteration but no longer do so. We have consciously stepped back from directing the activities and approaches of the community to increase the bottom-up element of the project. We proposed the LATAN community as a way of building opportunities for democratization of how the community works together to solve the problems. That entails a commitment to allowing the community to be fully democratic, whatever direction this takes it.

Trust and the Liverpool access to advice strategy

In the autumn of 2022, we worked with the LATAN organizations to draft a proposal to the LCC for a new citywide advice strategy to reflect the approach refined through the LATAN project. (The recommendations are further set out in Chapter 9.) Through a collaborative process we were able to agree outcomes and basic definitions, such as what constitutes legal advice. There was considerable scepticism about the usefulness of such a strategy, as well as about the suitability of the everyday legal problems framing that the research team proposed should be at its core. One of the attendees at the first meeting where we discussed the idea said, 'What does research conducted in Canada in the 1980s have to say to Liverpool in the 21st century?!'

The research team had to consider that choosing the everyday legal problems framing prioritizes some forms of legal advice but deprioritizes others. This created tensions between the different LATAN member organizations. Organizations that provide legal representation and specialist advice and casework can be deprioritized by this framing when compared with the existing approach to funding free legal advice that focuses on legal aid funding. This consequence can be reduced by emphasizing the need for a clear link to an advice level appropriate to the needs of an individual, whatever their particular legal problem and level of complexity. Developing the strategy also opened up discussions about the value of the network itself in light of the ongoing problems with capacity in the sector. Why should we be spending time on activities related to strategic collaboration and referral systems, when the fundamental problem is not enough money in the system? These are just a few examples from some of the challenging and constructive discussions that were had during the process of developing the strategy.

To ensure that the process was as participatory as possible, we invited all LATAN members to collaborate and offered several opportunities, via different means, to engage. We organized three workshops on the University of Liverpool campus to hold open discussions and work towards an agreement as to what should be included in the strategy. The LATAN committee (which we do not attend) also discussed the strategy at their meetings. This gave them an opportunity to discuss the strategy independently from us as lead researchers and with our particular framing of the idea. It was a demanding process but after considerable discussion and several iterations, we were able to build consensus across the network on the outline of a strategy. We then presented and discussed multiple drafts to the strategy working group before agreeing the version that was first presented to the Council in November 2023.

In the end, the strategy was developed and endorsed by 32 LATAN organizations. It was presented to the leader of the LCC, Councillor Liam Robinson, and others at meetings at the end of 2023 and early 2024. We assisted in the presentation of the advice strategy, but it was led by LATAN members (the CEOs of Shelter Liverpool and CAL) and by the coordinator and independent chair of LATAN. We felt that the organizations in the advice ecosystem should have lead roles in presenting and advocating for the strategy as this accorded with its ethos. This made the message stronger. Following these meetings, we received political agreement from Council Leader Robinson that the advice strategy should be implemented. At the time of writing in mid-2025, we continue to work with the Council towards its full implementation.

During this process we were able to build trust between the research team and LATAN. We believe that this was due to the highly participatory approach and quality of deliberation during the strategy development. It also built trust between organizations because they gained a deeper understanding of differing priorities and approaches to free legal advice they each hold because they were aired and examined in a positive environment. This whole process and agreement of the strategy capitalized on the trust that had developed between the network and the research team up to that point. It is unlikely that we would have had such strong engagement and reached a consensus without that.

Trust and Refernet

LATAN participants reported a need for a referral system and enthusiasm for the idea of building up referrals over time. They talked about the need to understand better where they could send clients with the confidence that client issues would be appropriately addressed: 'Um, so we've got to find a solution to make sure that clients know where to go and when to go on and we each know who is the best place to refer whoever to' (Interview A1). We decided that the implementation of a referral system would be beneficial to the network and would usefully provide a concrete focus around which people could coalesce in the early development of LATAN as trust was built up. Refernet was the referral system that we chose to implement, following discussions with the network. This was partly because CAL, who won the tender to be our third sector partner, was already using it.

One LATAN participant referred to the benefits of having an online referral platform before Refernet properly launched:

> I just … I think … you know … it needs, it needs something, because if you're all on there, then you can just make easy referrals, can't you? Because everything's there. It's up to your organization to log in and update your information. So it should always be up to date. (Interview A1)

Clients frequently present with a bundle of legal issues, which we discuss here as everyday legal problems, and organizations have differing capacity and capability to help clients with each of the issues in that bundle. Organizations often need to find referrals to help address the issues. Some need to refer externally, while some organizations can deal with issues in-house:

> Because often, not always … it is benefit issues or debt problems or financial issues [underlying the housing issue]. (Housing Focus Group)

> We get our referrals from a number of different sources … we identify what the reasons are and why they are in rent arrears, why are they in mortgage arrears. It could be benefit issues. Very often it is because of how the debt's being prioritized … And so, what we will do then is to speak to the judge and see if we could get that case adjourned. We can then sign that client up for full legal aid or full legal help, we can give them more in-depth advice with regards to get the issue resolved. But also, we can make the referrals to deal with the other issues which caused it … So, we will make a referral to our debt advisers who will usually look into options such as a debt relief order, and negotiations with the creditors, things like that … We can also help with the benefit issues. Quite often the issue's with the UC [Universal Credit], the

> transition from a legacy benefit, there's lots of different reasons why a client is in rent arrears and you know it is our job to try to identify what those issues are and try to resolve them. So, we rarely make referrals out. Because we do tend to have the team within and they can help with those issues. (Housing Focus Group)

Referrals to other sources of advice may be rare for this participant, but for most organizations, external referrals will be a lot more commonplace. Finding places to send these referrals is difficult, though. There simply is insufficient advice availability, compounded by insufficient appropriate specialist advice:

> But my difficulty always is, trying to refer people for higher levels of advice when nearly all the issues I deal with don't attract legal aid. And there isn't really any mechanism as such within the city for those referrals. It is a case of shopping around and trying to find it. So, it is quite difficult because many clients really can't afford the legal advice that they need and I can't give it ... it's casework [that is needed] ... it's just advising on a particular issue above my level. So, yeah, that's the main difficulty for me. It's also difficult and different, trying to find the advice that they actually need within the city. Although I do appreciate the other side of it because obviously my clients often have other issues as well. Domestic abuse or their accommodation, housing issues, benefits but ... the other places I can refer them ... don't really seem to take on some of the complex cases, in terms of social service support. (Immigration Focus Group)

Refernet was relatively successful as a referral system. Over the life of the funded period for Refernet, nearly 6,000 referrals were sent across the City. Despite this, and despite the enthusiasm for the concept of a referral system, in practice the system was difficult to embed into the everyday activities of the LATAN organizations. It is possible that the referral system was not as successful as it could have been because it represented an idea we brought in and implemented in an insufficiently participatory way. We developed the idea after local research pointed to an issue with referral fatigue and after discussions with the steering group, but perhaps this was insufficient. We then proposed Refernet. At least in concept, it solved the issue with referrals but perhaps that approach was not felt to be as useful by the rest of the community, so they voted with their feet. An overly top-down approach might have led to the wrong solution to the issue. Refernet implementation may also have suffered from the knowledge of how to use it being too concentrated in a few individuals, as discussed earlier, and then when individuals leave organizations the knowledge is lost. Also, we have had continued turnover in the crucial network development coordinator positions, again reflecting instability in staffing in the sector. We found that the referral system required this staffing support to run, and therefore could not support Refernet once that funded element of the project ended. On the other hand, it may simply have been too early in the development of LATAN to implement the referral system and the community might have organically developed it later on. At the time we imposed it, they had not yet built up the trust and relationships to make it successful. By the time we had built up the trust, the sunset period for Refernet funding was upon us. We are happy that we have helped to connect up those nearly 6,000 people to advice or other services to solve their problems. We do wonder if it couldn't have been more.

Enthusiasm does still exist to develop a referral system and several organizations have engaged in the process of understanding what might be best implemented to replace Refernet, which is no longer a viable option. Subsequent learning from this process suggests that a system that operates as both a directory of services and a referral system might be more appropriate, and we are pursuing funding to purchase such a system for the network. Combining these two functions would mean that a broader range of staff and organizations would be regular users of the system and help with its implementation. This would also benefit from not being so dependent on continued institutional memory in organizations that have massive staff turnover due to unstable funding streams. These same people do go from organization to organization, but this has not resulted in knowledge being built up across the sector. We do not yet understand why. It may be that we underestimated the resources required to implement such a system change across so many, diverse organizations. One of the attractions of the system preferred by LATAN members to replace Refernet is that the company provide greater technical support and resources than we had available. This would enable them to further support getting organizations up and running on the system, keeping details up to date and monitoring and prompting responses to referrals. Finally, the limited take up of the referral system is perhaps also to do with the funding scarcity created by austerity and the continued direct competition between organizations for those scarce resources. As one of the LATAN participants said when discussing why shared funding bids are difficult to manage:

> Because what they see is threat. So they think crap, we're gonna lose our ... advice contract here ... And instead of doing what would be in my personal view in the best of interests of Liverpool: open the doors, let's have a conversation about what need is out there, let's work with you, let's try and do this collectively, they are going no, no, no, our money's at risk here, we are closing it down. (Interview B1)

Conclusion

In this chapter we have considered the functioning of LATAN as a system, including the physical boundaries of the system that were imposed and the conceptual boundaries that were inherent, which dictated some of the system functions. We have also analysed the effect of trust to create positive or negative feedback loops that reinforce tendencies within the system. The ways that that trust has operated within the system over the five years of the LATAN project have been instrumental in its success and its failures.

8

The Role of Trust, Effective Participation and Everyday Legal Problems in Social Citizenship

Citizenship is fundamentally based on ideas of inclusion and exclusion. As Ruth Patrick (2017) said, 'An individual's sense of belonging and inclusion within their wider community and nation state is bound up in and contingent upon their citizenship status and practice' (Patrick, 2017: 15). In Chapter 3, we explained the influence of the social position that people are born in, work, live and grow in, and the further pathways that lead to health inequalities. We have highlighted the role that access to justice has in ameliorating the impact of social determinants of health. We argue that where people are unable to realize the social, civil and political rights that they are promised by law and the principles based on social citizenship, then their citizenship status loses its value. Policy decisions at national and local level have left people with a lesser status or a form of semi-citizenship, and in effect leave people excluded from their wider community, with a limited sense of belonging.

Access to justice, health inequalities and poverty are inextricably linked. The introduction of the welfare state just after the Second World War – including legal aid for the first time – and the new social form of citizenship that it heralded battled against inequality and the giant evil of 'want'. It was an attack on poverty. We have focused our discussion of these issues on the lived experience of citizenship for people in their everyday lives. Here we seek to locate this empirical evidence in relation to free legal advice within social, civil and political elements of the rights that make up social citizenship today.

This speaks to the heart of the Liverpool Access to Advice Network (LATAN) activities and research, which sit at the intersection between social and civil rights and the battle against poverty; at the intersection between the everyday legal problems that occur in people's lives and the ability to understand and resolve these issues. In other words, the interaction between the social rights that are promised as part of the welfare state – health, housing, economic security, education and so on – and the civil right of access to justice, which promises fair access to those rights. At this intersection sit trust and effective participation, which are key values of citizenship, and the everyday legal problems whose resolution can be undermined by a lack of these values. Through analysis of these three concepts this chapter reminds us of the importance of all three areas of rights – social, political and civil. As Mark Simpson said, 'Once in place, the three elements of citizenship are as interdependent as the legs of a three-legged stool – remove one and the other two cannot stand' (Simpson, 2022: 16).

We also seek to develop the understanding of social citizenship by emphasizing the importance of effective participation and trust as core values of a citizenship framework that delivers social rights (Marshall and Bottomore, 1992), and where people can resolve their everyday legal problems. Social citizenship is more often analysed through the lens of social rights – the welfare benefits system and social security (Dwyer, 2000; Taylor-Gooby, 2008; Patrick, 2017; Sigafoos and Organ, 2021) – whereas we also approach it from the perspective of civil rights and, in this final chapter, political rights. It is important to recognize the multi-rights framework of social citizenship and the interconnection between these different elements of engagement with the state if policies are to be effectively delivered and for citizenship to be meaningful. The chapter concludes by returning to the heart of this book and its bottom-up focus: the everyday legal problems that people experience and the importance of this conceptualization for social justice.

Is social citizenship relevant today?

Let us start by asking whether social citizenship is still relevant. Have social rights been so eroded by conditionality and individualization through concepts such as 'deservingness' and policy attacks on the welfare state and access to justice that we need to find a different name for citizenship and focus on access to free legal advice outside the concept of *social* citizenship (Sigafoos and Organ, 2021: 384)? Social citizenship has been in a state of flux from a legal, political and theoretical perspective for a number of years (Simpson, 2017), particularly because of the policy changes affecting the whole range of social determinants of health, such as housing, education and employment, during the years of austerity politics. These changes have eroded the social and economic security provided by the welfare system. There has been an increasing emphasis on work. We have taken a turn towards 'sticking plaster' policies to reduce poverty, such as the Household Support Fund (financial help administered through local councils for those who cannot afford essentials, like utilities or food) and the Winter Fuel Payment (£200 or £300 for older people in receipt of certain benefits). This further complexity and conditionality makes the overall provision of social security less effective.

Symptomatic of this erosion has been the steep rise in charitable activities trying to mitigate the effects of these policies related to the social determinants of health by taking on responsibilities formerly part of the welfare state. Many members of LATAN have tried to step into this gap. One of the most alarming developments has been the increase in food banks in the UK. The Trussell Trust, which is the largest network of food banks, reported that 3.1 million emergency food parcels were distributed in 2023–24 at their 1,699 locations, up from just a few hundred parcels in 2008. It is estimated that there are at least another 1,172 other independent food banks, with 72 food banks in Liverpool alone (Francis-Devine, 2024). For the people using these food banks and other anti-poverty services from charities it is hard to describe their citizenship as *social* citizenship. This reflects a return to a pre-welfare state approach that relied heavily on voluntary aid for those in poverty and whose purpose 'was to abate the nuisance of poverty without disturbing the pattern of inequality of which poverty was the most obviously unpleasant consequence' (Marshall and Bottomore, 1992: 27–8).

There have been numerous policy changes that have led to reduced social rights and have had negative effects on people's health, as we have established earlier in this book. Education and healthcare are largely free at the point of delivery, but we pay for dentists as soon as we turn 18, there are tuition fees at university, reduced tenancy rights, long healthcare waiting lists, paid school meals, insecure work contracts, a shortage of social housing, and so on and so on. This is not to mention the widespread erosion of the value of welfare benefits through policies such as the underoccupancy charge, better known as the 'bedroom tax' (a reduction in Universal Credit and housing benefit for social housing tenants who are deemed to have more bedrooms than they need), the introduction of Universal Credit, the introduction of the two-child limit (restricting child-related welfare benefits to the first two children in a house), the benefit cap, continual changes to disability benefits and more restrictive criteria, and strict sanctions for the smallest infractions, to name just a few. Even within the free education provision there is inadequate Special Educational Needs and Disabilities (SEND) provision in those free schools and there is ample evidence that children growing up in poverty have less educational attainment. One way of looking at this might be that there has been a shift away from the state fulfilling a right to education to just fulfilling a right to go to school. Evidence shows this is true for healthcare, as well: 'Hardship is making it harder to deliver the core functions of healthcare and education, not just in the most deprived areas but across Britain' (Bestwick and Schmuecker, 2024). There is a wide range of literature that has identified and analysed the negative impact of these policy changes (Fitzpatrick et al, 2019; Royston, 2023).

Despite these changes and the reality of poverty for millions in the UK and systemic health inequalities – as outlined in Chapter 3 – we still hear echoes of social citizenship in political discourse, particularly in relation to the National Health Service (NHS). The NHS remains a high-profile political issue and all the main parties promise to strengthen the NHS (even if the reality has been very different over the last 14 years). Health was the second most important issue in deciding which party someone voted for at the 2024 general election (Smith, 2024). We may still hear this political rhetoric in relation to social rights, but the social citizenship values of reciprocity, inclusion and trust (Taylor-Gooby, 2008; Sigafoos and Organ, 2021) have not been prioritized in the policy environment. Instead, the focus is on conditionality, deservingness and fragmentation of the provision of social support for people in crisis and on a day-to-day basis.

Due to the conceptual vagueness of citizenship, it is hard to know at what point social citizenship is no longer applicable; to know at what point it has been completely dismantled in policy terms and replaced by an alternative form of citizenship, such that we should stop talking about it, except in aspirational terms. Or, in other words, it is hard to know at what point *social* citizenship has no meaning for individual members of our political community. Edmiston's (2017) analogy to a heap of sand is illustrative of this point:

> If one grain of sand is taken away, a heap still remains. If another is removed, the same applies, and so on and so forth. However, at some point the collection of grains becomes so small that the sand can no longer, logically, be considered a heap. The difficulty comes in trying to define and identify the particular point at which this occurs. (Edmiston, 2017: 263)

From an individual perspective, research has shown that there are large sections of society for whom social citizenship is of very little relevance (Sigafoos and Organ, 2021). It is very hard to argue that there are enough grains left for a social citizenship 'heap'. The reshaping of citizenship has been so severe that for many people it has ceased to have meaning. This is particularly true for disabled people and for those that have fallen into poverty and destitution. The rapid increase in poverty levels, including the 3.8 million people living in destitution in the UK (Joseph Rowntree Foundation, 2024) are clearly not enjoying the promise of 'a modicum of economic security' that Marshall described as at least the minimum offering of post-Second World War UK citizenship (Marshall and Bottomore, 1992: 8). There has, though, been no political attempt to declare that the whole heap of social citizenship is to be swept away. Instead it has been an incremental removal of elements of social citizenship grain by grain.

We have previously argued that '[A]ccess to justice and welfare rights policies have undermined all three values of social citizenship [inclusivity, reciprocity and trust] to such an extent that … we are witnessing a *dismantling* of social citizenship, at least as it relates to the welfare rights at its core'(Sigafoos and Organ, 2021: 365). We continue to support this position in relation to welfare rights, but recognize that there are still some grains of social citizenship existent in practice (for some people). It still has some relevance to policy decisions today. However, the wide-ranging gaps in policy, the much-reduced promise of social security, and high levels of poverty, deep poverty and destitution means that its relevance is now more as a normative ideal and part of political rhetoric than as a strong empirical fact in people's everyday lives.

Despite all this, we remain hopeful, and LATAN is an exercise in finding concrete ways to stem the tide of social rights erosion. The next, final chapter, for example, focuses on the implementation of a new strategic approach to access to advice at a local authority level. This is an important public policy change that we believe will increase access to the remaining social rights. At national and local levels, access to justice should also be embedded in anti-poverty strategies. Resources provided by these policies should be adequate and targeted at areas based on need (for example based on levels of deprivation) to maximize the positive impact of these strategies to reduce health inequalities. In terms of the operationalization of these policies, fairer access to resources can be ensured by access to appropriate advice for the targeted population. This integration of advice and social policy will help give the concept of social citizenship a new, strengthened meaning in terms of social and civil rights. There is hope in strengthening the advice ecosystem in preparation for a time when greater resources can increase capacity in the sector.

The tendency to focus on social, rather than civil, rights is perhaps inevitable given that Marshall's framing of the new *social* citizenship was focused on the then recent incorporation of social rights into citizenship (Marshall and Bottomore, 1992: 29) as a means to reduce inequality. It is important to remember, however, that citizenship promises three groups of rights: social, civil and political. We analyse each of these in turn next, starting with the most recent addition, before moving on to the cross-cutting value of trust and finally the concept of everyday legal problems.

Social rights

Prior to the Second World War, 'Social rights were at a minimum and were not woven into the fabric of citizenship' (Marshall and Bottomore, 1992: 28), but after the war they were integrated into citizenship and there was a promise that an individual would not live below an acceptable standard of living, certainly not in poverty or destitution (Dwyer, 2000: 43). This promise has slipped from ensuring that people can participate fully in society with an acceptable standard of living to the provision of a safety net, and then in recent decades to a promise of an acceptable standard of living only for the deserving, and now even the 'deserving' are slipping into poverty and support is limited to only the undefined 'most vulnerable' in society. The rise of in-work poverty is a clear indication of this (Lohmann and Marx, 2018). Several successive governments have implemented policies that intentionally or unintentionally have had detrimental consequences for poverty and rising health inequalities, and have often shifted responsibility for this towards individual characteristics or behaviours.

Social rights – health, education, social and economic security and so on – sit in a complex legal environment. We have talked about social *rights*, but there has never been a general legal basis for them. Individual pieces of legislation generally set standards, which are implemented according to the ideology of the government in power. This is reflected in the general socio-economic, cultural and environmental conditions ring in the social determinants of health rainbow model discussed in Chapter 3. There is no provision in UK law that is comparable to the rights set out in the International Covenant on Economic, Social and Civil Rights, where Article 11, for example, states that, 'The States Parties to the present Covenant recognize the right of everyone to an adequate standard of living for himself and his family, including adequate food, clothing and housing, and to the continuous improvement of living conditions' (ICESCR, Article 11). This gives significant scope for complexity and probably raises the need for legal advice with regards to entitlement to them.

Furthermore, the receipt of welfare benefits has never been seen as a standalone right that someone can receive regardless of all responsibilities. Marshall himself stated the importance of responsibilities and duties, particularly the need to work. He said, for example, that:

> If citizenship is invoked in defence of rights, the corresponding duties of citizenship cannot be ignored … [some] duties are vague, and are included in the general obligation to live the life of a good citizen, giving such service as can promote the welfare of the community … Of paramount importance is the duty to work. (Marshall and Bottomore, 1992: 41, 45)

We can see this tension in the balance within the social rights system between social justice and market freedom, which has evolved over the decades to arrive in the third decade of the 21st century with a strong policy focus on work and conditionality. Work is viewed as the marker that you are deserving of support, and also as the route out of poverty, but it is a route that is a dead end for many (see Chapter 3). These policy developments 'embody a shift in the construction of poverty from a condition primarily characterized by lack of income to one mainly characterized by lack of employment' (Simpson, 2017: 652). This has led to a reduction in the amounts provided through welfare benefits, and increasing conditions tied to the receipt of benefits. One repudiation of the extreme policy focus on employment as the route out of poverty, and the discourse that frames people as either 'workers' or 'shirkers', is the high number of people working and receiving income support through the benefit system. In Liverpool, for example, 55 per cent of Universal Credit claimants are working (Liverpool City Council, 2024). This implies that the reduction in the value of welfare benefits, such as the basic rate of Universal Credit being set below the destitution threshold (Fitzpatrick et al, 2023), in order to force people into work, has not been matched by a drive to actually make work pay. Policies could raise income levels at work either through sufficient increases to the minimum wage or the strengthening of workers' rights.

The reintroduction of a welfare state that truly reflects the cost of living with dignity, and that seeks to reduce inequality rather than just offer a guaranteed minimum, would be a significant step towards rebuilding social citizenship values in the UK. Changes in policy could increase household income through raising in-work income and/or increasing the value of welfare benefits, such as raising housing benefit levels in line with rent rises, raising pension and benefit payment rates, removing the benefit cap, and removing the two-child limit, among many others. These are likely to increase significantly the monetary value of welfare benefits, reduce poverty and consequently have a positive impact on health, reducing health inequalities and facilitating people's ability to work. We strongly advocate for these changes. However, in the meantime, and alongside these changes, urgent action, such as developing the capacity and effectiveness of the free legal advice ecosystem, is needed to ameliorate and support access to what currently exists in the system, to what is promised as part of citizenship status.

Reducing income inequality would boost individuals' civic and social participation (Lancee and Van de Werfhorst, 2012), with benefits for health inequality. Civic participation is whether people take part in clubs and associations, even at neighbourhood level (Putnam, 2000; Pichler and Wallace, 2007; Lancee and Van de Werfhorst, 2012) and has also been termed formal social capital (Pichler and Wallace, 2007). Social participation, or informal social capital (Pichler and Wallace, 2007), is similar but involves participation in informal groups, such as with friends or family (Lancee and Van de Werfhorst, 2012).

The level of trust is a key driver. Uslaner and Brown argued: '[G]reater equality and higher levels of trust are two pathways to participation.

They are hardly the whole story, and they are not alternative accounts. Inequality may depress participation, either directly or indirectly, through its effects on trust' (2005: 869). As discussed in Chapter 3, in the influential book *The Spirit Level* (2009), Wilkinson and Pickett linked income inequality to a number of social and health problems. Among other issues, higher levels of inequality led to lower trust and lower participation, thereby weakening democratic institutions. In a later book, they drew a clearer connection to the literature on the social determinants of health (Pickett and Wilkinson, 2018). Greener (2025) added a further potential explanatory factor of the degree of integrative democracy, which captures the degree to which a political system incorporates a wide range of voices and interests. Higher integrative democracy can counter some of the negative health and social effects that can result from the status hierarchies caused by higher income inequality (Greener, 2025). This interaction seems important to us, and we will discuss political rights and participation later in this chapter for this reason. We will also return to the discussion of the crucial nature of trust as an overarching value (begun in Chapter 7).

Civil rights

For over a decade, cuts to free legal advice have reduced an individual's ability to access support needed to resolve everyday legal problems. Whatever the level and type of support that is offered through the welfare benefits system and however strong the rights of renters and workers, people may need advice to be able to access and/or activate them. The value of benefits is low and rights are weak in England and Wales, although if they were far higher and stronger, people would still need legal advice to ensure fair receipt of them. Our experience of, and research into, the welfare benefits system has highlighted well-documented problems with understanding what benefits are available, for whom and when, problems with the application processes (we train our students to do benefit checks and help with form-filling), and problems with accurate decision making in relation to benefit applications, sanctions decisions and medical assessments. Over 70 per cent of people that challenge these negative benefits decisions succeed at tribunal. At all stages of engaging with the welfare system, there is a potential need for free legal advice. It is true that the system could be designed better to reduce this demand for advice considerably, but no system is ever going to be perfect. The complexity and juridification of social rights mean that advice will always be needed to some degree without a fundamental system redesign in the UK. All these problems that lead to unfulfilled entitlements to welfare benefits relate to the civil right of access to justice and could be mitigated to some degree through providing more free legal advice.

The argument for free legal advice is an argument in favour of enabling people to get what they are promised by the state. In some ways this can feel like a lesser argument or just a temporary sticking plaster because in today's political climate, even if people get what the state has promised, many remain below the poverty line. Even if we are 'good' citizens that follow the governmental solution of work, we may still need to claim benefits and still be below the poverty line. This is an important element of the erosion of trust. Eighty-nine per cent of people referred to Trussell Trust food banks receive means-tested benefits and 20 per cent are from working households (Bull et al, 2023). The failings of the system in terms of accessing even the residual welfare benefits are evidenced by the £23 billion of unclaimed welfare benefits in 2023 (Ghelani et al, 2024). Not only does poverty exist for those claiming benefits and working, poverty is also caused by people's inability to access the limited support that is promised. Ensuring enjoyment of the civil right of access to justice will positively impact people's ability to fully realize their social rights as well. As is shown by Figure 3.4 in Chapter 3, access to justice can help reduce poverty and improve all the social determinants of health at several intervention points.

Free legal advice has dissipated dramatically following the Legal Aid, Sentencing and Punishment of Offenders Act 2012 (LASPO), which removed most legal aid funding for social welfare law (The Law Society, 2024), and the much reduced, non-strategic delivery of free legal advice at a local level in the wake of local authority funding cuts. Justice, though, did not even get on the list of concerns at the 2024 general election (YouGov, 2024), and when it was discussed it was usually in connection to courts and their waiting times. The close connection of access to justice and free legal advice to the social determinants of health and other social rights means, however, that it has to be addressed if anti-poverty strategies and other related policy goals are to succeed. Part of the reason for legal advice policy's lower profile is that it is very often supportive of other policy goals rather than an objective in its own right. It is the outcome of the advice that is important to people whose lives are affected by everyday legal problems, rather than the advice itself. Providing more and strategically allocated free legal advice is essential, though, as it can mitigate both the causes and consequences of poverty and health inequalities (as seen in Chapters 3 and 6).

Political rights: effective participation

We have explained in some detail the interaction between civil and social rights, which is so significant for the quality of a person's citizenship, and for their participation in society. Political rights is the third leg to the citizenship 'stool'. A person's 'citizenship status and practice' is also contingent on their enjoyment of their political rights. It is important to remember that although Marshall described their evolution over time, often divorced from each other, his approach to social citizenship in the 20th century was based on the interaction between these three areas of rights (Marshall and Bottomore, 1992). He recognized that each part of citizenship affects the others. Interventions in one area will have an impact on the others, as we have found in relation to providing free legal advice. Michael Lister expressed this well:

> Firstly, there is a practical argument that the exercise of one element of citizenship rights requires other citizenship rights. Or, to put it more simply, the effective exercise of political rights require civil rights, political rights require social rights, civil rights are predicated upon social rights and political rights and so on. (Lister, 2005: 473)

The purpose of this short section is to remind readers not to forget that social citizenship, indeed any form of citizenship, promises political rights as well as the civil and the social. This is an area that deserves further research. Understanding how participation is influenced by a person's access to their civil and social rights is a challenge, not least because of the wide range of factors that sit at the connection between poverty and participation (Dacombe, 2018). Marshall made clear that participation in political decision making and society more broadly is key to enjoying the status of citizenship: 'By the political element I mean the right to participate in the exercise of political power, as a member of a body invested with political authority or as an elector of the members of such a body' (Marshall and Bottomore, 1992: 9). Marshall refers here to the best known of our political rights, which is the right to vote in elections, and also the right to be a member of a political party or other organization with political authority, but full participation goes beyond this. Furthermore, if people are to participate fully then they need social rights as well, as described by Liebenberg: 'Full and effective participation in democratic processes requires that every member of society has access to the basic necessities of life … Social inclusion and participation in democratic institutions does not only depend on the guarantee of formal civil and political rights, but also on socio-economic rights' (1999: 59).

We believe that effective participation is central to evaluating the quality of someone's democratic participation and inclusion in society. This citizen-focusing criterion for democratic legitimacy is drawn from participatory democracy literature that emphasizes the reallocation of power away from traditional power-holders. This means it is an approach that fits with the bottom-up, everyday legal problems and community legal capital paradigm that underpins our exploration of the interaction between civil and social rights in this book.

So, what do we mean by effective participation? Robert Dahl in his seminal works on democratic theory listed effective participation as one of his five criteria for democratic legitimacy (Dahl, 1989, 2000). In the context specifically of participatory democracy, Murphy and Organ (2022) extended the understanding of this concept as follows:

> We understand effective participation to incorporate three fundamental elements of democratic legitimacy: '[E]xternal inclusion,' addressing the question of *who* participates; 'internal inclusion,' relating to *how* citizens participate; and 'impact,' which considers *what* happens after citizens participate. The question of impact is central to our understanding of effective participation … Even if a mechanism is fully inclusive, it must lead to influence over the policy-making agenda and its outcomes; effective citizen influence necessarily restricts the discretion of existing institutional decision-makers. (Murphy and Organ, 2023: 180–1)

This definition of effective participation focuses on the need for a political system with participatory processes that include everyone, are fair and lead to impact on decision makers. People in poverty and managing day-to-day crises are far less likely to have the resources to participate. Those that have been let down by the system are less likely to see any value in participating, even when they have the resources to do so. When they do participate, it is important it has a meaningful impact. As Antonio Floridia said, an enduring element of the participatory vision is that: '"real" participation – participation that is "truly effective" – is tied to the decision-making nature of the participatory process' (Floridia, 2017: 38). However inclusive and deliberative participation might be, it becomes almost meaningless for those who have participated if it does not influence subsequent decision making.

This is one of the key distinctions between engagement through consultations and effective participation. Consultations offer no promise of action, whereas effective participation does. This requires a considerable shift in the power dynamics of local authority decision making, and for significant levels of trust from politicians and council officers that it is appropriate for organizations and citizens to become decision makers. In turn, this builds trust in the political system, and where the subject of the participatory exercise relates to social rights it will build trust in the social welfare system too. If this happens, we believe that the benefits for government authorities in terms of using funds effectively and for residents and organizations in terms of strengthening communities and social security will be significant. The LATAN project has shown that without the guarantee of civil rights such as access to justice, socio-economic rights break down and social citizenship becomes meaningless. The converse is also true. Without the guarantee of socio-economic rights, as seen when people are in poverty or destitution, political and civil rights also break down. The subsequent failure to participate is a symptom of that exclusion.

A lack of political participation is closely related to poverty. There is a 'long-established empirical finding that inequalities in democratic participation are closely related to factors like poverty, social exclusion and low levels of education' (Dacombe, 2018: 54). Higher levels of income inequality are also linked to lower political participation (Solt, 2008). This is a cyclical process. Once people start to have low levels of participation, their influence on political decisions, which is already weak, gets weaker still, and there is even less chance of their interests being represented. When their interests are not represented, issues that they are facing are unlikely to improve and their participation is likely to drop further, all things being equal. In other words, those in poverty become increasingly politically voiceless and increasingly likely to remain trapped in poverty.

The reasons for this link between poverty and low political participation are complex. (For a summary of why poverty and low democratic participation rates are associated with each other see Dacombe, 2018). Although numerous studies have established the link between low participation and poverty, it is also important to recognize that the full range of social determinants of health are likely to have an impact on a person's decision or opportunity to participate in the political process. Perhaps the correlation is strong enough to think of the social determinants of participation in a similar way to the social determinants of health, to ensure the full range of institutional, cultural and social factors that influence participation are explored when thinking about how to strengthen participation.

Investment at the community level in a network of organizations, such as those in LATAN, and investing in maintaining these partnerships will reap rewards on civil, social and political fronts. In general, they are highly efficient and motivated organizations that can quickly engage their community in developing initiatives that will have positive social impacts. Policy initiatives could shift the focus to building political participation through community organizations, with expected secondary effects on poverty and access to justice. The process of developing new forms of participation can help build trust (although a lack of action by authorities following citizen participation can be counter-productive). In turn, this increased trust, and integration of expertise based on lived experience into the decision-making process, will reduce people's perceptions that legal capability barriers exist, which means improved problem resolution and raised living standards, and then, in turn, higher levels of participation.

Democratic participatory theory offers multiple new forms of participation – such as citizens assemblies, participatory budgeting and citizens initiatives (Smith, 2009; Alemanno and Organ, 2021). As part of the LATAN project we are trying a new form of democratic participation in 2025: Theatre

Informed Policy Making. This is a development of Forum and Legislative Theatre (Boal, 1999) that will help the implementation of Liverpool's new strategic approach to access to advice. People with experience of needing advice in Liverpool have developed a performance that highlights their experience of everyday legal problems and accessing advice and offers improvements in the free legal advice ecosystem. A panel of policy makers watch and comment on the issues and solutions offered and join discussion with the invited audience. This will contribute policy solutions and research into the connections between civil, political and social rights, and into new participatory forms of policy making. We hope that one outcome from the project will be a group of people with experience of everyday legal problems and poverty that have strengthened participation in Liverpool City Council (Council or LCC) decision making and greater ability to advocate for their community's interests. The introduction of Citizens Initiative Reviews in Oregon, USA, saw a similar strengthening of participation and advocacy beyond the initial project period (Gastil and Knobloch, 2020). If the wave of participatory and deliberative innovation (Smith, 2009; Alemanno and Organ, 2021) in democratic processes continues, there will be plenty of opportunity to understand better the connection between civil, political and social rights. There is some evidence that people do view democracy as a project that rests on providing social rights and security (Hooghe and Oser, 2018), but, again, more research is needed to understand the relationship between these different elements of social citizenship.

Despite the vagueness of citizenship as a concept and the state of flux that social citizenship has been in for several years, it is still a useful aspirational concept to underpin the theoretical explanation of why access to justice, free legal advice and LATAN really matter to people's everyday lives. The first part of this chapter has argued that all three elements of social citizenship matter. The current signs are not good for meaningful change in this policy space, but we can hope. If hope is to become reality, then the overarching value that policy makers need to consider and try to build is *trust*.

Trust

Trust is fundamental to all forms of political legitimacy, including democratic political legitimacy and legal legitimacy. Building trust in relation to social rights is an important part of the process of strengthening democracy and the value of citizenship, especially if we are to view democracy as a political form that rests on civil, political and also social rights, and that aims to reduce inequality and give a voice to everyone in society. In this section we discuss the value of trust that sits at the nexus of, and is important to, the three areas of rights: political (Warren, 1999), social (Vitale, 2024) and civil. Trust specifically in relation to LATAN was discussed in Chapter 7.

As indicated in Chapter 2, trust as a value of social citizenship is of fundamental importance to a citizen's potential enjoyment of the promises made within that citizenship framing. In other words, if people do not trust that they will get a fair outcome, then they are less likely to think resolution is worth pursuing. This is one of the main barriers in terms of legal capability. An important part of an advisor's role is to build trust in the process and the possibility of a fair outcome. In this way advisors act as trusted intermediaries. This is a role, also played by staff and volunteers in gateway organizations, that can be valuable in terms of reducing barriers to resolving everyday legal problems raised by a lack of public legal education and legal capability (Cohl et al, 2018). Our LATAN experience and research has highlighted the impact of policies on trust and the impact that this has, in turn, on people with everyday legal problems.

Trust is a critical value for social citizenship, but more than that it is at the core of the political system itself. Trust 'nourishes the legitimacy of the system as a whole … is essential to continued political legitimacy in any state other than the most authoritarian' (Taylor Gooby, 2008: 6). As we have previously argued: 'Trust and the fulfilment of its constituent expectations – fairness, pursuit of citizen interests, and competence – are essential to political legitimacy and citizenship in any form, social or otherwise' (Sigafoos and Organ, 2021: 384).

Within the evolving understanding of social citizenship, we have previously used Taylor-Gooby's (2008) framing based on the three values of reciprocity, inclusion and trust. This framing worked well in the context of access to welfare benefits generally and from the perspective of a particular group in society (for example people with disabilities). The LATAN research, however, has emphasized the particular importance of trust as a core value (see Chapter 7), distinct from the other two, across all policy areas, and indeed as a value for civil and political rights as well. Of the three social citizenship values, reciprocity and inclusion are largely focused on redistribution and the welfare state, but trust is different and transcends this focus on the welfare benefits element of social citizenship. Trust as a citizenship value is particularly relevant to our discussion in this book as it is focused on the civil as well as the social elements of citizenship. It is focused on how people access their social rights through resolving everyday legal problems and on fairness in the system.

Our research in previous years (Sigafoos and Organ, 2021) and during the LATAN project (as discussed in Chapter 7) has shown that a high number of people have very low levels of trust in relation to the enjoyment of their social rights and the systems and institutions around them, particularly the Department for Work and Pensions (DWP). They simply do not believe that the system will treat them or anyone else fairly. The system is illegitimate to them.

This lack of trust can be instrumental to creating negative feedback loops in systems (Stroh, 2015). In the case of LATAN this is particularly noticeable in relation to the welfare benefits system, where distrust leads to people not applying for or delaying application for welfare benefits and is the result of numerous stories of hardship and ill health stemming from system failures. This lack of trust between citizen and state, then, has several implications for the advice ecosystem. It undermines people's perceptions of their legal capability and increases the demand for free legal advice. Combined with stigma around claiming welfare benefits, this reduces the effectiveness of the system by leading to delays in applications and a greater degree of crisis at the point people seek help. Furthermore, the perception that there will be an unfair outcome reduces the likelihood that people will expend financial or other personal resources to resolve issues promptly, which also increases the likelihood of people falling into crisis. In turn, this increases costs that need to be spent on social support by local authorities. This lack of trust then delegitimizes the welfare system for people as claimants and contributors, which has a further corrosive effect on its effectiveness. This can all lead to further pressures on budgets, for example through increased appeal processes, and renewed calls for cuts to services to 'what we can afford', which then perpetuates the negative cycle of distrust, limited effectiveness and rising costs. This is true in other areas of social welfare law as well.

Trust is a core value of political, civil and social rights. It is particularly important to LATAN as the roles that its members play in the free legal advice ecosystem sit at the intersection between these groups of rights. This is most obvious because of the link between free legal advice and resolving income issues, but there is also a strong link to participation. Effective participation as a central principle of democratic legitimacy links the discussion, at least here in this chapter, to political rights and is a reminder of the intersecting nature of these rights. Looking for alternative means to develop participation at a local level, where trust is (at least somewhat) more likely to exist, will develop people's political rights in terms of effective participation that influences policy decisions, and will also feed back into trust in the delivery of social rights and in the use of legal avenues to resolve issues.

Free legal advice makes a particularly important contribution to strengthening trust as an element of civil rights in the citizenship settlement. We have argued throughout this book that free legal advice is an important means of increasing the fairness of social rights processes and enjoyment and ensuring that there is a fairer settlement for people as they seek to access the social support promised by the state. Fairness and trust go hand in hand. The strengthening of the interactions between the organizations and people involved in the social rights networks is an important means of developing the trust that is needed to underpin a positive cycle of improvement across the trilogy of social citizenship rights. As Vitale said: 'We can expect the relationships in the social rights network to be able to impact trust in the citizen–government relationship – including, in the right circumstances, to foster trust' (Vitale, 2024: 81).

People perform many different roles in LATAN's gateway and advice organizations that are at the heart of this social rights network, and these build relationships and trust that, in turn, foster trust in the citizen–government relationship. Recognizing the value of these roles and supporting their delivery will be advantageous for trust relationships in other elements of people's engagement with the government and local authorities, with subsequent benefits in terms of the effectiveness of these interactions. This quote summarizes this influence on other relationships: '[T]he citizen–government relationship exists in a network of relationships (the "social rights network"), and that trust in that relationship (and, for that matter, any trust relationship in the social rights network) ultimately depends on the other relationships constituting the network' (Vitale, 2018: 709). This makes the delivery of free legal advice particularly valuable. Within the social rights network the hundreds of voluntary and community sector (VCS) organizations in Liverpool play a particularly important role.

With the increasing residualization of welfare benefits, this importance has increased as these organizations have stepped in to fill the gaps caused by the withdrawal of the state or changes in policy. This means that the citizen–government relationship, including the LCC, is a three-way relationship between the citizen, the relevant authorities (often the DWP and the Council) and VCS organizations/civil society. The implication of this is that for the social rights network to function effectively there needs to be a relationship of trust between the Liverpool resident and the state, between the state, particularly the Council in this case, and VCS organizations, and between the Liverpool resident and the VCS organizations. As pointed out in Chapter 3, one of the five key factors that the *European Health Equity Status Report* stated as driving health inequalities between regions was social and human capital, including a lack of trust and political voice (WHO, 2019). To reduce poverty and health inequalities we must build trust across all areas of social citizenship and give a stronger political voice to those with everyday legal problems.

Everyday legal problems

We will conclude here by bringing the reader back to the heart of everything that has been discussed in this book, which are people's everyday legal problems and how they go about trying to resolve them. It is in the legal problems in people's everyday lives that the connection between law, social justice and poverty becomes tangible and most apparent, and where the social determinants of health are impacted. As we have indicated throughout this book, we now live in a world where social justice issues mean that people's day-to-day experiences are supported by a series of promises from the state, and there is a regulatory or legislative basis on which to challenge decisions that affect our lives. Law is now pervasive in people's everyday lives: 'We live in a "law-thick" world. Across our planet, everyday life plays out within a complex legal framework extending across almost all activities: commerce, education, employment, the environment, family life, and more. Problems that raise legal issues are everywhere. They are among the "wicked" problems of social policy' (Pleasence and Balmer, 2019: 140).

It is within this law-thick world that people's everyday lives play out. The social contract is supposed to provide social welfare and full, consistent participation for all in society. For many people in society, however, this is not the case and they fall into poverty or ill health, because of how limited the welfare state is or because of a lack of legal advice to help access it. This help for people's everyday legal problems is not the sole preserve of lawyers. We have a wide-ranging ecosystem of support for people to initiate action, progress and resolve their everyday legal problems. It is not just the importance of getting access to someone to give legal advice or to a system of justice that the everyday legal problems framing points towards. Importantly, it is also about the resolution of issues, about fair outcomes and the substantive element of access to (social) justice. One of the reasons that we believe that everyday legal problems as a concept is significant is that it points policy makers towards these thicker understandings of justice embedded in society and the reality of people's lives.

Policy makers must have a bottom-up focus on the everyday problems in people's lives and recognize them as complex bundles of issues, with legal and non-legal influences and outcomes. These issues cut across and interact between the full range of social determinants of health, linking between employment, housing, health, education and so on. The importance of good health to all in society, and to society as a whole, requires recognition that everyday legal and non-legal issues are interconnected, and a range of accessible support is necessary to help people avoid them and resolve them, and to maintain a decent level of income, a reasonable level of health and full participation in society. To achieve this, free legal advice must be delivered in a different way and be available to far more people than it is today.

If access to justice is to be meaningful and there is to be a fair regulatory framework, then policy must recognize these twin realities of 'ubiquitous' (Currie, 2009: 2) everyday legal problems and an advice ecosystem populated by organizations outside the legal profession. It should focus on facilitating people's ability to understand when and how social welfare law influences the social determinants of health in their lives and provide the legal advice that is needed to resolve everyday legal problems. In turn, this will combat poverty and health inequalities. The proposals in the next chapter for a new, strategic approach to access to advice are an important step in this direction.

9

No Wrong Door; Advice for All

> We'll bring those organizations together under an umbrella and define, you know, how we deliver advice … So that no wrong door … so no door of any advice or support organization was a wrong door. (Interview A2)

Liverpool's advice strategy: the context

In 2023, the Liverpool Access to Advice Network (LATAN) proposed an access to advice strategy to Liverpool City Council (Council or LCC). The new approach synthesizes the learning from the years of the LATAN project. Developed and endorsed by 32 LATAN organizations, it is intended to support LCC policy discussions and trigger the co-design of a truly inclusive Liverpool advice strategy. It is a blueprint for any local authority developing their strategic approach to free legal advice and as a guide to national access to justice policy. The guiding principles for the new strategic approach are discussed later in four main sections with recommendations, which are also highlighted in brief at the end of the chapter. This chapter is a manifesto for a new approach to access to advice that will build much-needed collaboration and capacity in the sector and maximize the effectiveness of scarce resources in an advice ecosystem where demand far outstrips supply.

The advice ecosystem and its hundreds of organizations are a valuable resource in the fight against poverty and health inequalities. They provide significant social and economic benefits to communities and residents in raising incomes and keeping people in work. Advice also provides significant savings to the public purse: 'In 2023, the provision of free specialist legal advice saved the Treasury approximately £9,100 per case. For the estimated ½ million people receiving free legal advice, this equates to a saving of around £4.5 billion in the first year' (Munro and Preece, 2024: 8).

This saving only relates to specialist legal advice. Further savings will have been made from the millions of people helped at a more general level of advice.

National and local authorities need to recognize and invest in the value of the advice ecosystem and acknowledge the positive economic impact of a well-functioning (because well-funded and effective) advice sector.

We believe that a cohesive, collaborative and accessible network of gateway and free legal advice providers will deliver earlier and more effective access to advice and help build capacity in the long term. This will help prevent and resolve the issues we describe as people's everyday legal problems: problems triggered by life events that occur every day across our communities. These sometimes complex issues often require social welfare legal advice (welfare rights, employment, special educational needs and disabilities (SEND), housing, immigration and so on) to break the negative cycle that these life events can trigger in people's lives.

We have already spoken throughout this book about our advocacy for improving 'the system', embedding policies that promote equitable distribution of power – which will be possible with the right mix of central government and local authority policies. We believe passionately that access to free legal advice is essential in the fight against poverty and health inequalities. Every local authority needs a cohesive and strategic approach to access to advice. Access to justice, specifically access to advice, is an important component in enabling people to tackle their everyday legal problems.

The Liverpool access to advice strategy as a policy document was developed in collaboration with LATAN members during a series of workshops and meetings in September and October 2023. It was presented to the leader of the LCC, Councillor Liam Robinson, and other key councillors and council officers at meetings at the end of 2023 and early 2024. We received political agreement that the advice strategy should be implemented. We continue to work with the Council towards its implementation.

We propose a strategic approach based on our years of experience with the LATAN project in Liverpool. We believe the recommendations are relevant to, and will benefit, all local authorities. This practice-focused final chapter is aimed specifically at policy makers at a national and local level and at improving the support for the valuable advice ecosystems that exist across the country. We believe that a strategic approach to free legal advice in all local authority areas will maximize the great work that is being done by voluntary and community sector (VCS) organizations and all legal advice providers to support people wrestling with the challenges of everyday legal problems.

VISION: no wrong door; advice for all

Collaboration is key to local advice services provision, so that wherever people are when they realize they have a problem that advice could help, or wherever they go to get support, that door opens up to all the services available in the advice network. No door is the wrong door.

A *universal, joined up system* of trusted gateway and advice providers will deliver the types and level of advice needed to reach people with particular legal needs and hard to serve populations. People will get advice as early as possible to reduce the likelihood of reaching crisis, and to enable them to respond to specific events.

Advice for all: the advice network has *capacity* to provide all people with the level and type of quality legal advice they need. This will require additional resources to increase the supply of advice.

Free legal advice strategy: implementation

The strategic approach to advice, when implemented, will engage with each of the three elements of a person's efforts to get advice to help resolve their everyday legal problems: *gateway*, *referral* and *advice provision*. A diverse range of organizations supports this journey at each stage so that: (1) people can recognize that legal advice could help the issue they have; (2) the organization they have been in contact with can refer them to someone that can provide that advice; and (3) the person gets the advice they need until their issue(s) is resolved. There are challenges for organizations in the advice network at each stage of this journey, particularly the capacity to meet the demand for advice. Fundamentally, more resource for advice funding is required. A more strategic approach to how this resource is shared will help mitigate some of the shortage but cannot compensate for it.

Our recommendations are grouped into five sections that explain the principles of the strategic approach and state what is needed. The first section focuses on the *advice network* and building a community of practice. The subsequent three sections focus on each element of a person's efforts to resolve an everyday legal problem: *gateway*, *referral* and *advice*. The fifth section – *Evidence base and identifying people's needs* – is focused on the importance of building the evidence base relating to free legal advice and increasing the ability to influence change.

The advice network and community of practice

Our strategic starting point is that a properly resourced advice network is needed. LATAN is a good example of what is possible. There needs to be a strong community of practice that can act as a positive voice for the advice ecosystem, drive further collaboration between organizations and the Council, and build an evidence base that can be used to effect positive change. Building this voice for the advice ecosystem will help give voice to those with everyday legal problems through embedding practices that advocate for clients to challenge the source of injustices in the system.

Building a community of practice, which is a process through which a group works together toward a common interest and engages in collective learning (Wenger-Trayner and Wenger-Trayner, 2015), will help to facilitate best practice between advice providers, and increase the ability of gateway organizations to identify advice needs and make referrals. This can be done, for example, through training, collaboration and knowledge exchange. This will also assist the development of a single city-wide referral system and help build on the multiple frameworks of quality standards that exist for advice providers in the UK.

A specific task of the advice network could be to take a lead role in implementing and developing the directory and referral system. It is important to note that an advice network needs to be staffed. At least a network coordinator and administrator are needed, but other roles, such as a social policy campaigns role and funding coordinator would also fit well.

What we need

- A well-resourced advice network supporting a strong community of practice built on shared objectives, learning and information.

Gateway

The first step in a person's journey to get advice is to recognize that they have a legal problem. 'No wrong door' means that any organization in the advice ecosystem, VCS, public or private organizations, can help people recognize an everyday legal problem and help them to access advice providers. This recognizes the value of organizations that do not give advice, or where it is only part of their remit, helping people identify that their problem may have a legal element and can be helped by advice. Low public legal education means that people are often unaware that their everyday legal problem could be helped by advice.

Developing close collaboration across a trusted network of VCS organizations as part of a network such as LATAN can help people take this first step towards resolving their problem, and reduce the impact of legal capability barriers. The trust that people have in their local community organizations means that they can give people confidence that they have the capability to pursue an issue that requires legal advice, and also that it is a fair process worth the effort to try to resolve an issue. Recognizing and helping to develop trusted intermediaries across the advice ecosystem is one way to help overcome these barriers to legal capability.

Multiple access points and a diversity of gateway organizations that cover a range of demographics are needed. This provides for different forms of advice seeking behaviour. It also facilitates access to advice for people with particular needs and from vulnerable groups, for example those with specific health needs, in a fully inclusive advice ecosystem. The breadth of the advice network is a particular strength in terms of accessibility and in terms of its ability to overcome all forms of exclusion, breaking down barriers such as those relating to digital access, language or disability.

'No wrong door' must also mean that the door opens to somewhere that has capacity to give someone advice at the right level. Ultimately, the aspiration is an appropriate and timely level of 'advice for all' that come through the door.

What we need

- A trusted integrated network of diverse gateway organizations where clients present with everyday legal problems.
- Development and funding of roles that recognize the value of the trust that people have in local organizations to overcome legal capability barriers.

Referrals

A referral is an important step in a person's journey to resolve an issue and can often be a point at which efforts to resolve everyday legal problems break down. Finding the advice that is available when needed (often at a point of crisis) is a challenge. The aim is that whenever an organization, be it VCS, health setting or any other, thinks that advice could help someone, they can find out whether advice is available and where. When available, they will know how to make an active client referral to a place giving relevant free legal advice. This is not just signposting, which can lead to referral fatigue and further trauma, but an active, managed, fully informed referral process. The referral system used needs to show service availability and enable communications and documentation to be transferred securely between organizations on behalf of the client. In Liverpool, LATAN has established data standards and referral protocols over the last three years for this purpose. There should be a single, administered, combined referral system and directory of services that can be accessed by all members of the advice ecosystem to an appropriate level. Self-referral by members of the public should also be available through the system. We have identified referral systems that can achieve this, but they need funding. A combined system of this sort will greatly increase the speed and quality of referrals. Through greater provision of information and widespread use, it should also ease pressure on other gateway points into the advice ecosystem. Alongside this electronic access point, further training for gateway organizations about referrals and initial contact with people with everyday legal problems would have significant gains in terms of public legal education and reducing legal capability barriers.

What we need

- An integrated, secure advice referral system with the online directory of VCS organizations and Council services, including a self-referral facility.
- Funding is needed for administration of the directory and to support the referral process.
- Development of the standards and referral protocols for gateway organizations.

Co-location of advice services

Co-location of advice and non-advice support services is a valuable means of targeting advice services at particularly vulnerable people. It is key to stopping the negative spiral of interconnecting everyday legal problems that people face and reducing their impact on the social determinants of health. Liverpool's Citizens Advice on Prescription project is a leading UK example of health–justice partnerships (HJPs), which are an important form of co-location of advice services in health settings. Co-location of advice services could be rolled out at other targeted organizations, such as schools, food banks and food pantries, community cafes and disability support groups. Developing new co-located advice services and building on Liverpool's experience of HJPs will help target advice to those that need it most, speed up referrals and reduce the negative spiral in the social determinants that unresolved everyday legal problems can cause.

What we need

- Co-located, cross-sector advice services along the lines of health–justice partnerships.
- An evidence base related to the co-location of advice services.

Advice provision

The third element in someone's efforts to resolve an everyday legal problem is, of course, to get the free legal advice that they need to address it, as early as possible at all levels of legal complexity. It is recognized that particular populations may need more or targeted support to make this happen. It is also recognized that areas of law have fluctuating demands depending on social and policy circumstances. The key areas of social welfare law identified are: welfare rights, debt/money advice, housing, employment, immigration,

SEND and family. Implementation of a free legal advice strategy should identify when and how differing areas of social welfare law should be targeted.

Perhaps the most important recommendation in the advice strategy is that every new anti-poverty strategy, programme or initiative, or others affecting the social determinants of health, should identify the advice needs that may be associated with their goals and hoped for outcomes. For example, a new housing strategy should recognize that there will be complexities and barriers to people's efforts to get access to limited social housing, and that people who are rough sleeping and homeless will need advice about their rights in various areas of social welfare law alongside the specific support to find them a home. In other words, all anti-poverty services should have a conscious link to advice services so that their delivery is in the design of the programme itself. This link to advice should recognize the different policy points at which advice can have an impact on someone's social determinants of health. This is discussed in Chapter 3 and illustrated by Figure 3.4. The availability of this advice will help target priority outcomes within a local authority's strategic goals. The recent 'Our Liverpool' project is a good example of this approach. Advice needs were identified and funded as part of an LCC project that had a broader aim of supporting the lives of vulnerable migrants, people seeking asylum and those with refugee status.

The VCS organizations that make up the advice ecosystem are a valuable resource available to assist with embedding advice in a local authority's programme design. They can share experiences of supporting people, as well as help identify the potential advice needs of the targeted population and how those needs could be provided for at all levels of complexity and specialization. It is important that a local authority identifies the key directorate with responsibility for each consultation and subsequent commissioning decisions. These decisions will be informed by the evidence base as outlined in the section 'Evidence base and identifying people's needs'.

The availability of advice services has reduced in recent years and there is high demand for the remaining services. Independence of advice services is important for people to trust the advice given. By maximizing the effectiveness of the advice sector so that people receive advice as promptly as possible, we can help prevent people from reaching crisis point and reduce the impact these crises have on local authority resources. It is important to note that the strategic focus on collaboration and supporting the connection of the advice network does not directly increase the capacity of advice providers. There is also a need for a long-term funding strategy to increase capacity and avoid the negative impacts that short-term funding has on organizational sustainability and advice provision.

What we need

- Development of a long-term network funding strategy to increase advice provision.
- Organizational collaboration to help maximize advice capacity and the use of scarce resources.
- Inclusion of appropriate independent advice and identification of resources for that advice when developing new local authority strategies or programmes.
- Identification of a key directorate with responsibility for ensuring appropriate independent advice is included in strategy and programme design.
- Involvement of organizations in the advice network in the design of advice services.

Evidence base and identifying people's needs

LATAN and its partners have worked to identify the everyday legal problems of people in Liverpool and to understand Liverpool's advice ecosystem in order to make recommendations to improve it. This has been done through multi-sector engagement between LATAN members, the universities, the Law Society and the Council, and through successfully applying for research funding. This extensive evidence base informs our proposal here for a new strategic approach to access to advice across all local authorities. We are confident that our proposed approach is generalizable to other areas, though obviously local efforts to implement it will identify the needs and resources of their advice ecosystem.

An evidence base is an important resource for planning the provision of advice, effectively prioritizing services, and being responsive to the changing social and policy environment. It is a driver for more effective participation of organizations in decision making. It is important that an evidence base continues to be developed through, for example, leveraging existing university research capacity and funding, and facilitating data sharing with local and national authorities. The recent evaluation of the effectiveness of the Citizens Advice on Prescription project is a good example of this collaboration (Aregawi et al, 2025). This will ensure that advice network decisions, particularly those relating to funding and allocation of resources, can be made using a strong evidence base.

Collective organizations such as LATAN and other advice networks need to harness their power to affect meaningful, positive change that affects 'the system' and thus the social determinants of health, and thereby challenge inequality at all levels of government. This will help reduce poverty and health inequalities through driving change at the macro rather than individual level. The local or regional authority, universities and the advice network should work together to facilitate research and inform and develop social policy campaigns. This will ensure evidence-based policy responses and make better use of scarce resources to meet people's advice needs.

Campaigns should seek to change policies that impact the prevalence and severity of peoples' everyday legal problems and their ability to access and receive advice. All stakeholders should share anonymized data and research to support campaigns and consultation responses. This social policy work will be part of a positive feedback loop helping to develop new local authority and national strategies and initiatives, such as anti-poverty, housing, and fair employment strategies that can have a positive impact on the social determinants of health.

What we need

- A regularly updated evidence base of people's advice needs and the existing advice ecosystem.
- Effective participation with advice networks in the allocation of resources and development and prioritization of advice provision.
- Resources for ongoing research into the advice sector, to coordinate evidence gathering and develop social policy campaigns.
- Collaboration between organizations to advocate for change.
- Alignment of data collection and data sharing across the network and local authorities.

Conclusion

We have seen in this book that there are a diverse number of organizations involved in a person's efforts to get advice in a limited, fragile and complex ecosystem. The seemingly high number of organizations that are stakeholders in the free legal advice sector must be set in the context of a sector that has suffered severe funding cuts in recent years, and where the majority of organizations act only as a gateway to the limited legal advice services that remain. Harnessing the value of this diverse network and their close engagement with the communities they serve is an important aim of the advice strategy.

Now is the ideal time to implement a new strategic approach to access to advice, in Liverpool as well as in every local authority. In Liverpool, the learning from the years of the LATAN project has laid the foundations for strong collaboration across the sector between all VCS organizations and advice providers. The advice sector is working together for the benefit of its clients in terms of access to and provision of advice, research and training, funding and social policy campaigns. This means that our proposed approach to advice provision is based on strong collaborative foundations and a good evidence base.

It can underpin policy responses to the everyday legal problems people are facing in their lives, and help local authorities to implement their wider strategic goals. We have summarized these recommendations in Box 9.1. We would strongly recommend that all local authorities take up the challenge of implementing this new strategic approach to access to free legal advice in order to revolutionize access to justice in their local area and maximize their efforts to fight poverty and health inequalities.

Box 9.1: Full list of recommendations for an effective advice network

1. A well-resourced advice network supporting a strong community of practice built on shared objectives, learning and information.
2. A trusted integrated network of diverse gateway organizations where clients present with everyday legal problems.
3. Development and funding of roles that recognize the value of the trust that people have in local organizations to overcome legal capability barriers.
4. An integrated, secure advice referral system with the online directory of VCS organizations and council services, including a self-referral facility.
5. Funding is needed for administration of the directory and to support the referral process.
6. Development of the standards and referral protocols for gateway organizations.
7. Co-located, cross-sector advice services along the lines of health–justice partnerships.
8. An evidence base related to the co-location of advice services.
9. Development of a long-term network funding strategy to increase advice provision.
10. Organizational collaboration to help maximize advice capacity and the use of scarce resources.
11. Inclusion of appropriate independent advice and identification of resources for that advice when developing new local authority strategies or programmes.
12. Identification of a key directorate with responsibility for ensuring appropriate independent advice is included in strategy and programme design.
13. Involvement of organizations in the advice network in the design of advice services.
14. A regularly updated evidence base of people's advice needs and the existing advice ecosystem.
15. Effective participation with advice networks in the allocation of resources and development and prioritization of advice provision.
16. Resources for ongoing research into the advice sector, to coordinate evidence gathering and develop social policy campaigns.
17. Collaboration between organizations to advocate for change.
18. Alignment of data collection and data sharing across the network and local authorities.

References

Abbot, S., Hobby, L. and Cotter, S. (2006) 'What is the impact on individual health of services in general practice settings which offer welfare benefits advice?', *Health and Social Care in the Community* 14 (1): 1–8.

Acheson, D. (2000) *Independent Inquiry into Inequalities in Health: Report,* London: The Stationery Office.

Addario, G., Vallgarda, L. and Khriakova, E. (2024) 'New poverty measure release: Below Average Resources (BAR)', National Centre for Social Research, [blog] 24 January. Available from: https://natcen.ac.uk/new-poverty-measure-release-below-average-resources-bar [Accessed 12 November 2024].

Adelman, C. (1993) 'Kurt Lewin and the origins of action research', *Educational Action Research*, 1(1): 7–24.

Adjei, N.K., Schlüter, D., Straatmann, V., Melis, G., Fleming, K., McGovern, R., et al (2021) 'Impact of poverty and family adversity on adolescent health: a multi-trajectory analysis using the UK Millennium Cohort Study', *The Lancet Regional Health – Europe*, 13(100279).

Advice Services Alliance and the Low Commission (2015) *The Role of Advice Services in Health Outcomes: Evidence Review and Mapping Study.* Available from: https://www.thelegaleducationfoundation.org/wp-content/uploads/2015/06/Role-of-Advice-Services-in-Health-Outcomes.pdf [Accessed 27 November 2024].

Advice Services UK (2011) 'Developing the Advice Quality Standard: definitions to help you understand the advice sector'. Available from: https://asauk.org.uk/wp-content/uploads/2013/08/Definitions-to-help-you-understand-the-advice-sector.pdf [Accessed 20 April 2025].

Albiston, C. and Sandefur, R. (2013) 'Expanding the empirical study of access to justice,' *Wisconsin Law Review*, 2013(1): 101–20.

Alemanno, A. and Organ, J. (2021) *Citizen Participation in Democratic Europe: What Next for the EU?*, London: ECPR Press.

Allmark, P., Baxter, S., Goyder, E., Guillaume, L., Crofton-Martin. G. (2013) 'Assessing the health benefits of advice services: using research evidence and logic model methods to explore complex pathways', *Health & Social Care Community*, 21(1): 59–68.

Almeder, R. (1986) 'A definition of pragmatism', *History of Philosophy Quarterly*, 3(1): 79–87.

Alston, P. (2018) 'Statement on Visit to the United Kingdom, by Professor Philip Alston, United Nations Special Rapporteur on extreme poverty and human rights', Geneva: United Nations Human Rights Office of the High Commissioner, 16 November, pp 1–24. Available from: https://www.ohchr.org/sites/default/files/Documents/Issues/Poverty/EOM_GB_16Nov2018.pdf [Accessed 30 November 2024].

Aregawi, G., Piroddi, R., Daras, K., Andersen De Cuevas, R., Abba, K., Gabbay, M., et al (2025) 'The impacts of Liverpool Citizens Advice on Prescription (CAP) on mental health outcomes – an instrumental variable (IV) approach', *SSM – Population Health*, 30: 101785.

Arendt, H. (1998) *The Human Condition* (2nd edn), Chicago: University of Chicago Press.

Ashton, M. (2024) *State of Health in Liverpool 2040,* Liverpool City Council. Available from: https://liverpool.gov.uk/media/y45lmvvm/health-in-liverpool-2040.pdf [Accessed 12 November 2024].

Bambra, C. (2016) *Health Divides: Where You Live Can Kill You,* Bristol: Policy Press.

Bambra, C., Bennett, N., McNamara, C., Munford, L. and Wickham, S. (2025) Public Health and Welfare Reform: Evidence Submission to the Work and Pensions Committee Pathways to Work Green Paper Inquiry, PTW0001. Available from: https://committees.parliament.uk/work/9065/get-britain-working-pathways-to-work/publications/ [Accessed 30 April 2025].

Bambra, C., Davies, H., Munford, L., Taylor-Robinson, D., Pickett, K., et al (2024) *Woman of the North*, Health Equity North, Northern Health Science Alliance. Available from: https://www.healthequitynorth.co.uk/app/uploads/Woman-of-the-North-report.pdf [Accessed 25 October 2024].

Barnard, C., Costello, F. and Fraser Butlin, S. (2024) *Low-Paid EU Migrant Workers: The House, the Street, the Town*, Bristol: Bristol University Press.

Barr, B. and Taylor-Robinson, D. (2016) 'Recessions are harmful to health: a government's response can be even more damaging', *BMJ (Online)*, 354(September): 1–2.

Barr, B., Higgerson, J. and Whitehead, M. (2017) 'Investigating the impact of the English health inequalities strategy: time trend analysis', *BMJ*, 358(July): 1–8.

Barr, B., Kinderman, P. and Whitehead, M. (2015) 'Trends in mental health inequalities in England during a period of recession, austerity and welfare reform 2004 to 2013', *Social Science & Medicine* (147): 324–31.

Baum, F., MacDougall, C. and Smith, D. (2006) 'Participatory action research', *Journal of Epidemiology & Community Health*, 60(10): 854–7.

Beardon, S. and Genn, H. (2018) *The Health Justice Landscape in England and Wales: Social Welfare Legal Services in Health Settings*, London: UCL Centre for Access to Justice. Available from: https://www.ucl.ac.uk/access-to-justice/sites/access-to-justice/files/lef030_mapping_report_web.pdf [Accessed 31 April 2025].

Bennett, D.L., Schlüter, D., Melis, G., Bywaters, P., Alexiou, A., Barr, B., et al (2022) 'Child poverty and children entering care in England, 2015–20: a longitudinal ecological study at the local area level', *The Lancet Public Health*, 7(6): 496–503.

Bertalanffy, L. von (1968) *General System Theory: Foundations, Development, Applications*, New York: George Brazillier.

Bestwick, M. and Schmuecker, K. (2024) *The Impact of Hardship on Primary Schools and Primary and Community Healthcare*, York: Joseph Rowntree Foundation. Available from: https://www.jrf.org.uk/deep-poverty-and-destitution/the-impact-of-hardship-on-primary-schools-and-primary-healthcare [Accessed 30 November 2024].

Beveridge, W. (1942) *Social Insurance and Allied Services (the Beveridge Report)* (Cmd. 6404), Norwich: The Stationery Office.

Blane, D. and Watt, G. (2012) 'GPs at the deep end: GP experience of the impact of austerity on patients and general practices in very deprived areas', University of Glasgow and Deep End Steering Group, Glasgow. Available from: https://www.gla.ac.uk/media/Media_232766_smxx.pdf [Accessed 27 November 2024].

Boal, A. (1999) *Legislative Theatre: Using Performance to Make Politics,* trans A. Jackson, London: Routledge.

Boyle, K. (2022) '*The access to justice journey'*, Briefing, Access to Justice for Social Rights: Addressing the Accountability Gap, Nuffield Foundation, London, May. Available from: https://www.nuffieldfoundation.org/wp-content/uploads/2019/11/Boyle-Briefing-The-Access-to-Justice-Journey_18MAY22.pdf [Accessed 30 November 2024].

Boyle, K. and Camps, D. (2022) 'A human rights lens: reclaiming the narrative for social rights as legal rights', in M. Adler (ed) *A Research Agenda for Social Welfare Law*, Cheltenham: Edward Elgar Publishing, pp 61–78.

Boyle, K. and Camps, D. (2024) 'Legal needs and access to justice', in N. Creutzfeldt, A. Kyprianides, B. Bradford and J. Jackson (eds) *Access to Justice, Digitalization and Vulnerability: Exploring Trust in Justice*, Bristol: Bristol University Press.

Boyle, K., Camps, D., English, K. and Ferrie, J. (2022) *The Practitioner Perspective on Access to Justice for Social Rights: Addressing the Accountability Gap*, London: Nuffield Foundation. Available from: https://www.,nuffieldfoundation.,org/wp-content/uploads/2019/11/Final-report-The-practitioner-perspective-on-access-to-justice-for-social-rights-1.pdf [Accessed 30 November 2024].

Bradbury, H. (2020) 'Introduction: how to situate and define action research', in H. Bradbury (ed) *The SAGE Handbook of Action Research*, London: Sage Publications, pp 1–12.

Bradshaw, J., Middleton, S., Davis, A., Oldfield, N., Smith, N., Cusworth, L., et al (2008) *A Minimum Income Standard for Britain*, York: Joseph Rowntree Foundation.

The Brain Charity (2024) *It's All in Your Head: Neurological Conditions: The Journey to and Impact of Diagnosis*. Available from: https://www.thebraincharity.org.uk/wp-content/uploads/2023/09/its-all-in-your-head-a-report-by-the-brain-charity-2023.pdf [Accessed 27 November 2024].

Braun, V. and Clarke, V. (2006) 'Using thematic analysis in psychology', *Qualitative Research in Psychology*, 3(2): 77–101.

Brigid Francis-Devine, B. (2024) *Food Banks in the UK*, Research Briefing, House of Commons Library.

Brown, G. (2001) 'Tackling child poverty: giving every child the best start in life', Press Release, Treasury Office. Available from: https://www.wired-gov.net/wg/wg-news-1.nsf/54e6de9e0c383719802572b9005141ed/64b3db7161aabe50802572ab004b4e97?OpenDocument

Bryman, A. (1988) *Quantity and Quality in Social Research*, London: Routledge.

Bryman, A. (2004) *Social Research Methods*, Oxford: Oxford University Press.

Bryman, A. (2006) 'Integrating quantitative and qualitative research: how is it done?', *Qualitative Research*, 6(1): 97–113.

Bull, R., Miles, C., Newbury, E., Nichols, A., Weekes, T. and Wyld, G. (2023) *Hunger in the UK 2023*, Salisbury: Trussell Trust. Available from: https://www.trussell.org.uk/publications/hunger-in-the-uk

Byrom, N. (2019) *Developing the Detail: Evaluating the Impact of Court Reform in England and Wales on Access to Justice*, London: Legal Education Foundation.

Campos, F.C. and Anderson, G.L. (2022) 'Paulo Freire's influence on participatory action research', in D. Burns, A. Howard and S.M. Ospina (eds) *The Sage Handbook of Participatory Research and Inquiry*, London: Sage Publications, pp 41–54.

Cappelletti, M. and Garth, B. (1978) 'Access to justice: the newest wave in the worldwide movement to make rights effective', *Buffalo Law Review*, 27: 181–292.

Cappelletti, M., Garth B. and Trocker, N. (1976) 'Access to justice, comparative general report', *The Rabel Journal of Comparative and International Private Law*, 40(3/4): 669.

Cappelletti, M., Garth, B. and Trocker, N. (1982) 'Access to justice, variations and continuity of a world-wide movement', *The Rabel Journal of Comparative and International Private Law*, 46: 664–707.

Carers UK (2024) 'Carers UK welcomes Carer's Allowance earnings threshold increase in Autumn Budget', *Carers UK*, 20 October. Available from: https://www.carersuk.org/press-releases/carers-uk-welcomes-carers-allowance-earnings-threshold-increase-in-autumn-budget/ [Accessed 24 November 2024].

Chang, H. (2021) 'Individual and collaborative autoethnography for social science research', in T.E. Adams, S. Holman Jones and C. Ellis (eds) *Handbook of Autoethnography* (2nd edn), New York: Routledge, pp 53–69.

Cheetham, M., Moffatt, S., Addison, M. and Wiseman, A. (2019) 'Impact of Universal Credit in North East England: a qualitative study of claimants and support staff', *BMJ Open,* 9(e029611).

Citizens Advice Liverpool (2024) 'Health programme', Citizens Advice Liverpool. Available from: https://www.citizensadviceliverpool.org.uk/citizens-advice-on-prescription-liverpool [Accessed 1 May 2025].

Clark, T., Foster, L., Sloan, L. and Bryman, A. (2021) *Bryman's Social Research Methods* (6th edn), Oxford: Oxford University Press.

Cohl, K., Lassonde, J., Mathews, J., Smith, C. and Thomson, G. (2018) *Trusted Help: The Role of Community Workers as Trusted Intermediaries Who Help People with Legal Problems, Part 1: Key Findings and Recommendations,* Toronto: Law Foundation of Ontario.

Cooper, K. and Stewart, K. (2013) *Does Money Affect Children's Outcomes? A Systematic Review,* Joseph Rowntree Foundation (ed), York: Joseph Rowntree Foundation.

Cooper, K. and Stewart, K. (2017) 'Does money affect children's outcomes? An update', CASE paper 203, Centre for Analysis of Social Exclusion. Available from: http://sticerd.lse.ac.uk/dps/case/cp/casepaper203.pdf

Cornford, T. (2016) 'The meaning of access to justice', in E. Palmer, T. Cornford, A. Guinchard and Y. Marique (eds) *Access to Justice: Beyond the Policies and Politics of Austerity*, Oxford: Hart Publishing, pp 27–40.

Coumarelos, C., Macourt, D., People, J., McDonald H.M., Wei, Z., Iriana, R. and Ramsey, S. (2012) *Legal Australia-Wide Survey: Legal Need in Australia*, Sydney: Law and Justice Foundation of New South Wales.

Craig, G. (2018) *Handbook on Global Social Justice*, Cheltenham: Edward Elgar Publishing.

Creswell, J.W. and Plano Clark, V.L. (2018) *Designing and Conducting Mixed Methods Research* (3rd edn), London: Sage Publications.

Creswell, J.W. and Poth, C.N. (2018) *Qualitative Inquiry and Research Design: Choosing among Five Approaches* (4th edn), London: Sage Publications.

Creutzfeldt, N., Kyprianides, A., Bradford, B. and Jackson, J. (eds) (2024) *Access to Justice, Digitalization and Vulnerability: Exploring Trust in Justice,* Bristol: Bristol University Press.

Currie, A. (2009) 'The legal problems of everyday life', in R. Sandefur (ed) *Access to Justice,* Sociology of Crime, Law and Deviance, Vol. 12, Leeds: Emerald Group Publishing, pp 1–41.

Currie, A. (2016) 'Nudging the paradigm shift, everyday legal problems in Canada', *Canadian Forum on Civil Justice,* 39. Available from: https://digitalcommons.osgoode.yorku.ca/cfcj/39 [Accessed 27 November 2024].

Dacombe, R. (2018) *Rethinking Civic Participation in Democratic Theory and Practice*, London: Palgrave Macmillan.

Dahl, R. (1989) *Democracy and Its Critics*, New Haven, CT: Yale University Press.

Dahl, R. (2000) *On Democracy*, New Haven, CT: Yale University Press.

Dahlgren, G. and Whitehead, M. (1991) 'Policies and strategies to promote social equity in health. background document to WHO – strategy paper for Europe', Stockholm: Institute for Future Studies. Available from: https://core.ac.uk/download/pdf/6472456.pdf

Dahlgren, G. and Whitehead, M. (2021) 'The Dahlgren–Whitehead model of health determinants: 30 years on and still chasing rainbows', *Public Health*, 199: 20–4.

Davis, A., Blackwell, C., Ellis, E., Padley, M., Stone, J. and Balchin, E. (2024) *A Minimum Income Standard for the United Kingdom in 2024*, York: Joseph Rowntree Foundation.

Denvir, C. and Selvarajah, A.D. (2021) 'Safeguarding access to justice in the age of the online court', *Modern Law Review*, 85: 25–68.

Department for Energy Security and Net Zero (2025) *Annual Fuel Poverty Statistics in England, 2025 (2024 data)*, Accredited Official Statistics, 27 March. Available from: https://assets.publishing.service.gov.uk/media/67e51e2cbb6002588a90d5d5/annual-fuel-poverty-statistics-report-2025.pdf [Accessed 18 June 2025].

Department of Health (1999) *Saving Lives: Our Healthier Nation*, The Stationery Office. Available from: https://assets.publishing.service.gov.uk/media/5a7b8c8240f0b62826a044aa/4386.pdf [Accessed 18 June 2025].

Department for Work and Pensions (2024) *Research and Analysis Summary: Review of the UK Material Deprivation Measures*. Available from: https://www.gov.uk/government/publications/review-of-the-uk-material-deprivation-measures/summary-review-of-the-uk-material-deprivation-measures#research-context [Accessed 1 May 2025].

Department for Work and Pensions (2025a) *Households Below Average Income Series: Quality and Methodological Information Report FYE 2023*. Available from: https://www.gov.uk/government/statistics/households-below-average-income-for-financial-years-ending-1995-to-2023/households-below-average-income-series-quality-and-methodology-information-report-fye-2023#introduction [Accessed 30 April 2025].

Department for Work and Pensions (2025b) *Below Average Resources: Developing a New Poverty Measure*. Available from: https://www.gov.uk/government/statistics/below-average-resources-developing-a-new-poverty-measure [Accessed 30 April 2025].

Department for Work and Pensions (2025c) *Official Statistics Below Average Resources: for Financial Years Ending 2001 to 2023*. Available from: https://www.gov.uk/government/statistics/below-average-resources-for-financial-year-2022-to-2023/below-average-resources-for-financial-year-2022-to-2023 [Accessed 30 April 2025].

Department for Work and Pensions (2025d) *Households Below Average Income: For Financial Years Ending 1995 to 2024, HBAI Summary Results*. Available from: https://www.gov.uk/government/statistics/households-below-average-income-for-financial-years-ending-1995-to-2024 [Accessed 30 April 2025].

Department for Work and Pensions (2025e) *Data Tables: Below Average Resources: for financial years ending 2001 to 2023*. Available from: https://www.gov.uk/government/statistics/below-average-resources-for-financial-year-2022-to-2023 [Accessed 30 April 2025].

Department for Work and Pensions (2025f) Pathways to Work: Reforming Benefits and Support to Get Britain Working Green Paper. GOV.UK.

Di Domenico, M., Haugh, H. and Tracey, P. (2010) 'Social bricolage: theorizing social value creation in social enterprises', *Entrepreneurship Theory and Practice*, 34(4): 681–703.

Dickerson, A. and Popli, G.K. (2016) 'Persistent poverty and children's cognitive development: evidence from the UK Millennium Cohort Study', *Journal of the Royal Statistical Society Series A: Statistics in Society*, 179(2): 535–58.

Diderichsen, F., Evans, T. and Whitehead, M. (2001) 'The social basis of disparities in health', in T. Evans and M. Whitehead (eds) *Challenging Inequities in Health: From Ethics to Action,* Oxford: Oxford University Press, pp 12–23.

Duncanson, K. and Henderson, E. (2021) *Courthouse Architecture, Design and Social Justice* (1st edn), London: Routledge.

Dwyer, P. (2000) *Welfare Rights and Responsibilities: Contesting Social Citizenship,* Bristol: Policy Press.

Edmiston, D. (2017) 'Welfare, austerity and social citizenship in the UK', *Social Policy and Society*, 16(2): 261.

Elliott, J. (1991) *Action Research for Educational Change*, Philadelphia, PA: Open University Press.

Fals Borda, O. (1979) 'Investigating reality in order to transform it: the Colombian experience', *Dialectical Anthropology*, 4(1): 33–55.

Fals Borda, O. (2001) 'Participatory (action) research in social theory: origins and challenges', in P. Reason and H. Bradbury (eds) *Handbook of Action Research: Participative Inquiry and Practice*, London: Sage Publications, pp 27–37.

Felstiner, W.L.F. Abel, R.L. and Sarat, A. (1981) 'The emergence and transformation of disputes: naming, blaming, claiming . . .', *Law and Society Review,* 15(3): 631–54.

Fetters, M.D., Curry, L.A. and Creswell, J.W. (2013) 'Achieving integration in mixed methods designs – principles and practices', *Health Services Research*, 6(2): 2134–56.

Fitzpatrick, C., McKeever, G. and Simpson, M. (2019) 'Conditionality, discretion and T.H. Marshall's "right to welfare"', *The Journal of Social Welfare & Family Law*, 41(4): 445.

Fitzpatrick, S., Bramley, G., Treanor, M., Blenkinsopp, J., McIntyre, J., Johnsen, S. and McMordie, L. (2023) *Destitution in the UK 2023*, York: Joseph Rowntree Foundation.

Floridia, A. (2017) *From Participation to Deliberation: A Critical Genealogy of Deliberative Democracy*, London: ECPR Press.

Flynn, A. and Hodgson, J. (eds) (2017) *Access to Justice and Legal Aid: Comparative Perspectives on Unmet Legal Need*, Oxford: Hart Publishing.

Francis-Devine, B. (2025) 'Income inequality in the UK', House of Commons Library, 15 April 2025, GOV.UK. Available from: https://commonslibrary.parliament.uk/research-briefings/cbp-7484 [Accessed 30 November 2024].

Francis-Devine, B. (2025) *Poverty in the UK: Statistics. House of Commons Library*. Available from: https://researchbriefings.files.parliament.uk/documents/SN07096/SN07096.pdf [Accessed 30 April 2025].

Francis-Devine, B., Malik, X. and Roberts, N. (2024) *Food Poverty: Households, Food Banks and Free School Meals. House of Commons Library*. Available from: https://researchbriefings.files.parliament.uk/documents/CBP-9209/CBP-9209.pdf [Accessed 18th June 2025].

Friere, P. (2005) *Pedagogy of the Oppressed: 30th Anniversary Edition*, trans M. Bergman Ramos, New York: Continuum.

Galanter, M. (1976) 'The duty not to deliver legal services', *University of Miami Law Review*, 30(4): 929–51.

Gastil, J. and Knobloch, K. (2020) *Hope for Democracy: How Citizens Can Bring Reason Back into Politics*, New York: Oxford Academic.

Genn, H. (1999) *Paths to Justice What People Do and Think About Going to Law*, London: Bloomsbury.

Genn, H. (2019) 'When law is good for your health: mitigating the social determinants of health through access to justice', *Current Legal Problems*, 72(1): 159–202.

Ghelani, D., Walker, R., Harkin, J., Ewan, R., Collins, K., Charlesworth, Z., et al (2024) 'Missing out 2024: £23 billion of support is unclaimed each year', Policy in Practice [blog]. Available from: www.policyinpractice.co.uk/publication/missing-out-2024/ [Accessed 30 April 2025].

Gilboe, S. and Curran, L. (2025) 'The role of justice in addressing the social determinants of health', *International Journal of Social Determinants of Health and Health Services*, 55(3): 249–61.

Graham, L. (2023) 'Reasserting the right to adequate clothing in International Human Rights Law', *Human Rights Law Review*, 24(1). https://doi.org/10.1093/hrlr/ngad039

Greener, I. (2025) 'Inequality and social harm: revisiting the Spirit Level debate by reproducing and updating it, as well as reanalysing the data with qualitative comparative analysis', *International Journal of Comparative Sociology*, 66(1): 92–111.

Greenwood, D. and Levin, M. (2007) *Introduction to Action Research* (2nd edn), London: Sage Publications.

Halliday, S. (2003) 'Duncan of Liverpool: Britain's first Medical Officer', *Journal of Medical Biography*, 11(3): 142–9.

Harding, M. (2021) 'Independence and accountability in the charity sector', in J. Picton and J. Sigafoos (eds) *Debates in Charity Law*, Oxford: Hart Publishing, pp 13–36.

Hayes, L. and Maynard, N. (2024a) *Without Access to Justice: The Work and Welfare Problems Driving Food Insecurity*, Liverpool: Feeding Liverpool. Available from: https://www.feedingliverpool.org/wp-content/uploads/2024/01/Without-Access-to-Justice-Report-2024-2.pdf [Accessed 27 November 2024].

Hayes, L. and Maynard, N. (2024b) '"Workers using foodbanks": the embedding of food insecurity at the nexus of welfare and employment laws', *Journal of Poverty and Social Justice*, 32(3): 318–42.

Heron, J. (1996) *Co-operative Inquiry: Research into the Human Condition*, London: Sage Publications.

Hesse-Biber, S.N. (2010) *Mixed Methods Research: Merging Theory with Practice*, London: The Guilford Press.

Hesse-Biber, S.N. (2015) 'Introduction: navigating a turbulent research landscape: working the boundaries, tensions, diversity, and contradictions of multimethod and mixed methods inquiry', in S.N. Hesse-Biber and R.B. Johnson (eds) *The Oxford Handbook of Multimethod and Mixed Methods Research Inquiry*, Oxford: Oxford University Press, pp 2–17.

Hirsch, D. (2023) *The Cost of Child Poverty in 2023*, London: Child Poverty Action Group.

HM Treasury and Hammond, P. (2018) 'Budget 2018: Philip Hammond's speech', October 29, GOV.UK. Available from: https://www.,gov.,uk/government/speeches/budget-2018-philip-hammonds-speech [Accessed 30 November 2024].

Hobson, F. (2020) 'The aims of ten years of welfare reform (2010–2020)', House of Commons Briefing Paper Number 9090, 18 December 2020.

Home Office (2024) *Family Policy: Family Life (as a Partner or Parent) and Exceptional Circumstances* (Version 21.0), London: The Home Office.

Home Office (nd) 'Asylum support: what you'll get'. Available from: https://www.gov.uk/asylum-support/what-youll-get [Accessed 27 November 2024].

Hooghe, M. and Oser, J. (2018) 'Social and political citizenship in European public opinion: an empirical analysis of T.H. Marshall's concept of social rights', *Government and Opposition*, 53(4): 595.

Houweling, T.A.J. and Grünberger, I. (2024) 'Intergenerational transmission of health inequalities: towards a life course approach to socioeconomic inequalities in health – a review', *Journal of Epidemiology and Community Health*, 78(10): 641–9.

Howard, S. (2024) 'GPs are being overwhelmed with housing and benefits requests, doctors warn', *BMJ*, 387.

Jacobson, J. and Cooper, P. (eds) (2020) *Participation in Courts and Tribunals: Concepts, Realities and Aspirations*, Bristol: Bristol University Press.

Joseph Rowntree Foundation (2024) *UK Poverty 2024: The Essential Guide to Understanding Poverty in the UK*, York: Joseph Rowntree Foundation.

Joseph Rowntree Foundation (2025) *UK Poverty 2025: The Essential Guide to Understanding Poverty in the UK*, York: Joseph Rowntree Foundation.

Kane, M., Thornton, J. and Bibby, J. (2022) 'Building public understanding of health and health inequalities', London: The Health Foundation, 14 March. Available from: https://www.health.org.uk/publications/long-reads/building-public-understanding-of-health-and-health-inequalities [Accessed 20 November 2024].

Kemmis, S. and McTaggart, R. (2005) 'Participatory action research: communicative action and the public sphere', in N.K. Denzin and Y.S. Lincoln (eds) *The Sage Handbook of Qualitative Research*, London: Sage Publications, pp 559–603.

Kesby, A. (2012) *The Right to Have Rights: Citizenship, Humanity, and International Law*, Oxford: Oxford University Press.

Kindon, S., Pain, R. and Kesby, M. (2007) 'Participatory action research: origins, approaches and methods', in S. Kindon, R. Pain and M. Kesby (eds) *Participatory Action Research Approaches and Methods: Connecting People, Participation and Place*, London: Routledge, pp 9–18.

Knigge, L. and Cope, M. (2006) 'Grounded visualization: integrating the analysis of qualitative and quantitative data through grounded theory and visualization', *Environment and Planning A: Economy and Space*, 38(11): 2021–37.

Kritzer, H. (2002) 'Stories from the field: collecting data outside over there', in J. Starr and M. Goodale (eds) *Practicing Ethnography in Law: New Dialogues, Enduring Methods*, New York: Palgrave Macmillan, pp 143–59.

Lai, E., Wickham, S., Law, C., Whitehead, M., Barr, B. and Taylor-Robinson, D. (2019) 'Poverty dynamics and health in late childhood in the UK: evidence from the Millennium Cohort Study', *Archives of Disease in Childhood*, 104(11): 1049–55.

Lancee, B. and Van de Werfhorst, H.G. (2012) 'Income inequality and participation: a comparison of 24 European countries', *Social Science Research*, 41(5): 1166–78.

Lane Scheppele, K. (2004) 'Constitutional ethnography: an introduction', *Law & Society Review*, 38: 389.

The Law Society (2024) 'Legal aid deserts', 21 February. Available from: https://www.lawsociety.org.uk/campaigns/civil-justice/legal-aid-deserts/ [Accessed 30 November 2024].

Lawton, E., Sandel, M., Morton, S., Ta, L., Kenyon, C. and Zuckerman, B. (2011) 'Medical–legal partnership: a new standard of care for vulnerable populations', in E. Tobin Tyler, E. Lawton, K.N. Conroy, M. Sandel and B. Zuckerman (eds) *Poverty, Health and Law*, Durham, NC: Carolina Academic Press, pp 71–97.

Legal Services Board (2020) *Reshaping Legal Services to Meet People's Needs: An Analysis of Legal Capability*. Available from: https://legalservicesboard.org.uk/wp-content/uploads/2020/02/PLE-Reshaping-Legal-Services.pdf [Accessed 1 May 2025].

Legal Services Board and the Law Society (2024) *Legal Needs of Individuals in England and Wales: Summary Report 2024*. Available from: https://legalservicesboard.org.uk/wp-content/uploads/2024/04/LN2023-Summary-report-18.04.24-updated.pdf [Accessed 30 November 2024].

Lévi–Strauss, C. (1967) *The Savage Mind,* Chicago: University of Chicago Press.

Lewin, K. (1946) 'Action research and minority problems', *Journal of Social Issues*, 2(4): 32–6.

Liamputtong, P. (2011) *Focus Group Methodology: Principles and Practice*, London: Sage Publications.

Liebenberg, S. (1999) 'Social citizenship – a precondition for meaningful democracy', *Agenda*, 15(40): 59–65.

Lister, M. (2005), 'Marshall-ing' social and political citizenship: towards a unified conception of citizenship, *Government and Opposition*, 40(4): 471–91.

Liverpool Access to Advice Network (LATAN) (2023) 'LATAN demand for advice and capacity survey 2023'. Available from: https://www.liverpoolaccesstoadvicenetwork.org.uk/_files/ugd/61ace9_26e438caaad745c28aa55349d97f44ca.pdf [Accessed 30 July 2025].

Liverpool City Council (2024) Briefing paper supplied at Anti-Poverty Strategy Meeting on 20th October 2024.

Living Wage Foundation (2024) 'What is the real living wage?', Living Wage Foundation. Available from: https://www.livingwage.org.uk/what-real-living-wage [Accessed 29 November 2024].

Lohmann, H. and Marx, I. (eds) (2018) *Handbook on In-work Poverty*, Northampton, MA: Edward Elgar Publishing.

Loopstra, R. (2018) 'Rising foodbank use in the UK: sign of a new public health emergency?', *Nutrition Bulletin*, 43(1): 53.

Loughborough University Centre for Research in Social Policy (2024) *Child Poverty Across the UK: A Briefing on the Local Child Poverty Statistics*. Loughborough University Centre for Research in Social Policy End Child Poverty. Available from: https://endchildpoverty.org.uk/wp-content/uploads/2024/06/End-Child-Poverty-Briefing.pdf [Accessed 1 October 2024].

Maani, N., Collin, J., Friel, S., Gilmore, A., McCambridge, J., Robertson, L. and Petticrew, M. (2020) 'Bringing the commercial determinants of health out of the shadows: a review of how the commercial determinants are represented in conceptual frameworks', *European Journal of Public Health*, 30(4): 660e4.

Magnussen, A.M. and Nilssen, E. (2013) 'Juridification and the construction of social citizenship', *Journal of Law and Society*, 40(2): 228–48.

Malterud, K. (2001) 'Qualitative research: standards, challenges, and guidelines', *The Lancet*, 358(9280): 483–8.

Mant, J., Newman, D. and O'Shea, D. (2024) 'Advising in a pandemic: the new era of "blended advice" in social welfare law', *Public Law* (1): 86–108.

Marmot, M., Allen, J., Boyce, T., Goldblatt, P. and Morrison, J. (2020) *Health Equity in England: The Marmot Review 10 Years On*, London: Institute of Health Equity. Available from: https://www.bmj.com/lookup/doi/10.1136/bmj.m693 [Accessed 27 November 2024].

Marmot, M., Allen, J., Goldblatt, P., Boyce, T., McNeish, D., Grady, M., et al (2010) *Fair Society, Healthy Lives: The Marmot Review: Strategic Review of Health Inequalities in England Post-2010*, London: London: Institute of Health.

Marshall, T.H. and Bottomore, T. (1992) *Citizenship and Social Class*, London: Pluto Press.

Mayo, M., Koessl, G., Scott, M. and Slater, I. (2015) *Access to Justice for Disadvantaged Communities*, Bristol: Bristol University Press.

McEvily, B., Perrone, V. and Zaheer, A. (2003) 'Trust as an organizing principle', *Organization Science*, 14(1): 91–103.

McIntyre, A. (2008) *Participatory Action Research*, London: Sage Publications.

Meadows, D. and Wright, D. (2009) *Thinking in Systems*, London: Earthscan.

Mertens, D.M. (2015) *Research and Evaluation in Education and Psychology: Integrating Diversity with Quantitative, Qualitative, and Mixed Methods* (4th edn), London: Sage Publications.

Ministry of Housing, Communities and Local Government (2019a) The English Indices of Deprivation 2019 (IoD2019). Available from: https://assets.publishing.service.gov.uk/media/5d8e26f6ed915d5570c6cc55/IoD2019_Statistical_Release.pdf [Accessed 27 November 2024].

Ministry of Housing, Communities and Local Government (2019b) File 1: Index of Multiple Deprivation (IMD2019) The English Indices of Deprivation 2019. Available from: https://www.gov.uk/government/statistics/english-indices-of-deprivation-2019 [Accessed 27 November 2024].

Ministry of Housing, Communities and Local Government (2019c) File 2: Domains of deprivation: The English Indices of Deprivation 2019. Available from: https://www.gov.uk/government/statistics/english-indices-of-deprivation-2019 [Accessed 27 November 2024].

Ministry of Housing, Communities and Local Government (2024) *Statutory Homelessness in England: Financial Year 2023–24*. Available from: https://www.gov.uk/government/statistics/statutory-homelessness-in-england-financial-year-2023-24/statutory-homelessness-in-england-financial-year-2023-24 [Accessed 29 November 2024].

Ministry of Justice (2019) *Legal Support: The Way Ahead*, London: The Stationery Office. Available from: https://assets.,publishing.service.gov.uk/media/5c5b3a0840f0b676e6ddc6dc/legal-support-the-way-ahead.pdf [Accessed 30 November 2024].

Ministry of Justice (2022) 'Pre-action protocols – civil procedure rules'. Available from: https://www.justice.gov.uk/courts/procedure-rules/civil/protocol [Accessed 8 April 2025].

Ministry of Justice (2023) 'Legal aid statistics: April to June 2023'. Available from: https://www.gov.uk/government/statistics/legal-aid-statistics-april-to-june-2023 [Accessed 30 November 2024].

Moffatt, S., White, M., Stacy, R., Downey, D. and Hudson, E. (2004) 'The impact of welfare advice in primary care: a qualitative study', *Critical Public Health* 14(3): 295.

Morris, D. (1999), *Charities and the Contract Culture: Partners or Contractors? Law and Practice in Conflict*, Liverpool: Charity Law Unit.

Morris, D. (2000) 'Charities in the contract culture: survival of the largest?' *Legal Studies*, 20(3): 409–27.

Morris, D. (2020) 'Commissioning of services by charities in the third decade of the contract culture: lessons learned (or not yet)', in J. Picton and J. Sigafoos (eds) *Debates in Charity Law*, Oxford: Hart Publishing, pp 231–56.

Morris, D. and Atkinson, K. (2003) 'Charities biting the hand that feeds: relationships with their funders', in D. Morris and J. Warburton (eds) *Charities, Governance and the Law: The Way Forward*, London: Keyhaven, pp 195–218.

Munford, L., Bambra, C., Davies, H., Pickett, K. and Taylor-Robinson, D. (2023) *Health Equity North: 2023*, Newcastle: Health Equity North.

Munro, R. and Preece, L. (2024) *The Value of Justice for All: Evaluating the Case for Funding the Free Specialist Legal Advice Sector,* A Report Commissioned by the Access to Justice Foundation and the Bar Council, Chelmsford: Pragmatix Advisory.

Murphy, B. and Organ, J. (2023) 'Global participatory democracy through a UN world citizens' initiative? Mapping the theoretical and institutional terrain', *German Law Journal*, 24(7): 1079.

National Centre for Social Research (nd) 'National Society for the Prevention of Cruelty to Children'. Available from: https://natcen.,ac.,uk/organisations/national-society-prevention-cruelty-children-nspcc [Accessed 30 November 2024].

National Council for Voluntary Organisations (2023) 'Financials', in *UK Civil Society Almanac 2023: Data. Trends. Insights*, 12 October, Available from: https://www.ncvo.org.uk/news-and-insights/news-index/uk-civil-society-almanac-2023/financials/where-do-voluntary-organisations-get-their-income-from/ [Accessed 29 November 2024].

Newman, D. and Gordon, F. (eds) (2023) *Access to Justice in Rural Communities Global Perspectives,* Oxford: Hart Publishing.

Newman, D. and Robins, J. (2024) 'Access to justice and the role of parliamentarians: what happens to those who fall through the justice gap?'. *Legal Studies*, 44(2): 221–41.

NHS England (2019) *Universal Personalised Care: Implementing the Comprehensive Model,* London: NHS England. Available from: https://www.england.nhs.uk/wp-content/uploads/2019/01/universal-personalised-care.pdf [Accessed 26 November 2024].

Nobleman, R.L. (2014) 'Addressing access to justice as a social determinant of health', *Health Law Journal*, 21: 49–74

Nowell, L.S., Norris, J.M., White, D.E. and Moules, N.J. (2017) 'Thematic analysis: striving to meet the trustworthiness criteria', *International Journal of Qualitative Methods*, 16(1): 1–13.

Nussbaum, M. (2007) 'Human rights and human capabilities', *Harvard Human Rights Journal*, 20: 21–4.

O'Cathain, A., Murphy, E. and Nicholl, J. (2007) 'Why, and how, mixed methods research is undertaken in health services research in England: a mixed methods study', *BMC Health Serv Res*, 7: 85.

OECD (Organization for Economic Cooperation and Development) (2024) 'Life expectancy', in *Society at a Glance 2024: OECD Social Indicators*, Paris: OECD Publishing, pp 98–9.

OECD/Open Society Foundations (2019) *Legal Needs Surveys and Access to Justice*, Paris: OECD Publishing.

Office for Budget Responsibility (2021) *Economic and Fiscal Outlook: October 2021*, London: Her Majesty's Stationery Office. Available from: https://obr.uk//docs/dlm_uploads/CCS1021486854-001_OBR-EFO-October-2021_CS_Web-Accessible_v2.pdf [Accessed 24 November 2024].

ONS (Office for National Statistics) (2024a) 'Statistical bulletin: Life expectancy for local areas in England, Northern Ireland and Wales: between 2001 to 2003 and 2021 to 2023 Subnational trends in the average number of years people will live beyond their current age measured by "period life expectancy"'. Available from: https://www.ons.gov.uk/peoplepopulationandcommunity/healthandsocialcare/healthandlifeexpectancies/bulletins/lifeexpectancyforlocalareasoftheuk/between2001to2003and2021to2023 [Accessed 18 June 2025].

ONS (Office for National Statistics) (2024b) 'Table 1: In Healthy life expectancy in England and Wales: between 2011 to 2013 and 2021 to 2023'. Available from: https://www.ons.gov.uk/peoplepopulationandcommunity/healthandsocialcare/healthandlifeexpectancies/bulletins/healthstatelifeexpectanciesuk/between2011to2013and2021to2023 [Accessed 22 April 2025].

Oquist, P. (1978) 'The epistemology of action research', *Acta Sociologica*, 21(2): 143–63.

Organ, J. and Sigafoos, J. (2017) 'What if there is nowhere to get advice?', in A. Flynn and J. Hodgson (eds) *Access to Justice and Legal Aid: Comparative Perspectives on Unmet Legal Need*, Oxford: Hart Publishing, pp 161–78.

Organ, J. and Sigafoos, J. (2018) *The Impact of LASPO on Routes to Justice*, Manchester: Equality and Human Rights Commission.

Organ, J., Sigafoos, J. and Wickham, S. (2021) 'How legal advice can ameliorate the unequal health impact of Covid-19', *Journal of Social Security Law*, 28(1).

Organ, J., Sigafoos, J., Wickham, S. and Schenwi-Dim, G. (2020) *Access to Legal Advice for All: Essential to Reduce Social and Economic Impacts of COVID-19*, Heseltine Institute for Public Policy. https://doi.org/10.17638/03106591

Paradies, Y., Ben, J., Denson, N., Elias, A., Priest, N., Pieterse, A., Gupta, A., Kelaher, M. and Gee, G. (2015) 'Racism as a determinant of health: a systematic review and meta-analysis', *PLoS One*, 10(9): e0138511.

Parmet, W., Smith, L. and Benedict, M. (2011) 'Social determinants, health disparities and the role of law', in E. Tobin Tyler, E. Lawton, K.N. Conroy, M. Sandel and B. Zuckerman (eds) *Poverty, Health and Law*, Durham, NC: Carolina Academic Press, pp 3–37.

Patrick, R. (2017) *For Whose Benefit? The Lived Experiences of Welfare Reform*, Bristol: Policy Press.

Pearce, A., Dundas, R., Whitehead, M. and Taylor-Robinson, D. (2019) 'Pathways to inequalities in child health', *Archives of Disease in Childhood*, 104(10): 998–1003.

Pereira, A and Rappaport, J. (2022) 'The participatory research of Orlando Fals Borda', in D. Burns, A. Howard and S.M. Ospina (eds) *The Sage Handbook of Participatory Research and Inquiry*, London: Sage Publications, pp 55–68.

Petrou, S., Fraser, J. and Sidebotham, P. (2014) 'Child death in high-income countries', *The Lancet*, 384(9946): 831–3.

Pichler, F. and Wallace, C. (2007) 'Patterns of formal and informal social capital in Europe', *European Sociological Review*, 23: 423–35.

Pickett, K. and Wilkinson, R. (2009) *The Spirit Level: Why More Equal Societies Almost Always Do Better*, London: Penguin Books.

Pickett, K., Taylor-Robinson, D., Alexiou, A., Alrouh, B., Atkins, R., Ayadurai, C. et al (2021) *The Child of the North: Building a Fairer Future after COVID-19*, The Northern Health Science Alliance and N8 Research Partnership. Available from: https://www.thenhsa.co.uk/app/uploads/2022/01/Child-of-the-North-Report-FINAL-1.pdf [Accessed 1 June 2023].

Pickett, K., Wilkinson, R., Gauhar, A. and Sahni-Nicholas, P. (2024) *The Spirit Level at 15: The Enduring Impact of Inequality*. York: University of York.

Pleasence, P. and Balmer, N. (2014) *How People Resolve 'Legal' Problems*, Cambridge: PPSR.

Pleasence, P. and Balmer, N. (2019) 'Justice and the capability to function in society', *Daedalus*, 148(1): 140–9.

Pleasence, P., Balmer, N.J. and Denvir, C. (2017) 'Wrong about rights: public knowledge of key areas of consumer, housing and employment law in England and Wales', *Modern Law Review*, 80(5): 836–59.

Popay J., Kowarzik U., Mallinson S., Mackian, S. and Barker, J. (2007) 'Social problems, primary care and pathways to help and support: addressing health inequalities at the individual level. Part I: the GP perspective', *Journal of Epidemiology & Community Health*, 61: 966–71.

Putnam, R.D. (2000) *Bowling Alone: The Collapse and Revival of American Community,* New York: Simon and Schuster.

Rappaport, J. (2020) *Cowards Don't Make History: Orlando Fals Borda and the Origins of Participatory Action Research*, Durham, NC: Duke University Press.

Rappaport, J. (2024) 'Participatory research as activism: Orlando Fals Borda and the Latin American tradition of engaged research', in L. Cox, A. Szolucha, A.A. Lozano and S. Chattopadhyay (eds) *Handbook of Research Methods and Applications for Social Movements*, Cheltenham: Edward Elgar Publishing, pp 387–99.

Rathbone, A., Foster, M. and Nyikavaranda, P. (2022) *Addressing the Skills Gap within Advice Services,* Legal Advice Group. Available from: https://londonlegalsupporttrust.org.uk/wp-content/uploads/2022/05/Addressing-skills-gap-report-final.pdf [Accessed 30 November 2024].

Reason, P. and Bradbury, H. (2008) 'Introduction', in P. Reason and H. Bradbury (eds) *Sage Handbook of Action Research: Participative Inquiry and Practice*, London: Sage Publications, pp 1–10.

Reece, S., Sheldon, T., Dickerson, J. and Pickett, K. (2022) 'A review of the effectiveness and experiences of welfare advice services co-located in health settings: a critical narrative systematic review', *Social Science & Medicine*, 296(1): 114746.

Renwick, C. (2023) 'The family life of Peter and Ruth Townsend: social science and methods in 1950s and early 1960s Britain', *Twentieth Century British History*, 34(4): 634–56.

Rice, L. and Sara, R. (2019) 'Updating the determinants of health model in the Information Age', *Health Promotion International*, 34(6): 1241–49.

Richmond, C. (2002) 'Sir Douglas Black', *BMJ*, 325(7365): 661.

Robinson, E., Stone, J. and Padley, M. (2025) *Households Living Below a Minimum Income Standard: 2008–2023*, York: Joseph Rowntree Foundation.

Royston, S. (2023) *Broken Benefits: What's Gone Wrong with Welfare Reform*, Bristol: Policy Press.

Sandefur, R. (2019) 'Access to what?', *Daedalus*, 148(1): 49–55.

Sen, A. (1999) *Development as Freedom*, Oxford: Oxford University Press.

Senge, P.M. (1990) *The Fifth Discipline: The Art and Practice of the Learning Organization*, New York: Doubleday.

Sidebotham, P., Fraser, J. Freemantle, J., Petrou, S., Pulikottil-Jacob, R., Cutler, T. et al (2014) 'Understanding why children die in high-income countries', *The Lancet*, 384(9946): 915–27.

Sigafoos, J. and Organ, J. (2021) 'What about the poor people's rights: dismantling social citizenship', *Journal of Law and* Society, 48(3): 362–85.

Simpson, M. (2017) 'Renegotiating social citizenship in the age of devolution', *Journal of Law and Society*, 44(4): 646.

Simpson, M. (2022) *A Socio-legal Perspective on Social Citizenship: In Social Citizenship in an Age of Welfare Regionalism: The State of the Social Union*, Oxford: Hart Publishing.

Simpson, M., McKeever, G. and Fitzpatrick, C. (2023) 'Legal protection against destitution in the UK: the case for a right to a subsistence minimum', *Modern Law Review*, 86(2): 465–97.

Smith, G. (2009) *Democratic Innovations: Designing Institutions for Citizen Participation*, Cambridge: Cambridge University Press.

Smith, M. (2024) 'General election 2024: what are the most important issues for voters?', YouGov, UK. Available from: https://yougov.co.uk/politics/articles/49594-general-election-2024-what-are-the-most-important-issues-for-voters

Social Metrics Commission (2023) *Measuring Poverty 2023: A Report of the Social Metrics Commission,* Social Metrics Commission. Available from: www.socialmetricscommission.org.uk [Accessed 10 June 2024].

Solt, F. (2008) 'Economic inequality and democratic political engagement', *American Journal of Political Science*, 52: 48–60.

Sommerlad, H. (2018) 'Law and social justice', in G. Craig (ed) *Handbook on Global Social Justice*, Cheltenham: Edward Elgar Publishing, pp 285–302.

Sommerlad, H. and Sanderson, P. (2013) 'Social justice on the margins: the future of the not for profit sector as providers of legal advice in England and Wales', *Journal of Social Welfare & Family Law,* 35(3): 305.

Song, H., Zhang, A., Barr, B. and Wickham, S. (2024) 'Effect of Universal Credit on young children's mental health: quasi-experimental evidence from Understanding Society', *Journal of Epidemiology and Community Health,* 78(12): 764–71.

Stalford, H. (2024) 'Children's rights and access to justice', *The International Journal of Children's Rights*, 32(2): 231–3.

Stark, J.L. (2014) 'The potential of Deweyan-inspired action research', *Education and Culture*, 30(2): 87–101.

Stroh, D.P. (2015) *Systems Thinking for Social Change: A Practical Guide to Solving Complex Problems, Avoiding Unintended Consequences, and Achieving Lasting Results*, London: Chelsea Green Publishing.

Summers, D. (2009) 'David Cameron warns of "new age of austerity"', *The Guardian* 26 April 2009. Available from: https://www.theguardian.com/politics/2009/apr/26/david-cameron-conservative-economic-policy1 [Accessed 24 November 2024].

Takle, M., Solstad Vedeler, J., Schoyen, M.A., Klette-Bøhler, K. and Falch-Eriksen, A. (eds) (2023) *Citizenship and Social Exclusion at the Margins of the Welfare State*, London: Routledge.

Tashakkori, A. and Teddlie, C. (eds) (2010) *Sage Handbook of Mixed Methods in Social and Behavioral Research* (2nd edn), London: Sage Publications.

Taylor-Gooby, P. (2008) *Reframing Social Citizenship*, Oxford: Oxford University Press.

Taylor-Robinson, D., Lai, E., Wickham, S., Rose, T., Norman, P., Bambra, C., et al (2019) 'Assessing the impact of rising child poverty on the unprecedented rise in infant mortality in England, 2000–2017: time trend analysis', *BMJ Open*, 9(e029424).

Teddlie, C. and Tashakkori, A. (2003) 'Major issues and controversies in the use of mixed methods in the social and behavioural sciences', in A. Tashakkori and C. Teddlie (eds) *Handbook of Mixed Methods in Social and Behavioural Research*, London: Sage Publications, pp 3–50.

Teitelbaum, J. and Lawton, E. (2017) 'The roots and branches of the medical–legal partnership approach to health: from collegiality to civil rights to health equity', *Yale Journal of Health Policy, Law, and Ethics*, 17(2): 343–77.

Tominey, E., Baxter, A., Cheetham, M., Marimpi, M., Morris, S., Munsford, L. et al (2024) 'We can't tackle the mental health crisis without reforming social security', LSE British Politics and Policy, [blog], 30 October. Available from: https://blogs.lse.ac.uk/politicsandpolicy/we-cant-tackle-the-mental-health-crisis-without-reforming-social-security/ [Accessed 30 October 2024].

Townsend, P. (1979) *Poverty in the United Kingdom: A Survey of Household Resources and Standards of Living*, Harmondsworth: Penguin Books.

Townsend, P. and Davidson, N. (1982) *Inequalities in Health: The Black Report*, Harmondsworth: Penguin Books.

Uslaner, E. and Brown, M. (2005) 'Inequality, trust, and civic engagement', *American Politics Research*, 33(6): 868–94.

Vitale, D. (2018) 'A trust network model for social rights fulfilment', *Oxford Journal of Legal Studies*, 38: 706–32.

Vitale, D. (2024) *Trust, Courts and Social Rights: A Trust-Based Framework for Social Rights Enforcement*, Cambridge: Cambridge University Press.

Wagner, C., Carmeli, C., Jackisch, J., Kivimäki, M., van der Linden, B., Cullati, S. et al (2024) 'Life course epidemiology and public health', *The Lancet Public Health*, 9(4): 261–9.

Warren, M. (ed) (1999) *Democracy and Trust,* Cambridge: Cambridge University Press.

Watkins, D. (2022) 'Reimagining the relationship between legal capability and the capabilities approach,' *International Journal of Public Legal Education*, 5(1): 4–36.

Watt, D. (2007) 'On becoming a qualitative researcher: the value of reflexivity', *The Qualitative Report*, 12(1): 82–101.

Webster, R. (2016) *Payment by Results: Lessons from the Literatu*re, Geneva: Oak Foundation.

Wenger-Trayner, E. and Wenger-Trayner, B. (2015) 'Introduction to communities of practice: a brief overview of the concept and its uses'. Available from: https://www.wenger-trayner.com/introduction-to-communities-of-practice/ [Accessed 8 April 2025].

Wheeldon, J., Ahlberg, M. and Liamputtong, P. (2019) 'Mind Maps in Qualitative Research', in P. Liamputtong (ed) *Handbook of Research Methods in Health Social Sciences*, Singapore: Springer, pp 1113–29.

Whitehead, M., Barr, B. and Taylor-Robinson, D. (2020) 'The BMJ Opinion', 'Covid-19: We are not "all in it together" – less privileged in society are suffering the brunt of the damage', [blog], 22 May. Available from: https://blogs.bmj.com/bmj/2020/05/22/covid-19-we-are-not-all-in-it-together-less-privileged-in-society-are-suffering-the-brunt-of-the-damage/ [Accessed 27 November 2024].

Whitehead, M., Taylor-Robinson, D. and Barr, B. (2021) 'Poverty, health, and Covid-19: yet again, poor families will be hardest hit by the pandemic's long economic fallout', *BMJ:* 372–6.

Whitworth, D. and Smith, A. (2024) 'Unpaid carers being forced to repay £250m to DWP in allowance overpayments', BBC, 18 May, Available from: https://www.bbc.co.uk/news/uk-69031180 [Accessed 24 November 2024].

WHO (World Health Organization) (2013) 'Social determinants of health: key concepts'. Available from: https://www.who.int/news-room/questions-and-answers/item/social-determinants-of-health-key-concepts [Accessed 1 November 2024].

WHO (World Health Organization) (2019) *Healthy, Prosperous Lives for All: The European Health Equity Status Report*, Copenhagen: WHO Regional Office for Europe.

WHO (World Health Organization) (nd) 'Social determinants of health: overview'. Available from: https://www.who.int/health-topics/social-determinants-of-health#tab=tab_1 [Accessed 30 November 2024].

Wickham, S., Anwar, E., Barr, B., Law, C. and Taylor-Robinson, D. (2016) 'Poverty and child health in the UK: using evidence for action', *Archives of Disease in Childhood*, 101(8): 759–66.

Wickham, S., Whitehead, M., Taylor-Robinson, D. and Barr, B. (2017) 'The effect of a transition into poverty on child and maternal mental health: a longitudinal analysis of the UK Millennium Cohort Study', *The Lancet Public Health*, 2: 141–8.

Wickham, S., Bentley, L., Rose, T., Whitehead, M., Taylor-Robinson, D. and Barr, B. (2020) 'Effects on mental health of a UK welfare reform, Universal Credit: a longitudinal controlled study', *The Lancet Public Health*, 5(3): 157–64.

Wilding, J. (2023) *The Legal Aid Market*, Bristol: Policy Press.

Wiley, L.F., Yearby, R., Clark, B.R. and Mohapatra, S. (2022) 'Introduction: what is health justice?', *Journal of Law, Medicine and Ethics*, 20(4): 636–40.

Wilkinson, R. and Pickett, K. (2009) *The Spirit Level: Why More Equal Societies Almost Always Do Better*, London: Penguin Group.

Wilkinson, R. and Pickett, K. (2018) *The Inner Level*, London: Allen Lane.

Woodhead, C., Collins, H., Lomas, R. and Raine, R. (2017) 'Co-located welfare advice in general practice: a realist qualitative study', *Health and Social Care*, 25(6): 1794.

YouGov (2024) *Legal Needs of Individuals in England and Wales: Summary Report 2024*, London: Legal Services Board and the Law Society. Available from: https://legalservicesboard.org.uk/wp-content/uploads/2024/04/LN2023-Summary-report-18.04.24-updated.pdf [Accessed 1 May 2024].

Zucker, L.G. (1986) 'Production of trust: institutional sources of economic structure, 1840–1920', *Research in Organizational Behavior*, 8: 53–111.

Index